WOMEN ENTREPRENEURSHIP IN INDIA

Women
Entrepreneurship
in India

By

R. Vasanthagopal and Santha S.

New Century Publications
New Delhi, India

NEW CENTURY PUBLICATIONS
4800/24, Bharat Ram Road,
Ansari Road, Daryaganj,
New Delhi -110 002 (India)

Tel.: 011 – 2324 7798, 4358 7398, 6539 6605
Fax: 011 – 4101 7798
E-mail: indiatax@vsnl.com
www.newcenturypublications.com

Editorial office:
34, Gujranwala Town, Part-2,
Delhi - 110 009

Tel.: 27247805, 27464774

First Published – **September 2008**

ISBN: 978-81-7708-182-4

Published by New Century Publications and printed at Salasar
Imaging Systems, New Delhi

Designs: Patch Creative Unit, New Delhi

PRINTED IN INDIA

ABOUT THE BOOK

Any strategy aimed at economic development will be lop-sided without involving women who constitute half of the world population. Evidence has unequivocally established that entrepreneurial spirit is not a male prerogative. Women entrepreneurship has gained momentum in the last three decades with the increase in the number of women enterprises and their substantive contribution to economic growth. The industrial performance of Asia-Pacific region propelled by foreign direct investment, technological innovations and manufactured exports has brought a wide range of economic and social opportunities to women entrepreneurs.

In this dynamic world, women entrepreneurs are an important part of the global quest for sustained economic development and social progress. In India, though women have played a key role in the society, their entrepreneurial ability has not been properly tapped due to the lower status of women in the society. It is only from the Fifth Five Year Plan (1974-78) onwards that their role has been explicitly recognised with a marked shift in the approach from women welfare to women development and empowerment. The development of women entrepreneurship has become an important aspect of our plan priorities. Several policies and programmes are being implemented for the development of women entrepreneurship in India.

The present work deals with various dimensions of women entrepreneurship in India. It also explains the experience of other countries in this regard.

AUTHORS' PROFILE

Dr. R. Vasanthagopal is a Selection Grade Lecturer in the Post-graduate Department of Commerce and Research Centre, The Cochin College, Kochi. After his Masters Degree in Commerce from Kerala University, he obtained M.Phil. in Commerce and Ph.D. in industrial relations from the same University. He specialises in finance, industrial relations and socio-economic issues. He has published several research articles in reputed Commerce and Management journals. He has participated and presented papers in various regional, national and international seminars.

Dr. Santha S. is a Senior Scale Lecturer in the Post-graduate Department of Commerce in St. Peter's College, Kolenchery, Ernakulam. She secured her Masters Degree in Commerce and Ph.D. in women entrepreneurship from M.G. University, Kottayam. Her areas of specialisation are finance and women issues. She has published several articles in reputed national journals and participated in national and international seminars.

PREFACE

Though the Constitution of India provides equal rights and privileges for men and women and makes special provisions for women to improve their status in society, strong patriarchal traditions are followed and women's lives are shaped by social customs. The need to bring women into the mainstream of development has been a national concern since Independence in 1947 and their status has improved in the last few decades with the enactment of pro-women legislations and implementation of women-specific development programmes.

For sustained economic development and social justice, socio-economic status of women should be improved along with that of men. Socio-economic freedom gives the women the right to determine the course of their lives. Entrepreneurship enhances the women's social standing. The entrepreneurial activity is dependent on several complex economic, social and psychological factors. Thus, for any attempt made to understand the entrepreneurial activity among women, an analysis of their socio-economic origins is necessary.

The degree of entrepreneurial activity depends to a certain extent upon the socio-economic status of an entrepreneur. The socio-economic status of rural and urban women is different in India and there are several categories of rural women, based on religion, caste, education and income.

Women entrepreneurship is gaining momentum and has become a pressing need of the day in a developing country like India. Economic development of a country is generally equated with its industrial development. It is the entrepreneur who stands at the centre of the industrial activity and assumes various roles of a country's development process. Large, medium and small industrial units play a mutually complementary role in the integrated and harmonious growth of the industrial sector as a whole. However, small enterprises outnumber the larger ones in every country and play a vital role in the process of industrialisation by contributing significantly to employment, production and exports.

Regarding entrepreneurship, much literature has been published. Since women entrepreneurship is a recent phenomenon, only very few efforts have been made to explore women entrepreneurship in India. By and large, these studies have focused on women more as workers and less as entrepreneurs. This necessitates more studies on women entrepreneurship, so as to implement effective policy measures in this regard.

The present work deals with various dimensions of women entrepreneurship in India. It also explains the experience of other countries in this regard. Moreover, it examines in detail the activities and problems of women entrepreneurs in two important States of India, viz. Kerala and Tamil Nadu.

August 5, 2008

CONTENTS

1

Women Entrepreneurship:
An Introduction

Entrepreneurship plays an imperative role in the growth of any society. Development of entrepreneurship culture and qualitative business development services are the major requirements for industrial growth. Entrepreneurship emerges from an individual's creative spirit into long-term business ownership, employment creation, capital formation and economic security. Entrepreneurial skills are essential for industrialisation and for alleviation of mass unemployment and poverty.

As technology speeds up lives, women are an emerging economic force, which cannot be neglected by the policy makers. The world's modern democratic economy depends on the participation of both sexes. Global markets and women are not often used in the same sentence, but increasingly, statistics show that women have economic clout-most visibly as entrepreneurs and most powerfully as consumers. Today, women in advanced market economies own more than 25 per cent of all businesses and women-owned businesses in Africa, Asia, Eastern Europe, and Latin America are growing rapidly. In some regions of the world, transformation to market economy, women entrepreneurs is a growing trend. However, in India, the actual participation of women in income generating activities is quite unsatisfactory, only eight per cent of the small scale- manufacturing units are owned and operated by women.

1.1 Concept of Women Entrepreneurship
Entrepreneurship is an economic activity which is undertaken by an individual or group of individuals.

Entrepreneurship can be defined as the making of a "new combination" of already existing materials and forces; that entrepreneurship throws up as innovations, as opposed to inventions and that no one is entrepreneur for ever, only when he or she is actually doing the innovative activity.

Women entrepreneurship is the process where women organise all the factors of production, undertake risks, and provide employment to others. The definition of women entrepreneurship has never been differentiated on the basis of sex and hence could be extended to women entrepreneurs without any restrictions. A woman entrepreneur is a person who is an enterprising individual with an eye for opportunities and an uncanny vision, commercial acumen, with tremendous perseverance and above all a person who is willing to take risks with the unknown because of the adventurous spirit she possesses.

Thus, a woman entrepreneur is one who starts business and manages it independently and tactfully, takes all the risks, faces the challenges boldly with an iron will to succeed. Women entrepreneurship is an economic activity of those women who think of a business enterprise, initiate it, organise and combine the factors of production, operate the enterprise and undertake risks and handle economic uncertainty involved in running a business enterprise.

1.2 Evolution of Women Entrepreneurship

Although women form a very large proportion of the self-employed group, their work is often not recognised as "work". The prevailing 'house-hold strategy' catalyses the devaluation of women's productive activities as secondary and subordinate to men's work. Women's contributions vary according to the structure, needs, customs and attitudes of society. Women entered   entrepreneurial activities because of poor economic conditions, high unemployment rates and divorce catapult. In Babylonia, about 200 B.C., women were permitted to engage in business and to work as scribes.

By 14th century, in England and France, women were frequently accepted on a par with men as carpenters, saddlers, barbers, tailors and spurriers. Dressmaking and lace making guilds were competed more with men for some jobs, but were concentrated primarily in textile mills and clothing factories. In 1950, women made up nearly 25 per cent of both industrial and service sectors of the developing countries. In 1980, it increased to 28 per cent and 31 per cent respectively. Meanwhile, in 1950, 53 per cent of females and 65 per cent of males of industrialised countries were in non-agricultural sectors. As a result of the economic crisis of the 1980s and the commercialisation and modernisation of the economy, women lost employment in agriculture and industries. This pushed women in urban areas to find out a suitable solution for generating income, which resulted in the emergence of self-employment, largely in micro-businesses.

1.3 Importance of Women Entrepreneurship

Women perform an important role in building the real backbone of a nation's economy. There is considerable entrepreneurial talent among women. Many women's domestic skills such as people and time management and household budgeting are directly transferable in the business context. Women have the ability to balance different tasks and priorities and tend to find satisfaction and success in and from building relationships with customers and employees, in having control of their own destiny, and in doing something that they consider worthwhile. They have the potential and the will to establish and manage enterprises of their own. These qualities and strengths of women are to be tapped for productive channels. But simultaneous creation and development of small business among women is a difficult task. Even though women's contributions to business are one of the major engines of global economic growth, too often, women do not have access to basic business education, commercial credit and marketing opportunities. Maintenance of proper quantitative balance among various economic activities is one of the principal functions of the economic system, which should operate to give equal freedom of choice to men and women.

The process of economic development would be incomplete and lopsided, unless women are fully involved in it. The orientation of a society as a whole, regarding desirability that women should play an equal part in the country's development, is a very important precondition for the advancement not only of women, but the country as a whole. The highest national priority must be for the unleashing of woman power which is the single most important source of societal energy. Women entrepreneurs should be regarded as individuals who take up roles in which they would like to adjust their family and society, economic performance and personal requirements. "Emancipation of women is an essential prerequisite for economic development and social progress of the nations."

In the closing years of the 21st century, multi- skilled, productive and innovative women entrepreneurs are inextricable for achieving sustained economic growth. Globalisation of industrial production and economic interdependence have become the torch-bearers for all international co-operations. In the dynamic world which is experiencing the effects of globalisation, privatisation and liberalisation, women entrepreneurs are likely to become an even more important part of the global quest for sustained economic growth and social development. The economic status of woman is now accepted as an indication of the society's stage of development. Women (especially rural women) are vital development agents who can play a significant role in the economic development of a nation, but they should have an equal access to productive resources, opportunities and public services.

It has also been realised in the last few years that the widespread poverty and stunted economic growth can be overcome only by gainful and sustainable economic participation of women. National development will be sluggish, if the economic engine operates only at half power. Women in Enterprise Building has emerged as an agenda for many policy makers, researchers, and trainers and as well as for associations and organisations involved in women development. If women acquire skills, they can carve a niche for themselves in the outside world too. This is the reason why women entrepreneurship development has become a subject of great concern and serious discussion in recent times.

1.4 Women Entrepreneurship in India

Women entrepreneurship in India represents a group of women who have broken away from the beaten track and are exploring new vistas of economic participation. Women in India entered business due to pull and push factors. Their task has been full of challenges. In spite of the family opposition, many women have proved themselves independent and successful entrepreneurs. The emergence of women entrepreneurs and women-owned firms and their significant contributions to the economy are visible in India and these businesses are ready for continued growth in the future. In India, women constitute half of the total population (495.74 million), but their participation in the economic activity is very low. Female Work Participation Rate was 25.7 per cent in 2001.

In India, women are relatively powerless with little or no control over resources and little decision making power. Women in the informal sector are found to be home-based workers, engaged in the petty manufacture of goods, either on piece rate basis or on own account, petty traders and petty shopkeepers or service specialists. Studies reveal that 89 per cent of India's women workers toil in the informal sectors in sub-human conditions. Over 2/3 of the enterprises are self owned and have a fixed capital of less than Rs. 50. Over 4/5 of the women workers in this sector earn less than Rs. 500 p.m.

The income earned by women in this sector is said to be about ¼ of that of a woman in the organised sector."

Nowadays women are well-educated with technical and professional qualifications. Many of them have medical, management and similar degrees and diplomas. Many entered their family business as equal partners. Women set up their own clinics or nursing homes, small boutiques, small manufacturing enterprises and entered garment exports. They have their own personal choices and the courage to undertake new ventures. However, many have to face family antipathy and do not get adequate support from their family.

1.5 Evolution of Women Entrepreneurship in India

In India, women's participation in economic activity is common from time immemorial. Women had significant role in the society across centuries and geographical boundaries. The role of women has gone through several transitions. It took centuries for women's roles to move in the present direction. There are some regions where women live in a barbarian era, chained and shackled to the social taboos, restrictions and lakshmana rekhas of others who frame a code of conduct. At the same time there are other regions where women fight for and win freedom and opportunity to play their roles in a new context with new occupations and a new way of life. As regards the ancient industries of India, family was the unit of production where women played an important role in the production process. Even in Mohenjodaro and Harappa culture, women shared a responsible position with men and helped in spinning and clay modelling and other simple arts and crafts. Women played a very pivotal role in creating household utility requirements and agricultural activities and weaving during the Vedic Period. In the traditional economy, they played vital roles in agriculture industry and services. [1]

They were the makers of intoxicant soma-juice, a skilful task. In the 18th century, women had a significant role in economy and a definite status in the social structure. The arrival of East India Company, introduction of Zamindari system in northern India and Ryotwari system in Southern India resulted in weakening of corporate character of the village community which affected women's work and status in agricultural economy. The destruction of the Indian handicrafts and household industries paved the way for emergence of the industrial revolution in England. A series of mechanical inventions, large scale production of standardised machine made goods and foreign capital etc. made large masses of working women from their traditional occupations and reduced their status to unskilled and unwanted workers.

At the beginning of the British Period, women in South India performed manuring operations and also engaged in dairy occupations. They were also engaged in spinning. Some of them were also found in salt industry and quick lime production. In Northern India, women engaged in various activities like agriculture, carrying water for wealthy families, collecting and drying the dung for fuel, washing clothes of the people in the vicinity, producing leaf plates, glass ornaments, leather goods, lac ornaments, preparing ghee and butter, retailing vegetables and fish at the weekly markets, mid-wifery, singing and dancing etc. Spinning was the women's main occupation in the first decade of the 19th century. In Assam, spinning and weaving were done at home by women. Women's informal trading activities in the international distribution system have been well documented since early 1950s. After the advent of the British rule, women were able to participate in economic and social life. However, only a very small percentage of women could avail themselves of the educational facilities and pursued an independent career.

During 19th century and early 20th centuries there was relatively limited use of women in textile mills. Women's role was upset only after the advent of the industrial revolution. Many of their tasks formerly undertaken in the house were removed to the factory with the introduction of power driven machinery in textiles, sugar and rice mills, the status of the women was reduced to that of unskilled wage earners. Because of all these changes, women's original creative talent and skills were unutilised or under utilised. Their important role in the economy was undermined which in turn hindered their growth and development. The Green Revolution has led to increased demands for casual labour, dispossession of small landholders from their land and consequently, pushing out of women from such small landholdings to become wage earners.

Though many of the tasks performed by males are getting mechanised, the women continue to toil in labour intensive jobs like rice transplantation, cleaning and storage of grain in post-harvest operations, picking of leaves and fruit, hand shelling groundnut, picking out cotton seed, etc. Women get limited job opportunities in modern occupations/trades as they do not have access to the training required for new technologies. In many areas where multiple crops are grown, the workload of women has increased. In industry, women continue to be employed mostly on unskilled jobs. The average earning of a regular salaried woman worker continues to be less than that of a man. An emerging phenomenon in the rural scene is the "single-parent rural family", due to large-scale migration of men seeking employment in urban areas. The woman has to assume the role of head of the household and responsibility for the support and care of children and also of the elders in the rural family. Her income is inadequate to meet the family's needs; thus, there is tension in the family, as remittances from the men-folk are mostly irregular as also meager, given the high cost (and many temptations) of urban living. [2]

The women entrepreneurs of 1950s, 1960s, and 1970s had accepted both their social and occupational roles. They tried to balance their dual responsibilities. During 1950s, some women gave up their education and undertook entrepreneurial activities as there was no income generating males in their families. Some others took charge of the businesses of their husbands due to illness or death of their husbands and in certain cases the businesses were taken and managed by their relatives and women lived as their dependents. During 1960s many women had adequate education and they were largely unarticulated. Some of them took the beginning steps to start small individual home-based enterprises. It was only from 1970 onwards that the Government took   systematic efforts to promote self-employment among women.

Women entrepreneurship in India became popular in the late 1970s and now more and more women are emerging as entrepreneurs in all kinds of economic activities. Many women after their education became professionals with lot of aspirations and ambitions. According to the 1971 Census, the total female working population is about 13.8 per cent of the total work force. The official statistics show that only six per cent of the female population is in regular employment where as 94 per cent is self-employed. The women who constitute a large portion of the self–employed are predominantly rural, poor, and illiterate: they are also very active. 1980s provided the real breakthrough for women in many fields and many frontiers. Many had education in highly sophisticated technology and profession.

In India, the use of a wider definition of the term "economic activity" resulted in an upward revision of the estimated 13 per cent of economically active women to 88 per cent. During the last four decades, a number of schemes and policies were introduced in the country to develop and encourage new women entrepreneurs. The National Perspective Plan for Women, 1988-'00 shows the fact that 94 per cent of women workers worked in the unorganized sector and 83 per cent of them were engaged in agriculture and allied activities like dairy, animal husbandry, sericulture, handicrafts, handlooms and forestry. [3]

During the 1990s, women were capable, competent, confident and assertive and had a clear idea about the ventures to be undertaken and they succeeded in them. Many women entered   large-scale enterprises of their parents or husbands and proved their competence and capabilities. Women acquired high self-esteem and the capability of solving the problems independently through economic independence.

In the 21th century women are becoming experts in all the fields especially in telecom and IT. Their status has been changed with the impact of growing liberalisation, industrialization, and social legislation. With the growing awareness about business and the spread of education, they have entered in non-traditional higher levels of activities like engineering, electronics and energy and acquired expertise in these fields. Many of the new industries are headed and guided by women. However, in India a large number of highly educated women do not seek employment. Marriage and family have always been the first choice for most Indian women. Female role prescriptions have created mind blocks. Men are more likely to engage in entrepreneurial activities. The number of men in autonomous start-up category is twice that of women, thrice in the category of manageresses. [4]

1.6 Organisations Promoting Women Entrepreneurship

- **National Resource Centre for Women (NRCW):** An autonomous body set up under the National Commission for Women Act, 1990 to orient and sensitise policy planners towards women's issues, facilitating leadership training and creating a national database in the field of women's development.
- **Women's India Trust (WIT):** WIT is a charitable organisation established in 1968 to develop skills of women and to earn a regular income by providing training and employment opportunities to the needy and unskilled women of all communities in and around Mumbai.
- **Women Development Corporation (WDC):** WDCs were set up in 1986 to create sustained income generating activities for women to provide better employment avenues for women so as to make them economically independent and self- reliant.

- **Development of Women and Children in Urban Area (DWCUA):** DWCUA was introduced in 1997 to organise the urban poor among women in socio-economic self-employment activity groups with the dual objective of providing self-employment opportunities and social strength to them.
- **Association of Women Entrepreneurs of Karnataka (AWAKE):** AWAKE was constituted by a team of women entrepreneurs in Bangalore with a view to helping other women in different ways–to prepare project report, to secure finance, to choose and use a product, to deal with bureaucratic hassles, to tackle labour problems etc.
- **Working Women's Forum (WWF):** WWF was founded in Chennai for the development of poor working women, to rescue petty traders from the clutches of middlemen and to make them confident entrepreneurs in their own right. The beneficiaries are fisher women, lace makers, beedi making women, landless women, labourers and agarbathi workers.
- **Association of Women Entrepreneurs of Small Scale Industries (AWESSI):** It was founded in Ambattur in Chennai in 1984 to promote, protect and encourage women entrepreneurs and their interests in South India, to seek work and co-operate with the Central and State Government services and other Government agencies and to promote measures for the furtherance and protection of small-scale industries.
- **Women's Occupational Training Directorate:** It organises regular skill training courses at basic, advanced and post advanced levels. There are 10 Regional Vocational Training Institutes (RVTIs) in different parts of the country, besides a National Vocational Training Institute (NVTI) at NOIDA.
- **Aid The Weaker Trust (ATWT):** ATWT was constituted in Bangalore by a group of activists to impart training to women in printing. It is the only one in Asia. Its benefits

are available to women all over Karnataka. It provides economic assistance and equips girls with expertise in various aspects of printing and building up self-confidence.

- **Self- Employed Women's Association (SEWA):** SEWA is a trade union registered in 1972. It is an organisation of poor self- employed women workers. SEWA's main goals are to organise women workers to obtain full employment and self- reliance.

- **Women Entrepreneurship of Maharashtra (WIMA):** It was set up in 1985 with its head office in Pune to provide a forum for members and to help them sell their products. It also provides training to its members. It has established industrial estates in New Mumbai and Hadapsar.

- **Self-help Groups (SHGs):** An association of women, constituted mainly for the purpose of uplifting the women belonging to the Below Poverty Line (BPL) categories to the Above Poverty Line (APL) category. The major activities of the group are income generation programmes, informal banking, credit, unions, health, nutritional programmes etc.

- **Women Development Cells (WDC):** In order to streamline gender development in banking and to have focused attention on coverage of women by banks, NABARD has been supporting setting up of Women Development Cells (WDCs) in Regional Rural Banks and Cooperative Banks.

1.7 Financial Institutions Assisting Women in India

For the past several years, financial institutions have been playing a pivotal role in giving financial assistance and consultancy services to women entrepreneurs. These institutions include:

- National Small Industries Corporation (NSIC).
- All-India Development Banks (AIDBs), viz. IDBI, IFCI, ICICI, IIBI, IDFC and SIDBI.

- Specialised Financial Institutions (SFIs), viz. Exim Bank and NABARD.
- Investment Institutions, viz. LIC, GIC, NIC, NIA, OIC, UII and UTI.
- Regional/State-Level Institutions, viz. NEDFI, SIDCs and SFCs.
- Commercial Banks.
- Co-operative Banks etc.

1.8 Successful Indian Women Entrepreneurs

Rita Singh, founder of the M'escos (Mid-east Shipping Company) group, is one of the first woman entrepreneurs in the business world who exports trendy M'escos shoes and owns a fleet of state-of-the-art- helicopters and ships, and Rs.450 crore steel plant. Recently Indira Vishnampet, The CEO and founder of Hydus, Inc. (Houston), a solutions provider in enterprise integration and enterprises data management has been rewarded as the Outstanding Woman Entrepreneur for the year 2007 for her professional achievements.

Mrs. Vibha Bahl, founder and Managing Director Fun Foods, India, who started her career in 1984 as businesswoman by taking homemade flavored yoghurt to Diwali Mela and they ended up selling like hot cakes. Now she has three factories and a range of 120 products to her credit. Betsy Fein, the president of Clutter buster, was once serving as human resource director, started with a shoestring budget has now flourished and is a recognised industry leader. Smt. Shanaz Hussain, Beauty Clinical Cosmetics, is the famous woman entrepreneur who won India's highest honor Padma Shree in the field of natural beauty and anti-ageing treatments. [5]

Other successful women entrepreneurs in India are Smt. Sumati Morarji—Shipping Corporation, Smt. Sharayu Daftary—Automobile Radiators, Smt. Yamutai Kirloskar—Mahila Udyog Limited, Smt. Vimal Pitre—Surgical Instruments, Smt. Manik Vandrekar—Leather Crafts, Smt.

Radanika Pradhan—Plastic Industries, Smt. Gogate—Drugs, Smt. Swati Bhatija—Engineering Industry, Smt. Prerang Thakore—Jayant Vitamins Limited, Smt. Nargis Wadia—Inter Publicity, Smt. Neena Malhotra—Exports, Smt. Rajani Aggarwal—Engineering, Smt. Wadia—Fabrics, Smt. Weheeda Rehman—Fast Foods and Smt. Kiran Mazumdar Shaw—Biocon Industries.

Surveys conducted demonstrate that women's primary entrepreneurial activity is focused on the small and medium enterprise (SME) sector. In 2003, approximately 60 per cent entrepreneurs are small-scale entrepreneurs, 15 per cent represent the large-scale manufacturers and the remainder comprise of cottage and micro entrepreneurs. They work in a wide range of sectors, from trade and services, to tailoring, beauty parlours, and printing. [6] However, the involvement of women entrepreneurs in the production sector is minimal and the development of this sector is rather slow. Though there is a steep rise in the number of women entrepreneurs in general in the last few years, there are very few in the field of engineering unlike in Information Technology. In India, home based work has increased from 35 per cent in 2000 to 51 per cent in 2005. To day, piece- rate home based workers are engaged even by international chairs of production in industries like garments, foot wear, electronics, plastic, foot balls and also in national or local markets in industries like bidi, agarbati and textiles, craft work like weaving and basket work, as also agri-processing are now being done on a sub contracted basis. [7]

Women setting up micro enterprises, SMEs, or formal large-scale businesses all encounter varying degrees of difficulty in obtaining capital, collateral, and fair lending terms. Women suffer because of ignorance of their legal rights, strong social resistahce in getting women their due share, lack of legal safeguards and absence of strong women's associations especially in rural areas which can protect their interests. Programmes for encouraging entrepreneurship among women are doomed to fail or at best to succeed partially when taken up in isolation.

In large cities where land prices have shot up, fledgling women entrepreneurs find it difficult to commute long distances to outlying areas, which are poorly connected. In most cases, enterprises defined as being run by women are controlled and managed by men. Women face constraints in training, availability of finance and other facilities like land, industrial plots and sheds etc. banks and money lenders are reluctant due to the risk involved in the business and the high operational costs. Women face marketing problems. As women are accepting a subordinate status, as a result they lack confidence of their own capabilities. Many have to face family antipathy and do not get adequate support from their family. Even at home, family members do not have much faith in women possessing the abilities of decision-making. [8] Bankers' pessimistic view of women's credit worthiness fosters a reluctance to grant credits. This constitutes another obstacle to female entrepreneurship. But women have proved to be better payers than their male counterparts in many countries, including Denmark, Sri Lanka, Bangladesh, Kenya and in rest of India. [9]

The participation of women in SSI sector has been identified in three different roles-as owners, as managers and as employees. The Government of India defined a woman enterprise as 'an SSI or a SSSBE managed by one or more women entrepreneurs in proprietary concerns, or in which she/ they individually or jointly have a share capital of not less than 51 per cent as partners/ share holders/ Directors of Private Limited Company/ Members of Co-operative Society'. The role of women entrepreneurs in the economic development can be analysed on the basis of their participation in industrial activities.

1.9 Concluding Observations

In India, women are relatively powerless with little or no

control over resources and little decision making power. However, Indian women play an important role in agricultural production, fishery, forestry/natural resources, artisan production, silk production and home based manufacturing, dairying, animal husbandry and other related activities such as storage, marketing of produce, food processing etc. Large number of female labour is engaged in the plantation sector also. According to the 1981 Census, about 54 per cent of rural women and 26 per cent of urban women are engaged in marginal occupations in order to supplement the family income by collection of fish, firewood, cow dung, maintenance of kitchen gardens, tailoring, weaving and teaching. According to the World Bank Report 1991, "Gender and poverty in India", prepared by the World Bank in collaboration with the Govt. of India, women contribute heavily to the Indian economy, forming1/3 of the total labour force in India, women head 1/3 of the rural families, and women's economic productivity is critical for the 60 million Indian households below poverty line.

Women in the informal sector are found to be home-based workers, engaged in the petty manufacture of goods, either on piece rate basis or on own account, petty traders and petty shopkeepers or service specialists. It is estimated that India is home to 92 million working women, though 90 per cent of them are working in the unorganised sector. The female Work Participation Rate (WPR) increased from 14.2 per cent in 1971 to 22.3 per cent in 1991. Women's share in the organised sector meanwhile, increased from 11 per cent in 1971 to 15.9 per cent in 1997. [10] The Female Work Participation Rate was 25.7 per cent in 2001. [11] However, the Economic Survey 2000-'01, Government of India observes that in National Income

Accounting "a significant part of the contribution of a larger section of society, especially, women, towards the economy remains unrecognised in quantitative terms or at best under-valued because of the restricted definition of economic activity in National Income Accounting. Only market-oriented activities are considered 'economic'. Their work is also characterised by a high degree of casualisation and is subject to seasonal variance in supply and demand. Lack of organisation and labour intensive nature of their work has also increased their invisibility and powerlessness. But the quantification of this activity, in terms of work-hours contributed, or its income-generating equivalent was not attempted or recorded. Their work is also characterised by a high degree of casualisation and is subject to seasonal variance in supply and demand. Lack of organisation and labour intensive nature of their work has also increased their invisibility and powerlessness.

Studies reveal that 89 per cent of India's women workers toil in the informal sectors in sub-human conditions. In urban areas, nearly 40 per cent of women workers are engaged in providing services, followed by 30 per cent in trade 15 per cent in manufacturing, 3 per cent in construction and 5 per cent in primary activities 57 per cent women work outside the home and 43 per cent with in the home. 60 per cent of those working outside homes are either mobile or operate from pavements without pucca structures at their work place which make them vulnerable to the vagaries of weather, spelling irregularity of work and income. Over 2/3 of the enterprises are self owned and have a fixed capital of less than Rs. 50. "Over 4/5 of the women workers in this sector earn less than Rs.500/-p.m. The income earned by women in this sector is said to be about ¼ of that of a woman in the organised sector." [12] In India, and in many other developing countries, self- employment and employment are the two major forms of work and of earning livelihood. The work of self-employed can be divided in to three categories:

- Home based workers who produce products such as beedis, garments, textiles, footwear, food products and handicrafts either on their own as artisans, or on a piece rate from a contractor or middleman.

- Small petty traders, vendors and hawkers who sell household goods or vegetables, fruits, eggs, fish and other food in market place or move with a head load or a pushcart from village to village or in the streets.
- The providers of services and manual labour engaged in agriculture, construction, transportation, cleaning, laundering, health, catering or domestic help.

Nearly 90 per cent of employment in India falls into these three categories which is described as informal sector. [13]

Women entrepreneurship in India represents a group of women who have broken away from the beaten track and are exploring new vistas of economic participation. Women in India entered business due to pull and push factors. Their task has been full of challenges. Some women became entrepreneurs due to the absence of income generating male in the family. In such families the women gave up their education and ambition for themselves and became the income generators for their families. The traditional women were mainly engaged in business like pickles, pappad, soap, garments, curry powder, incense sticks, soaps, washing powder, jam, fruit juices, squash, preparing dabbas and reaching them etc. which either do not require any formalised training or are developed from a hobby or an interest into a business.

Small business has been a leader in offering women the opportunity for economic expression through entrepreneurship. However, women in the North East enjoy a special status in the society because of their entrepreneurial desire and ability, hard working nature and matrilineal society in some areas of the region.   Moreover, women of the region enjoy a comparatively higher status in society because of the liberal social outlook of the region. They contribute significantly to the development of the society.

The emergence of women entrepreneurs and women-owned firms and their significant contributions to the economy are visible in India and these businesses are ready for continued growth in the future. Their participation in remunerative work in the formal and non-formal labour market has increased significantly in the past decade. As per 1981 census, out of the total number of self- employed persons, women account for only 5 per cent. The majority of self employed women were engaged in the unorganised sector like agriculture, handicrafts, handloom and cottage industries. During 1988-89 there were more than 1,53,000 women entrepreneurs claiming 9 per cent of the total 1.5 million entrepreneurs in India. Only 12 per cent of the total self employed women were in the organised sector. [14] There were more than 2,95,680 women entrepreneurs claiming 11.2 per cent of the total 2.64 million entrepreneurs in India during 1995-96. This is almost double the percentage of women (5.2 per cent) among the total population of self-employed during 1981.

The number of women entrepreneurs has increased especially during 1990's. Official statistics reveal that women constitute 60 per cent of the rural unemployed and 56 per cent of the total employed. A large number of highly educated women are house makers. Marriage is the only career for the most Indian women. Those who employed, confine their activities in the areas like teaching, office work, nursing etc. The number of men in autonomous start-up category is twice that of women, thrice in the category of entrepreneurs and four times in the category of women-managers. [15]

Traditionally, youth in India from business families have learnt the business techniques from the older generation. Most the Indian women entrepreneurs were either housewives or fresh graduates with little or no previous experience of running a business. Family run business in India is going through a stage of transition due to the effects of globalisation, privatisation, spatial mobility, social legislation and liberalisation. Women's income is becoming very necessary to households of all types in the wake of globalisation and changing economic structures. In recent years, there was a significant growth in industry and technology.

Nowadays, women are well-educated with technical and professional qualifications. Many of them have medical, management and similar degrees and diplomas. Many entered their family business as equal partners. Women set up their own clinics or nursing homes, small boutiques, small manufacturing enterprises and entered garment exports. They have their own personal choices and the courage to undertake new ventures. Women in rural areas are engaged in selling eco-friendly bags, dolls, soft toys, handicrafts, solapur chappals, sanitary material, plates and cups of areca leaves, decorative items, chocolates, ice-creams etc. In urban and semi urban areas they are engaged in selling designer saris, doing mirror work, furniture making, land scalping, tailoring and embroidery work, fashion designing, mobile laundries, screen printing, cyber cafe, driving schools, supplying household articles, beauty parlours, DTP, manufacture and export of food products, interior designing etc. Entrepreneurship in the animation industry is a new area where women entrepreneurs have greater scope for development. Women entrepreneurs manufacturing solar cookers in Gujarat, small foundries in Maharashtra and TV capacitors in Orissa have proved that women can excel men in any field if they are given the opportunities and thus the entrepreneurship of women is evident in endless ways. [16]

Notes

1. Sen Gupta Padmini, *Women in India*, Information Services of India, New Delhi, 1964, p. 5.

2. Planning Commission, Government of India, Seventh Plan-Five Year Plans, Sectoral Policies and Programmes, New Delhi, 1985-90.

3. P.V. Narasaiah and Ramakrishnaiah K., DWCRA Programme in Cuddapah District: An Evaluation- *SEDME*, 31-3 September, 2004, p. 43.

4. Malathi V Gopal, *Role Conflicts of Women Entrepreneurs*, Indian Institute of Management, NISIET, Government of

India,Hyderabad, 2005, p. 54.

5. www.shahnaz-husain.com

6. www. Justin.org

7. Renana Jhabvala, South Asian Policy Conference on Home Based Workers, *Vikasini,* Vol. No. 22, No.1, Jan-March, 2007, pp.13-14.

8. www.iimahd.ernet.in

9. vandana.shukla@timesgroup.com

10. Press Information Bureau, Government of India.,2000

11. Census of India, 2001, Chapter 18, Gender and development, Economic Review, 2001, p3.

12. Gender and Poverty in India, *World Bank Report,* 1991.

13. Ela Bhatt, Toward Empowerment, *World development,* Oxford, U.K, 1989, Vol.17, No.7, pp.1059-1989.

14. Women Entrepreneurship in India: Challenges and Achievements, Published by nisiet, An organisation of Ministry of SSI Government of India, Yousuf guda, Hyderabad 2005 p. 103.

15. Manimala Mathew, Srinivas Prakhya, J, Malathi V.Gopal, Joseph Shields, Global Entrepreneurship Monitor, Indian Institute of Management, Bangalore , 2001, p. 54.

16. Vasant Desai P, Entrepreneurial Development Volume-1, Himalaya Publishing House- Bombay, 1991, p. 103.

2

Women Entrepreneurship:
Studies in India and Abroad

There is a growing interest in entrepreneurship, particularly women entrepreneurship, the world over. A number of studies have been undertaken in other countries as well as in India to investigate the various aspects of women entrepreneurship. These studies clearly indicate that women entrepreneurship is indispensable for the overall development of the nation.

2.1 Studies Abroad

Several studies conducted in the West have highlighted the different aspects of women entrepreneurship. The core area covered by individual researchers and institutions includes: reasons for women entrepreneurship, characteristics and status of women entrepreneurs, scope of activities of women entrepreneurs, involvement of various agencies in the development of women entrepreneurship and problems of women entrepreneurs.

2.1.1 Reasons for Women Entrepreneurship: Schwartz (1979) [1] in an exploratory study of 20 female entrepreneurs found that their prime motivations for starting a business were the need to achieve, the desire to be independent, the need for job satisfaction, and economic necessity.

Sinfield (1981) [2] observed that with high levels of long-term unemployment in various 'female sectors' of the economy, proprietorship is becoming an important means of employment for many women.

Goffee and Scase (1983) [3] feel that those women who are economically marginalised because of the lack of opportunities for paid employment may have no option but to start their own businesses as a source of earnings.

Huntley (1985) [4] used a case study approach to explore the life events and experiences that had influenced women to choose entrepreneurship as a career alternative. Most ventured into entrepreneurship because of a desire to be independent and to be in control of their lives. They defined their own measurement of success, i.e. succumbing to social expectations and definitions. They were looking for a balance of personal and professional interests and admitted to career satisfaction which transcended other aspects of their lives.

Shane, Kolvereid and Westhead (1991) [5] observed that women were   driven by entrepreneurship more by the need for achievement than by monetary reasons.

Allen and Truman (1999) [6] pointed out that the alternative options in the mainstream labour market could be very limiting for women while entrepreneurship may be a positive escape route.

Shaver, Gartner and Gatewood (1995) [7] stated that 'Women decide to become entrepreneurs for such reasons as self-fulfillment and as a way to actualise personal goals that focus on family'.

Meanwhile, Morrison, White and Van Velsor (1987) [8] who had a different view about the reason for women entrepreneurship, observed that in the West, women were increasingly turning to entrepreneurship as a way of coping with the 'glass ceiling' that seems to prevent them from reaching top managerial positions in organisation.

2.1.2 Characteristics and Status of Women Entrepreneurs: Swatko (1981) [9] found that non-traditional females preferred enterprising vocations and aspired for occupations employing a greater percentage of males than traditional females. But, Peter Berger and Richard J. Neuhas (1978) [10] in their study 'The Role of Small Business' have stated that when the business women have been organised by voluntary organisations in such countries as India and the Philippines, they have developed leadership and other skills of great value to their families and their communities. In the search for social and economic equity it may well be these organised businesswomen who will be the impetus for change.

Aldrich and Sakano (1995) [11] in a study of five industrial nations in the late 1980s have found that men simply do not include women in their business advisory circles, only 10 per cent of the people mentioned by men as being relied upon for advice and assistance were women. Nearly 40 per cent of the advisor networks of women business owners were women. Thus, men were involved in mainly same–sex networks, dealing almost entirely with other men, whereas women were involved in mainly cross-sex networks, dealing mostly with men, but with a high proportion of women as well.

Alsos and Ljunggren (1998) and Ljunggren (1999) [12] have identified the following differences between men and women in connection with their initial deliberations on establishing a self-owned enterprise. In the survey, the persons were observed for 12 months up to the start of the enterprise. No significant differences were found between women's and men's activities when weighing the reasons for and against the establishment of an enterprise. Women were slightly more active in asking for loans from public sources. The total decision-making process from the time when the idea was conceived to the time when the project was started was almost the same for men and women. The women spent longer periods of time between each step and activity in the decision-taking. The women prepared a business plan and started marketing much later in the process than the men – but they applied for loans much earlier than the men. The women were less willing than the men to engage staff.

Aurora (formerly Busygirl) and Korn Ferry/Future Step conducted a research study on 'Vanishing talent: Risk, reward and recognition' (2002) [13] by taking a sample of 350 + UK executives to find out if more women than men were leaving corporate organisations for entrepreneurial ventures, and if so, what choices they were making about women's views on corporate life and entrepreneurial ventures. Across the findings, women heavily sought recognition, reward and re-invention. The research indicates that women enjoy calling the shots in business. Women who took the leap from corporate life to start a business venture say they are extremely satisfied. They found that 99 per cent of women entrepreneurs cite being able to fulfill their personal vision as extremely rewarding while for men it is a combination of time for family, recognition for accomplishments, taking risks without repercussions, and not needing to fit in. However 85 per cent men and 88 per cent women cite the 'lack of a benefits package' as a less satisfying aspect of leaving corporate life to start their own business. Other top reasons for both men and women entrepreneurs leaving corporate life are to take risk with new ideas and to test personal limits, and to have more strategic input into decisions. Men identify money as the second most popular reason to change jobs, along with opportunities for strategic input, whereas women rank it fifth, behind risk, recognition and spending more time with the family.

Palmer (1985) [14] found that most assistance (credit, technical assistance and training) has been directed to men, or male dominated activities where the income generating activities of women have been ignored, they have often been seen, implicitly or explicitly, as having only marginal importance.

MacDonald (1986) [15] conducted a study to compare the perceptions of successful women entrepreneurs with those of the less successful ones. Conclusions drawn were: net profit is a factor of success in the opinion of more successful women entrepreneurs and not in that of less successful ones, length of time in business is a prediction of success; both successful and less successful women entrepreneurs perceive the same traits and characteristics necessary for success; Having entrepreneurial parents does not influence the success of the women entrepreneurs.

Hisrich and Brush (1986) [16] stated that in order to get a full picture of the personality and motivations of the women entrepreneurs, a comparison of entrepreneurial characteristics with those of the typical woman executive is a must. The person making a career as a company executive usually has experience or expertise in her specific area, is conservative, cautious, logical and averse to risk; these attributes are necessary for performing the more "custodial" tasks required within an organisation, such as controlling cash, people or assets. In contrast, the woman entrepreneur is an individualist, creative, enthusiastic, instinctive and adaptable. She must deal with very real and immediate problems like meeting payroll, hiring and firing employees and pacifying creditors often in the face of little cash, instability and few assets. An entrepreneur is not a cog in the wheel and cannot take the time to make lengthy studies or spend weeks seeking advice before making a decision. Her concern is for growth and creating assets. The rewards can be great both financially and psychologically, but the drawbacks can mean sacrifices personally, emotionally and financially. A high energy level is essential for the women entrepreneurs' need to inspire and motivate her employees. This calls for self-confidence, flexibility, persistence, independence and determination to succeed etc.

Sextan and Kent (1981) [17] reported the results of a study comparing the characteristics of female entrepreneurs and executives. The study was conducted on 45 female executives and 48 female entrepreneurs. The results show that female entrepreneurs are marginally less educated than female executives; though the younger female entrepreneurs are better educated, they tend to place slightly higher emphasis on their job than their family. The executives view their ability to work with people as the greatest factor of success, while the entrepreneurs tend to view hard work and persistence as more important. Entrepreneurs tend to follow their fathers who are engaged in business, although they do not acknowledge their fathers as role models. In contrast executives do not follow in their fathers' footsteps. Executives tend to be older and have demonstrated more job stability than female entrepreneurs and executives tend to be more similar than dissimilar.

Hisrich and O'Brien (1982) [18] studied how the characteristics of women entrepreneurs varied according to the type of business. Female entrepreneurs in the non-traditional business areas (finance, insurance, manufacturing and construction) differed from their counterparts in more traditionally female business areas (retail and wholesale trade). The latter group had particular difficulty in gaining access to external financial sources - from banks, informal investors or venture capitalists.

Hisrich and Brush (1986) [19] made a comparison of the motivations, business skills, occupational backgrounds and personality traits of male and female entrepreneurs from research evidence and data. They found that in some respects, women entrepreneurs possess very different motivations, business skill levels and occupational backgrounds which are very different from their male counterparts. The start-up process of a business for women entrepreneurs is also different from that of males, especially in terms of support systems, sources of funds and problems. Men are often motivated by the drive to control their own destinies to make things happen. In contrast, women tend to be motivated by a need for independence and achievement that results from the frustration they feel at not being allowed to perform in the job at the level they are capable of. Both men and women entrepreneurs feel that their best solution to these problems is to venture out alone.

The typical woman entrepreneur resembles her male counterpart in most personality characteristics like being highly energetic, independent, competitive, self confident, perfectionist, flexible, very goal-directed and generalist. However, women entrepreneurs see themselves as only moderately social which probably reflects the view that overly social behaviour can be detrimental to a woman's business image. Sociable woman is often considered less serious about her business, whereas the sociable man is often considered just good. Women entrepreneurs also see themselves as far less anxious than their male counterparts, probably because, unlike their male counterparts, they are not the sole support of the family, and have both emotional and financial support from the spouse. Men, however, have been found to be more confident and less flexible and tolerant than women, which could result in different management styles.

Brydon and Chant (1989) [20] observed that overall status, bargaining position and income of women who are wage earners, self-employed traders, artisans or farmers are higher than those of women who are confined to domestic or subsistence activities. But even when women bear the costs and risks of setting up an enterprise, they may not control the benefits. Thus, it is not enough to increase the capacity of women to generate income; they must also be able to control their returns and protect their sources of income and assets.

Sundin and Holmquist (1988), Carter and Allen (1997) [21] have described the features of enterprises established by women. It is stated that in women-owned enterprises the management style is more feminine, participative and open in the internal communication, and with less hierarchy than in traditional enterprises. Women-owned enterprises are highly structured, built up formally, and planning oriented. It is also found that women-owned enterprises have other types of goals –including success goals- quite different from male-owned enterprises.

Epstein Scarrlett (1990) [22] stated that female petty–entrepreneurs are reported by Metraux for the Meribal Valley, Haiti, where there are a large number of young girls or women who set up their stand along roads or paths, in a hut or at the foot of a tree, to sell thread, matches, candies, fruits, vegetable cereals, spices and tobacco.

Williamson (1986) [23] conducted an in-depth study of Joyce Eddy, a successful female entrepreneur, with the purpose of gathering biological material of a successful female entrepreneur to provide a role model for existing and would be female entrepreneurs. It is found that Joyce was successful despite her shortcomings and in regard to personal characteristics and requirement often equaled entrepreneurial success. The study concluded that there is no formula for entrepreneurial success. But, Taylor (1988) [24] in his study found that self-confidence and a drive for autonomy are the major part of the make-up of an entrepreneur. The drive for autonomy seems to be the common characteristic of all successful entrepreneurs, including women.

Marlow (1997) [25] demonstrates that as a consequence of their background, Scandinavian women set up business in the service sector with little use of advanced technology, with relatively small preliminary expenses, relatively low prospects of income, and lower growth potential.

BT/Aurora women entrepreneurs and ICT research (2004) [26] conducted an online survey researching their knowledge, usage and attitudes towards computers and technology over 2,000 women entrepreneurs. They found that female entrepreneurs are a tech savvy bunch. 66 per cent own a portable data device, 99 per cent know exactly what broadband is and what it can bring to their businesses. 28 per cent of women in business use friends, family and other women for their technology and telecom advice. 17 per cent women business owners use consultants, 17 per cent use the Internet, and 8 per cent use Business Link. 87 per cent of women surveyed said broadband would be vital to their business growth.

Tripp (1992) [27] made a study in the United Republic of Tanzania about self-employment amongst women. It is revealed that there has been a tremendous increase in self-employment amongst women. The upper and middle income groups of women working in this sector were earning up to ten times the amount that lower income women were able to earn.

Centre for Women's Business (2000) [28] in a study pointed out that in Washington DC women-owned firms established within the past decade are making substantial contributions to the economy and are poised for continued growth in the future. They have reached the same level of business achievement as women-owned firms started in the past, and are more likely to be oriented toward future growth than their predecessors. Thirty-eight per cent of women business owners who have started their firms within the past decade have already achieved at least US$ 5,00,000 in annual revenues.

According to Nina McLemore, (2000) [29] Chair of the Center for Women's Business Research and President of Regent Capital, 'The new generation of women entrepreneurs appears to be narrowing the business revenue gap; it appears that among business started within the past decade, there is no significant gender difference in the share of firms with $500000 or more in revenues. Women-owned businesses established in the last decade are making significant economic contributions, at the same overall level as their predecessors.'

Sharon Hadary (2004) [30] gathered through the Center's extensive research initiatives almost three-quarters of those who expanded their business achieved or exceeded their goals. Women-owned business with US$ 1 million or more in revenues is more likely than smaller business owned by women to have large corporations and Government as their customers. Women-owned businesses are just as financially strong and creditworthy as the average US firm, with similar performance on bill payment and similar levels of credit risk, and are just as likely to remain in business.

2.1.3. Scope of Activities of Women Entrepreneurs: Hirata and Humphrey (1990) [31] have found in their study that older married men with children tend to resist entering informal sector occupations and continue to aspire to formal sector jobs. This might be in quite separate spheres of women where there is no possibility of direct competition with them. Again, Jockes, (1991) [32] observed that over 80 per cent of self-employed women are in agriculture and sales, compared to only 50 per cent of men, with them engaging a range of other informal sector activities.

In the meantime, ILO Report (1994) [33] pointed out that in Asia, women commonly dominate in hawking and trading activities. More recently, there has been an increase in their involvement in micro and small scale production activities and home-based activities, as self-employed or piece rate workers.

2.1.4. Involvement of Government Agencies and Financial Institutions: Van der and Romijn (1987) [34] made a study on small enterprises run by women. They found that business association and service agencies set up for supporting small enterprises also limit women access to their services.

Lycklama A. Nijeholt (1987) [35] in a study 'The fallacy of integration: The UN strategy of integrating women into development revisted', states that programmes have nevertheless declared themselves in favour of integrating women into overall development. She points to a misperception, since women are in fact integrated in society, though not always into development programmes. The failure lies with the programmes, not with the women.

Hilhorst Harry Oppenoorth (1992) [36] conducted an exploratory study on 'Financing women's enterprises-Beyond barriers and bias'. The epilogue highlights the need for more information on the effectiveness of financial interventions for poor women. It is emphasised that for any economic gains, financial interventions have to be selected according to the potential of women for making improvements in their position with respect to decision-making. Financial intervention in household based production is to be preceded by location, specific analysis, and taking gender into account. It is also stated that women must be able to control their returns and protect their sources of income. It is suggested that persons who design and implement the programmes that make credit available to women, should also be aware of effects on women's status and visibility and specifically the influence on the extent of their decision making role. A flexible approach is to be exercised in the administration of credit for women.

Haan (1994) [37] stated that in Africa and Asia, the community based training approach of the ILKO for self-employment and income-generation provide them with new skills of particular usefulness in secondary activities to supplement the household income. It increased their income, level of nutrition and involvement in community affairs among women.

Mayoux (1998) [38] in her research paper 'Women's Empowerment and Micro Finance Programmes: Approaches, Evidence and Ways, Forward' states that Micro Finance schemes have improved the perception of women's contribution to household income and family welfare and increased women's participation in decision making in the household, resulting in overall improvement in attitudes towards women in the household community.

2.1.5 Problems of Women Entrepreneurship: Schwartz (1979) [39] in an exploratory study of 20 female entrepreneurs found that the major problem encountered during start-up was credit discrimination and the subsequent problem was underestimating operating and/or marketing costs.

Hisrich and Brush (1984) [40] conducted a nationwide in-depth survey of 468 women entrepreneurs. They found that the biggest business start-up problems of the 'typical' woman entrepreneur were finance, credit and lack of business training. Her greatest operational problem was lack of financial planning experience.

Buvinic and Berger (1990) [41] in their study stated that to restrict financial support to manufacturing means imposing an additional barrier to the economic participation of women, given their predominance in trading activities.

Tovo (1991) [42] observes that self-employed women face

several problems common to all small-scale entrepreneurs, which include limited access to capital, inputs and markets. Often a large number of small enterprises share one market segment, causing competition to be fierce and prices to be low. The products of small enterprises can be extremely dependable on a limited number of suppliers and wholesalers. This renders the entrepreneur economically vulnerable and often exposes her/him to exploitation.

Berik (1987) [43] in his study states that the tasks and influence of women who work in family-based enterprises are determined by local customs including gender roles, their age groups, position in their family, which includes specification of their bargaining power. Their participation in decision-making is often weak and their work is undervalued, even though women contribute significantly to the household income. He also states that working in family based-enterprises could limit the time available to women for more profitable self-employment.

Van der and Romijn (1987) [44] made a study on small enterprises run by women. They found that business headed by women is consistently worse off than others. Women generally have fewer resources than men, and are impeded by lower levels of education and literacy, and by restricted physical and occupational mobility. They have limited access to profitable activities, and their skills are often common to large numbers of other women, so that work in these areas is generally competitive, oversubscribed and poorly paid. Women have little contacts and less bureaucratic know-how and bargaining power than men, which limits their productivities and profitability.

Neider (1987) [45] conducted a study on female entrepreneurs in Florida. The study revealed that tension between personal life and career was a major problem for these women. Husbands were generally not much involved in their wives' businesses and were not supportive of them.

Bequele and Boyden (1988) [46] state that the dynamics

and continuity of women's enterprises are often influenced by household composition and the life-cycle, which in turn determine labour availability, financial and kinship obligations and household needs. The presence of child labour, for example, is crucial in terms of the potential to increase household income.

Brush   (1992), Cromie and Hayes (1988) [47] observe that women entrepreneurs' ambitions as regards their enterprise and their job are affected by their family responsibilities.

McKee (1989) [48] indicates that poor women prefer to expand only to the limits of their own labour and management capabilities on the assumption that their basic consumption needs have already been met.

Holt and Ribe (1990) [49] reveal that enterprises run by women tend to be small even by the standards of the informal sector. They are usually run on a part time basis to allow women to attend to their other obligations. Generally extra labour is not contracted, although the enterprise may depend heavily on the unpaid labour of children.

Gianotten et al. (1990) [50] cite   examples where men have reacted with violence to changes in women's economic status, as when women sought to reduce their unpaid obligations to men in favour of their own work. Husbands may start to obstruct their partners enterprise if the earnings become greater than their own.

Downing (1991) [51] observes that expansion of enterprise increases the risk. It is only possible to take risk where there is a secure source of income, such as from wage employment, ensuring that the basic consumption needs can be met.

Stolen (1991) [52] points out that when the man's contribution to the household decreases, women need assistance to ensure that their husbands become more 'integrated' into household production and family life. A reduction in the man's contribution not only restricts the capacity of the woman to save and invest in her enterprise but also leaves her with the sole responsibility of maintaining her dependents.

Brush (1992) [53] observes that woman's domestic responsibilities and limited mobility chances at work, together with other institutional factors such as sexism and patterns of childhood and socialisation combine to produce a different way of approaching business ownership.

Hisrich and Brush (1994) [54] point out that women also bear most of the responsibility for childcare and home management and these responsibilities often lead to work-family conflicts. This, combined with problems arising from lack of prior employment and managerial experience faced by many women, may result in differences between male and female entrepreneurs in terms of market entry choices, start-up problems and other issues.

White (1991) [55] in his study states that in West Java, if women's enterprises grow in scale and capitalisation, quite commonly husbands, who previously played only a minor, if any, role in the enterprise, impose themselves as managers, the women being relegated to the status of unpaid family member.

Lyberaki and Smyth (1990) [56] observes that many women entrepreneurs decide not to expand their enterprises so as to avoid visibility and various regulations, taxes, etc. In large enterprises, division of labour is more complex and management skill is more crucial. Work also becomes more demanding and less compatible with women's other activities and obligations and may have to be legally registered. Women want to avoid all these problems.

Tinker, cited by Downing (1991) [57] points out that most female entrepreneurs appear to select a lateral growth pattern, increasing the number, rather than the size, of the enterprises in which they are engaged. But, Tinker, (1995) [58] in a study 'Women in micro-and small-scale development' points out that credit is not the only barrier to entering business. The literature indicates that feminist or anti-feminist perspectives, management skills, understanding organisational structures and training/re-training issues are hurdles as well.

Khondkar (1998) [59] conducted a study in Bangladesh about women's access to credit. It is stated that women run the risk of losing control of the loans to male relatives because they are culturally excluded from participating in markets outside their homes to buy inputs and to sell outputs.

Ljunggren (1999) [60] feels that women encounter barriers in the initial phase – and perhaps they are more uncertain about the viability of the project. There may also be fewer women than men who actually want to start their own businesses.

Richard Kibombo and Samuel K. Kayabwe (2000) [61] who conducted a detailed study on economic empowerment of women through the use of Information and Communication Technologies (ICTs) reveal that there is an overall poor usage of ICTs by women entrepreneurs as a means of communication with the exception of telephone services. They mostly rely on the local network of fellow entrepreneurs to receive information relating to their businesses. It is found that there is the poor usage of ICTs for enterprise development purposes. Entrepreneurs need information regarding credit facilities and as how to improve products/services in order to improve their business.

Bruce (1989) [62] observes that lack of capital is not the only factor that may impede the growth of women enterprises. Women are more likely to work in low return sectors than men, so their profits are lower; women often spend a relatively high proportion of their profit on household needs and generally have less access than men to use of household funds for investments.

Aldrich et al. (1989) [63] found significant differences in the sex composition of networks for men and women entrepreneurs in the USA and Italy. They observe that structural constraints found in the work place, in marriage and family roles and in organised social life restricted the social networks of women business owners. Women owned businesses are typically much smaller and limited to a particular sector of the economy, viz. Retail and Services, as well as the lower status position of the job market. Essentially, women appear to be left out of the informal, strong tie networks that provide men entrepreneurs with access to the resources and support needed for the success and survival. Women entrepreneurs are thus left with challenge of meeting their own needs through formal, weak tie-channels.

Moser (1992:97) [64] finds that women in Guayaquil are mainly engaged in selling, dressmaking and personal services, whereas men are engaged in selling, tailoring, carpentry, personal services and mechanics.

Sexton and Bowman-Upton (1990) [65] made an in-depth study of the possible disadvantages of women entrepreneurs. Their findings indicate that men and women business owners differ on only two of nine psychological traits relevant to entrepreneurship. Women entrepreneurs scored lower on risk taking and endurance (energy level).

2.2 Studies in India

Considering the importance of the discipline, quite a large number of studies covering different aspects of women entrepreneurship have been undertaken by individual researchers and institutions in India.

2.2.1. Reasons for Women Entrepreneurship: Beena and Sushma (2003) [66] conducted a study on 'Women Entrepreneurs Managing Petty Business: A Study from the Motivational Perspective'. The study reveals that the reasons for starting their enterprises are monetary returns and need to support family. Krishnaveni Motha (2004) [67] in a study on women entrepreneurship in rural areas of India also observed that the majority of women entered the entrepreneurial field to supplement family income and due to other reasons such as economic necessity, non- availability of government jobs, etc.

Mohiuddin Asghari (1983) [68] conducted a study on

'Entrepreneurship Development Among Women'. The study observed that women became entrepreneurs due to the following reasons: (i) economic needs, (ii) as a challenge to satisfy some of their personality needs (power, achievement, novel experience, etc.), (iii) educated women like to utilise their knowledge gained, (iv) family occupation and (v) as a leisure time activity.

Shah and Hina (1987) [69] analysed the application forms of 300 women who undertook entrepreneurship development programme and 60 women trainees who later became entrepreneurs to find out their motivations for becoming an entrepreneur. Among the motives to become an entrepreneur are economic needs, utilisation of own experience and education, the support and interests of the husband and family, availability of free time and finance, desire to be independent, personal ego and satisfaction of doing something on one's own.

Singh and Senguptha (1985) [70] conducted a study on 45 women who were attending the entrepreneurial development programme held in November-December 1983 to identify the factors that prompted women to start their own business. The study observed that more educationally qualified women perceived entrepreneurship as a challenge, ambition fulfillment and for doing something fruitful, whereas those less educationally qualified perceived entrepreneurship as a tool for earning quick money.

Seenivasagalu (2001) [71] conducted a comparative study on 'Women Entrepreneurs and Executives' in Chennai city. It is revealed that women entrepreneurs are mainly motivated by 'education and previous experience'. It is recommended that promotion of women entrepreneurship is a better solution for unemployment and involvement of women in economic activities.

Singh, Sehgal, Tinani and Senguptha (1986) [72] in an exploratory study of successful women entrepreneurs examined their motivations. The study reveals that the five dominant motivating factors rank-wise for women entrepreneurs venturing into entrepreneurship are to keep busy (rank 1), to fulfill ambition (rank 2), to pursue one's own interest (rank 3), by accident or circumstances beyond control (rank 4) and to earn money (rank 5) .

Paramjeet Dhillon (1993) [73] conducted a detailed study on 'Motives and characteristics of successful women entrepreneurs' by selecting a sample of 40 women entrepreneurs who got assistance from the SISI, Okhla and AEPC and Nehru Place. It was found that women entrepreneurs had varied motives for establishing an enterprise. The most important motives were 'fulfillment of ambition and pursuit of own interest'.

Lokeswara Choudary (1999) [74] carried out a study on women entrepreneurs of Vikram Sarabhai Industrial Estate in Chennai city. It is revealed that the factors which motivated the entrepreneurs to undertake business are: (i) previous experience, (ii) to work independently, (iii) to supplement family income and (iv) to get economic independence. But, an exploratory study on women entrepreneurs of Hyderabad and Secunderabad cities conducted by Aravinda and Renuka (2001) [75] revealed that the most common motivational factors influencing the women entrepreneurship were: (i) self-interest in that specific area of enterprise, (ii) inspiration from other success or achievement, (iii) self-respect, (iv) advice of family members and (v) economic necessity. The facilitating factors in the maintenance of the enterprise were: (i) self-interest, (ii) experience, (iii) family-help and (iv) support.

Sumi Guha (1999) [76] in a study 'Entrepreneurship and empowerment of women' examined the economic and social background of women entrepreneurs. The study revealed that the main reason behind the inclination of women towards self-employment is the lack of job opportunity and increasing cost of living.

Nirmala Karuna D'Cruz (2003) [77] conducted a study titled 'Constraints on Women Entrepreneurship Development in Kerala: An Analysis of Familial, Social, and Psychological Dimensions'. The study reveals that it is not the aspiration of women that has made them entrepreneurs; they have taken up this career in the absence of any other means of contributing to family income. Again, most of them started business only after all their attempts to secure a regular, secure and salaried job failed.

ESCAP study (1991) [78] on occupation pointed out that geographical relocation of industries from developed to developing countries in recent years has been a prime factor in facilitating the increased participation of women, as gathered from the UN report.

2.2.2 Characteristics of Women Entrepreneurs: Singh and Senguptha (1985) [79] conducted a study on 45 women who were attending the entrepreneurial development programme held in November-December 1983 to determine the characteristics of women who were at the threshold of starting their businesses. The conclusions drawn from the study were majority of the potential entrepreneurs had clarity about their projects, but needed moral support from male and other family members for setting up their enterprises. Women entrepreneurs preferred to combine their need for excellence with emotional dependency. They had inner uncertainty of their own capabilities and needed male support to pave their way either with money, business know-how or moral support.

Jayasree (1997) [80] studied the entrepreneur's access to household resources in Madras and Pondicherry by selecting a sample of 140 women entrepreneurs. She found that the major and foremost source of finance mobilisation was from family and personal saving only. Members of the family played greater roles in decision making, starting and checking the work routine and financial management.

Krishnaveni Motha (2004) [81] in a study about women entrepreneurship in rural areas of India observed that many women themselves were running the enterprises effectively and belonged to low socio- economic groups. The study also revealed that women entrepreneurs who received family support could manage the enterprise more effectively.

Shah and Hina (1987) [82] in their study on women entrepreneurship observed that the distinctive feature of women entrepreneurs is need for achievement, self-sufficiency in terms of internal and external resources awareness, initiative taking, problem solving and risk taking.

Anna (1989) [83] in an exploratory study on women entrepreneurship in industrial manufacturing sector of Kerala states that no single community group is engaged in all the different trade lines. But Christian women have proved to be more enterprising. More than 50 per cent of women entrepreneurs of the sample group are housewives. The older the units, the lower the educational level of entrepreneurs and most of them are from semi-urban areas and belong to the middle class. It is also found that most of the units were tiny in terms of capital investment, labour employed and the sales turnover.

Dharmaja, Bhatia and Saini (1999) [84] in their article 'Women Entrepreneurs - Perceptions, Attitudes and Opinions' pointed out that the majority of women entrepreneurs started their business units in the age span of 26 to 35 years, which indicates that this age group is most suitable for venturing into self-employment. The majority of women had no previous experience in business. Most of them had good educational background and had no income before the establishment of the enterprise, but belonged to urban background. They feel that women belonging to non-business family background are also not lagging behind. Women possess in good measure the qualities of endurance and sustained efforts to nurture their enterprise. A majority of the women had set up manufacturing units. There was a lack of information and knowledge regarding various schemes of the Government for women entrepreneurs.

Radhika Sachdev (1999) [85] in her article stated that a typical profile of a woman owned enterprise is low-risk venture, less employment generation, low-capital investment, operations restricted to a saturated market and product selection and extension of a domestic activity.

Seenivasagalu (2001) [86] conducted a comparative study on 'Women Entrepreneurs and Executives' in Chennai city. The conclusions drawn from the study were: the majority of women units are registered manufacturing units which are sole proprietorship firms, less than 3 years old. The majority of the women entrepreneurs are doing business in rented buildings and very few supply their products to Government departments. Women entrepreneurs face medium and sometimes high competition and have achieved normal increase in capital investments, sales turnover and net profit over the establishment year. It is revealed that women executives are educationally and economically better off than women entrepreneurs, whereas women entrepreneurs are participating more in socio-cultural activities.

Mathialagan (2002) [87] conducted a socio-economic study on women entrepreneurs of Chennai city. He stated that socio-demographic and economic variables play a significant role in shifting the women folk into a new stream of life. Women entrepreneurs prefer service sector. Of all the communities, backward class tops the first list.

Small Industries Extension Training Institute, Hyderabad (1974) [88] in a study cited that younger age, formal education, urban background, experience in industry, high level of aspiration, taking and adoption of inclination were some of the characteristics that were positively associated with the quality of entrepreneurship.

Nagendra P. Singh and Rita Sen Gupta (1985) [89] conducted an exploratory study on 'Potential Women Entrepreneurs, Their Profile, Vision and Motivation'. It is revealed that women are as effective as men in business and industry.

Paramjeet Dhillon (1993) [90] conducted a detailed study on 'Motives and characteristics of successful women entrepreneurs' by selecting a sample of 40 women entrepreneurs to get assistance from the SISI, Okhla and AEPC, Nehru Place. It was found that the most important factor for the success of the entrepreneur is 'commitment to work'. The women entrepreneurs are willing to take high personal risks, but moderate risk in delegation of authority and responsibilities to employees and they have a high need for achievement, independence, orientation, ability for decision making, future planning and good time-management in a better manner than in male-dominated manufacturing industries. The competition between men and women in male-oriented entrepreneurial activities is on unequal terms, rendering success for women difficult.

Lokeswara Choudary (1999) [91] carried out a study on women entrepreneurs of Vikram Sarabhai Industrial Estate in Chennai city. It is found that hardwork, achievement, motivation, self-confidence, etc. played a major role in keeping the entrepreneurial job successful.

Saraswathi Amma and Sudarsanan Pillai (2000) [92] in a study on women entrepreneurs in garment industries in Kerala pointed out that all successful women entrepreneurs had strong family support and enjoyed personal freedom and majority of the women were concentrated in urban areas. They emphasised the need for EDP for helping women in non-traditional, high-skill and male-dominated activities.

Mathialagan (2002) [93] conducted a socio-economic study on women entrepreneurs of Chennai city. Risk taking, innovation, self-confidence and achievement motivation are considered as the more vital attributes for the success in entrepreneurship.

Chittawadagi (2004) [94] in his study 'women entrepreneurship in cooperative banking sector' observed that women entrepreneurs with professional competence and leadership qualities are able to mobilise deposits and invest the same profitably.

2.2.3. Scope of Activities of Women Entrepreneurs:

Anil Kumar (2004) [95] made a study about enterprise location: choice of women entrepreneurs by selecting a sample of 120 women entrepreneurs in Haryana state, India. It was found that most of the women entrepreneurs wanted to operate their businesses 'near the homes' followed by 'near the market'.

Choudhury, Shashi Baijal and Asokan (1997) [96] in a study on 'Banks and Women's Enterprise Development-A Comparison of Approaches in India and U.K.' found that women entrepreneurs preferred service and retail trading activities.

Savitri Ramamurthy (1988) [97] in a pilot study on women entrepreneurs in Delhi pointed out that 40 per cent of them had ventured into non-traditional areas such as engineering, consultancy, chemicals, circuit-breakers, amplifiers, transformers, microphones, etc.

Kerala Women's Commission (2002) [98] conducted a study on 'Status of Women in Kerala'. It was noted that women entrepreneurs have started owning IT centers and electronic items manufacturing units/firms, printing press, hollow bricks production units, etc in recent times. It is stated that women entrepreneurs have started shifting to modern lines of activities/enterprises.

Beena and Sushma (2003) [99] made a study on 'women entrepreneurs managing petty business: A study from the motivational perspective' by taking a sample of 30 women entrepreneurs of Andhra Pradesh. They found that women entrepreneurs were engaged in activities like selling vegetables, leafy vegetables, flowers etc. perhaps due to the following reasons: agricultural activities are predominant in our country, these women have migrated from villages where they were involved in farming, familiarity of the products and their potential making them opt for this business. Selling fruits, flowers and vegetables requires minimum technical skill, but requires high lungpower. Laundry, selling snacks and tea are skill based and are determined by caste and tradition.

2.2.4. Involvement of Government Agencies and Financial Institutions: Some studies stressed the need for effective implementation of development policies by the Government agencies.

Narasaiah and Ramakrishnaiah (2000) [100] made an evaluation of DWCRA programme in Cuddapah district by selecting a sample of 9 DWCRA groups in Rayachoty. They found that the DWCRA members were confronted with many serious problems in the areas of production, finance and marketing. The entrepreneurial development programmes to enhance the entrepreneurial skills were not properly implemented and no concrete efforts were made to identify suitable and viable training programmes for women entrepreneur development.

Seenivasagalu (2001) [101] conducted a comparative study on 'Women Entrepreneurs and Executives' in Chennai city. It was found that lack of awareness, inadequate Government assistance and lack of favourable women entrepreneurship environment were the causes for poor responses in the case of women becoming entrepreneurs.

Sulochana A. Nadkarni (1981) [102] conducted a study on 'Women, Entrepreneurship and Economic Development' in Pune city. She found that the development plans and supportive services had generally overlooked the need to devise plans to help women to overcome constraints and difficulties.

Aruna Prasad, Shashi Raja Gopal, Tara Appachoo and Narayan Prasad (1984) [103] in their research paper 'A Review of the Economic Schemes for the Development of Women in the Past Decade with Special Reference to Karnataka State' highlighted some of the aspects relating to the various schemes introduced specially for women. They found that the utilisation of both the economic schemes and the welfare schemes by the women is rather poor because of lack of awareness. They suggested that schemes for the economic development of women could really achieve their target only when there is efficient implementation, periodical evaluation and follow-up and there should be readiness to introduce changes in them according to the expressed needs of the beneficiaries.

The first national conference of women entrepreneurs held at New Delhi in November 1987 [104] emphasised the need for developing women entrepreneurs and for priority to women in the allotment of land, factory sheds, sanction of power, licensing, etc. which in turn facilitate the overall development of the country.

Shanta Kohli (1991) [105] has found that there is a presumption that government must analyse the current status and the potential role of women in the process of industrialisation with a view to bringing a positive change, which would result in sharing responsibilities and benefits by either sex. It is emphasised that adequate legislation for social facilities, health provisions, maternity and social security benefits would enhance women's involvement in the development process of the country.

Tara S. Nair (1996) [106] in her study 'Entrepreneurship Training for Women in the Industrial Rural Sector: A Review of Approaches and Strategies' made an attempt to review the strategies and approaches followed in the country over the past four decades. It is revealed that development strategies targeted at women cannot hence be fitted coercively in to conventional, one-dimensional and deterministic moulds like the anti-poverty paradigm that a typical state-sponsored sectoral programme cannot take care of such a synergistic approach. It is emphasised that the 'over aggregative' and 'misleading' categories of income and class are to be rejected and the importance of gender as crucial parameter not only in analytical exercises, but also in policies and programmes is to be recognised.

Saraswathy Amma and Sudarsanan Pillai (1998) [107] in a study/observed that many schemes and programmes are now available to attract women as prospective entrepreneurs sponsored by governmental and non-governmental agencies. They made proposals and suggestions to incorporate the effect of the advances in technology and changes in economic policies of the Government in entrepreneurship development programmes.

Dharmaja, Bhatia and Saini (1999) [108] in their article 'Women Entrepreneurs - Their perceptions about business opportunities and attitudes towards entrepreneurial support agencies (A study of Haryana State)' stressed that there was a lack of information and knowledge regarding various schemes of assistance launched by the Government of India.

Anjaneya Swamy and Deepak Raajan (2003) [109] in their working paper on women entrepreneurs point out that a multi-pronged approach needs to be adopted to motivate the women to pursue entrepreneurial activities.

Sosamma (1999) [110] Secretary, Small Industries Department, Chennai, pointed out that the Government was keen on the development of women entrepreneurs and a variety of schemes were available to them for setting up an industrial venture. Besides concentrating on setting up 'Traditional Units', typically meant for them, women should go in for other areas too.

Kerala Women's Commission (2002) [111] conducted a study on the 'Status of Women in Kerala'. In this study the status of women in development programmes in Kerala was also analysed by taking a sample of 412 different entrepreneurial development units of Kannur district. It is revealed that the encouragement of officials in the case of Government programmes and the encouragement from the responsible field staff of NGOs programmes were the most influential factor that prompted the idea of starting the enterprises by women.

Choudhury, Shashi Baijal and Asokan (1997) [112] in a study on 'Banks and Women's Enterprise Development-A Comparison of Approaches in India and the U.K.' found that in both India and the U.K, commercial banks continue to be the major source of finance for small firms. In India, compared with the U.K., the share of women entrepreneurs is not significant despite various women-specific schemes and incentives. In the U.K. clearing banks do not have women specific schemes/incentives. But in India, banks have 'women wings' to cater exclusively to the needs of women entrepreneurs.

Chittawadagi (2004) [113] in his study 'Women Entrepreneurship in Cooperative Banking Sector' observed that the bank is playing a vital role in the integration of women for their economic emancipation and for developing women entrepreneurship.

2.2.5 Problems of Women Entrepreneurship: Lokeswara Choudary (1999) [114] carried out a study on women entrepreneurs of Vikram Sarabhai Industrial Estate in Chennai city. The study observed that most of them had the following constraints, viz. lack of proper training, experience, lack of encouragement from the society, inadequate Government assistance, more competition, inadequate knowledge and experience in management of various factors.

Singh, Sehgal, Tinani and Senguptha (1986) [115] in an exploratory study on successful women entrepreneurs examined the types of problems encountered by them to reach the level of success and to identify the operational problems they are currently facing. 18.7 per cent women entrepreneurs perceived no operational problems, whereas 81.3 per cent indicated problems of varied nature, like managing works (23 per cent) marketing (20.5 per cent) recovery of dues (17.9 per cent), financial (10.2 per cent) and mobility (13 per cent) etc. Only 44 per cent felt that women had to fight harder in the entrepreneurial world to succeed. Only 35 per cent experienced role conflict, as these women had children between 10 and 15 years and were not able to fulfill their role as a mother.

Surti and Sarupriya (1983) [116] investigated the psychological factors affecting women entrepreneurs. They examined the role of stress experienced by women entrepreneurs, the effect of demographic variables, such as marital status and type of family on stress and how women entrepreneurs cope with stress. Results indicated that unmarried subjects experienced less stress and less self-role distance than married subjects. Subjects from joint families tended to experience less role o stress than subjects from nuclear families, probably because they share their problems with other family members. External locus of control was significantly related to role stress and fear of success was related to result inadequacy and role inadequacy dimensions of stress. While many subjects used intra persistent coping styles that is, taking action to solve problems, avoidance oriented coping styles were more common than approach oriented styles of coping.

Gupta and Srinivasan (1992) [117] pointed out that the failure of many women co-operatives in 1971 engaged in basket making is an example of how the scarcity of raw materials sounds the death-knell of enterprises run by women.

Nirmala Karuna D'Cruz (2003) [118] conducted a study on the 'Constraints on Women Entrepreneurship Development in Kerala: An Analysis of Familial, Social and Psychological Dimensions'. The study reveals that the biggest problem was reportedly in areas of procurement of raw materials and canvassing of orders. Staying away from home for long hours, particularly late in the evening, attending meetings, meeting and discussing with government officials and taking care of family problems alongside all these responsibilities were reported to be a serious burden along with lack of facilities and time to attend to their familial roles, rent payment and additional labour cost.

Papisetty Rama Mohana Rao (2004) [119] in his study 'Problems of women micro entrepreneurs in Chennai with special reference to access to credit' found that inadequate infrastructure, high labour mobility, shortage of electricity and delayed realisation of debtors etc. were the main problems faced by the women entrepreneurs. It is also revealed that access of credit has been the exclusive privilege of the rich and powerful. Women micro entrepreneurs suffered due to lack of recognition in the community. They have limited access to resources such as credit and improved means of production and marketing skills.

Choudhury, Shashi baijal and Asokan (1997) [120] in a study on 'Banks and Women's Enterprise Development - A Comparison of Approaches in India and the U.K.' found that both in India and the U.K., the main difficulty that women entrepreneurs face when starting up of the business is the burden of family responsibilities.

Balu and Seenivasagalu (1999) [121] in a study 'Innovation, Creativity and Women Entrepreneurs' found that as women entrepreneurs were doing small businesses, where there was no scope for innovation, their innovative skills were not adequately used, though they possessed such skills. There was a long gap between creativity and women entrepreneurship. Creativity was also not successfully utilised by them.

Mathialagan (2002) [122] conducted a socio-economic study on women entrepreneurs of Chennai city. Regarding the constraints of women entrepreneurs, the personal factor seems to influence more in the service sector where as the environmental factors influence manufacturing and trading factors.

Mallika Das (1999) [123] made an exploratory study of women entrepreneurs in Tamil Nadu and Kerala. The study examined the problems faced by women in initiating, running and succeeding in business and differences between the experiences of women from the developing and developed worlds. The study also underscored the difficulties faced by women in getting funds for setting up business and meeting the working capital requirements. The women in the study differ from western counterparts in family background, marital status, incubator organisations issues and environmental factors (support services).

The Department of Economics and Statistics, Government of Kerala (1984) [124] conducted a study on women's industrial programme in Kerala. The main objective of the study was to assess the involvement of manpower in this field and to analyse the difficulties and problems faced by the women entrepreneurs, which impede the growth and smooth functioning of units. It was supported by the views of 275 women entrepreneurs of Kerala. It revealed that nearly 82 per cent of women's industrial units were functioning throughout the year. Women's units are still in their infancy and they face the problems of (i) capital, (ii) raw materials, (iii) marketing, (iv) competition and (v) availability of power.

Hariram and Chitra Narayanan (1992) [125] pointed out that women had only vague ideas about wanting to do something and who were grouping for a foothold. What they need is a pointer towards EDPs, the first step in learning what business is all about. It would help if bankers did not attempt to confuse her further and treat that confusion with contempt.

Dhanalakshmi (1995) [126] carried out a study on women entrepreneurship which seeks to examine the problems faced by women entrepreneurs in Madurai. It is stated that women who have interest in business should take the first step and are courageous enough to face the ups and downs, their families should encourage them and the financial institutions should be liberal in financing the venture conducted by women.

Savithri (2002) [127] made a comparative study of women executives and women entrepreneurs in Chennai city to gauge the stress on women executives and women entrepreneurs and the factors influencing stress, the stress level, its impact on them, etc. It is found that stress played a role in a wide range of common ailments, such as headache, allergy and skin diseases, blood pressure, ulcer, diabetes and heart diseases. Stress affects sleep, productivity and growth. Workload also causes stress. Women entrepreneurs develop stress when there is labour problem, wastage and loss occurring in the organisation, feeling that they do not have enough time to do everything that is required. For women executives stress originates from personality, family and organisation. Both the parties are affected physically, psychologically and then create stress in the family and in the organisation. It is also found that women entrepreneurs in the trading and service sectors have more stress than women entrepreneurs in other areas.

On the basis of the review of these studies, it can be deduced that women entrepreneurs are playing a very significant role in the development of a country, but at the same time, they are facing disparate problems which are detrimental to the development of women entrepreneurship. Thus, there is need for more specific studies on women entrepreneurship using structured questionnaires and appropriate tools, so that the various aspects of women entrepreneurship could be understood in the larger context. This can then become the basis of designing interventions to address this problem.

Notes

1. E.B. Schwartz, 'Entrepreneurship: A Female Frontier', *Journal of Contemporary Business* (Winter), pp. 47-76, 1979.

2. A. Sinfield, in Martin Robertson, *What Unemployment Means*, Oxford: U.K., 1981.

3. R. Goffee. and Scase R, 'Business Ownership and Women's Subordination: a Preliminary Study of Female Proprietors', *Sociological Review*, Vol.31, 1983.

4. R.L Huntley, 'Women Entrepreneurs and Career Choice', *Dissertation Abstracts International (Part A)* ,46, 1755-A, 1985.

5. S. Shane, Kolvereid. L and Westhead. P, 'An Exploratory Examination of the Reasons Leading to New Firms Formation Across Country and Gender', *Journal of Business Management*, XXXV-1, 1991.

6. H. Allen, Anderson et al, *Effective Entrepreneurship*, Blockwell Publishers Inc., USA, 1996.

7. www.ebst.dk/publikationer

8. A.M. Morrison., White R.P. and Van Velsor E. along with the Centre for Creative Leadership, *Breaking the Glass Ceiling: Can*

Women Reach Top of America's Largest Corporations?, Reading M.A. Addison Wesley Publishers, Inc., 1987.

9. Swatko, Breaking in 'Experience in Male Dominated Professions', *Women and Theory* 2(3) pp. 67-69, 1981.

10. Peter Berger and Richard Neuhas J, *To Empower People*, The American Enterprise Institute, 1978.

11. Aldrich and Sakano, 'Entrepreneurship in Global Context', Sue Birley and Macmillan, *World Development*, Vol. 17, No. 7, pp. 979-991, 1997.

12. www.ebst.dk/publikationer

13. www.auroravoice.com

14. I. Palmer, *The Impact of Agrarian Reform on Women, Women's Role and Gender Differences in Development*, Monograph, No.6, West Hartford, Kumarian Press, 1985, p. 55.

15. J.L. MacDonald, 'The Traits and Characteristics of Women Entrepreneurs: Criteria for Predicting Success in Business Management', *Dissertation Abstracts International (Part-A)*, 46(8), 2169-A, 1986.

16. R.D. Hisrich and Brush, *The Women Entrepreneur: Characteristics, Skills, Problems and Prescriptions for Success*, in D.I. Sexton and. Simlor R.W (eds.) The Arts and Science of Entrepreneurship, Cambridge, Mass, Ballinger, 1986.

17. Sextan and Kent, *The Art and Science of Entrepreneurship*, Cambridge, Mass, Ballinger, 1981.

18. R.D. Hisrich and O'Brien 'The Women Entrepreneur as a Reflection of Type of Businesses' Frontiers of Entrepreneurship Research, *Proceedings of the 1981 Conference on Entrepreneurship*, Welleslay, Mass, Bobson College, 1982, pp.54-67.

19. R.D. Hisrich and Brush, 'The Women Entrepreneurs: Characteristics, Skills, Problems and Prescriptions for Success', in D.I. Sexton and Simlor R.W. (eds.), *The Arts and Science of Entrepreneurship*, Cambridge, Mass, Ballinger, 1986.

20. L. Brydon, and Chant. S, *Women in the Third World, Gender Issues in Rural and Urban Areas*, Aldershot, Edward Elgar Press, 1989, p. 327.

21. www.ebst.dk/publikationer

22. T. Epstein Scarrlett, 'Female Petty Entrepreneurs and their Multiple Roles', Oxford and I BH Publishing Co. Pvt. Ltd, 1990.

23. L.C. Williamson, Joyce Eddy A., 'Successful Female Entrepreneurs'. *Dissertation Abstracts International (Part A)*, 46(9),

2739-A, 1986.

24. R.R. Taylor, *Exceptional Entrepreneurial Women: Strategies for Success*, Praeger Publishers, New York, 1988.

25. www.ebst.dk/publikationer.

26. www.auroravoice,com/research.asp.

27. Tripp, Bridge, Briefings on Development & Gender, *Report No.15*, p.29, Dec., 1993.

28. www.auroravoice.com

29. Nina McLemore, Center for Women's Business Research, *National Association of Women Business Owners,* Orange County Chapter P.O. Box 1714, Tustin, CA 92781, 2000.

30. www.womensbusinessresearch.org

31. Hirata and Humphre, BRIDGE, Briefings on Development & Gender, *Report*, No.15, p. 27, December, 1993.

32. Jockes, Bridge, Briefings on Development & Gender, *Report*, No.15, p.27, December, 1993.

33. *ILO Report*, Women in the Informal Sector-Overview – Gender, Poverty and Employment Turning Capability into Entitlements -ILO: The Changing Role of Women in the Economy, Employment and Social Issues, Geneva, 1994.

34. Van der and Romijn, *Entrepreneurship and Small Enterprise Development for Women in Developing Countries,* An Agenda of Unanswered Questions, Management Development Branch, ILO, Geneva, 1987, p.90.

35. Lycklama A. Nijeholt, 'The Fallacy of Integration: The UN strategy of Integrating Women in to Development Revisted'. *Netherlands Review of Development Studies*, Vol.1, pp. 57-71, 1987.

36. Hilhorst Harry Oppenoorth, *Financing Women's Enterprises - Beyond Barriers and Bias,* Royal Tropical Institute, The Netherlands Intermediate Technology Publication, U.K., UNIFEM - U.S.A., 1992.

37. H.C. Haan, Community-Based Training for Employment and Income Generation, Geneva, ILO, 1994.

38. Mayoux, Linda, 'Women's Empowerment and Micro-Finance Programmes: Approaches, Evidence and Ways Forward', *Discussion Paper,* Open University, Milton Keynes, U.K., 1998.

39. E.B. Schwartz,' Entrepreneurship: A Female Frontier', *Journal of Contemporary Business (Winter)*, 1979, pp.47- 76.

40. R.D. Hisrich and Brush C.G, 'The Women Entrepreneur; Management, Skills and Business Problems'. *Journal of Small*

*Business Management ,*22 January, pp.30-37, 1984.

41. M. Buvinic and Berger. M, 'Sex Differences in Access to a Small Enterprise Development Fund in Peru', *World Development,* Vol.18, No.5, pp. 695-705, 1990.

42. M. Tovo, 'Micro Enterprise Among Village Women in Tanzania'. *Small Enterprise Development,* Vol. 2 No.1, pp. 20-31, 1991.

43. G. Berik ,'Women Carpet Weavers in Rural Turkey: Pattern of Employment, Earnings and Status', *Women, Work and Development,* International Labour Office, Geneva, No.15, p.112, 1987.

44. Van der and Romijn, Entrepreneurship and Small Enterprise Development for Women in Developing Countries. An Agenda of Unanswered Questions, Geneva ILO, Management Development Branch p. 90, 1987.

45. L. Neider, 'Á Preliminary Investigation of Female Entrepreneurs in Florida', *Journal of Small Business* Management, XXV-3, 1987.

46. A. Bequele and Boyden, Combating Child Labour, Geneva, ILO, 1988, p. 226.

47. www.ebst.dk/publikationer

48. K. Mc Kee, 'Micro Level Strategies for Supporting Livelihoods Employment and Income Generation of Poor Women in Third World: The Challenge of Significance', *World Development* , Vol. 17, No. 7, pp. 993-1006, 1989.

49. S.L. Holt and Ribe. H, *Developing Financial Institutions for the Poor: Reducing Gender Barriers,* Policy, Research and External Affairs Division, World Bank, Washington, 1990, p. 36.

50. V. Gianotten, Riofrio. G, Bueningen C Van and Van Kooten C. Las mugeres del grupo destinatario: La mujer en programas de promicion urbana en el peru.lima, Informe de evaluacion DGIS-CEBEMO,1990, p. 68.

51. J. Downing, 'Gender and the Growth of Micro Enterprises', *Small Enterprise Development,* Vol. 2, No.1, pp. 4-13, 1991.

52. K.A Stolen, 'The Social and Cultural Context: Women and Development Assistance', *Paper Presented at the Symposium Sharing Poverty or Creating Wealth? Access to Credit for Women's Enterprises,* Amsterdam, The Netherlands, 7th-9th January, p. 14, 1991.

53. Brush, 'Entrepreneurship in a Global Context', *World*

Development, Vol. 17, No.7, pp. 979-991, 1997.

54. R. Hisrich and Brush. C, 'The Women Entrepreneur: Management Skill and Business Problems', *Journal of Small Business Management,* XX11-1, 1994.

55. B. White, 'Studying Women and Rural Non-farm Sector Development in West Java', *Project Working Paper Series*, No.B-12, Institute of Social Studies and Banding Research Project Office, New York, U.S.A, p. 45, 1991.

56. A. Lyberaki and Smyth, I., 'Small is Small: The Role and Functions of Small Scale Industries'. In: M.P. Van Dijik and Secher Marcussen .H (EDS.), Industrialisation in the Third World: The Need for Alternative Strategies Frank cass, London, 1990, pp. 125-145.

57. Tinker, cited by Downing 'Gender and the Growth of Micro Enterprises'. *Small Enterprise Development*, Vol.2, No.1, pp.4-13, 1991.

58. I. Tinker, *Women in Micro and Small-Scale Development*, West View Press, U.S.A, 1995, p. 31.

59. Khondkar, Mubina, 'Women's Access to Credit and Gender Relations in Bangladesh', *Ph.D. Thesis*, University of Manchester, U.K.,1998.

60. www.ebst.dk/publikationer

61. Richard Kibombo and Samuel K Kayabwe, 'A Baseline Study on Economic Empowerment of Women Through the Use of ICTs in Uganda', *Final Report,* Compiled for the Council for Economic Empowerment of Women of Africa (CEWA), Uganda Chapter-IDRC, October, 2000.

62. J. Bruce, 'Home Divided'. *World Development*, Vol.17, No. 7, pp. 979-991, 1989.

63. Aldrich et al, In 'Entrepreneurship in a Global Context', Sue Birley and Macmillan, Routledge, London & New York, *World Development*, Vol.17, No.7, pp. 979-991, 1989.

64. Moser, Bridge, Briefings on Development & Gender, *Report No.15*, p. 27, December, 1993.

65. Sexton and Bowman-Upton, *Entrepreneurship in Global Market-Strong Ties, Weak Ties and Strangers,* Sue Birley and Macmillan, 1997, p.4.

66. C. Beena and Sushma. B, 'Women Entrepreneurs Managing Petty Business-A Study from the Motivational Perspectives', *Southern Economics*, Vol. 42, No. 2, May 15, pp. 5-8, 2003.

67. Krishnaveni Motha, 'Women Entrepreneurship in Rural Areas of India', *SEDME* , Vol.No.31, No. 3, pp. 8-32, Sep., 2004.

68. Mohiuddin, Asghari, 'Entrepreneurship Development Among Women, Retrospects and Prospects', *SEDME*, 10 (1), 1983.

69. Shah and Hina, *Fostering Women Entrepreneurs in India*, Mittal Publications, Delhi, 1987.

70. N.P. Singh and Senguptha R. 'Potential Women Entrepreneurs; Their Profile, Vision and Motivation- An Exploratory Study', *Research Report Serial-1*, New Delhi, NIESUBUD, 1985.

71. R. Seenivasagalu, 'Women Entrepreneurs and Executives- A Comparative Study', *Ph.D. Thesis*, Madras University, Madras, March, 2001.

72. N.P. Singh, Sehgal P., Tinani M. and Senguptha R., 'Successful Women Entrepreneurs-Their Identity, Expectation and Problems - An Exploratory Research Study', *Research Report Serial II*, New Delhi/MDI Collaboration, 1986.

73. Paramjeet Kaur Dhillon, *Women Entrepreneurs, Problems and Prospects*, Blaze Publishers & Distributors Pvt. Ltd., New Delhi, 1993.

74. Y. Lokeswara Choudary, 'Women Entrepreneurs - A Case Study of Vikram Sarabhai Industrial Estate in Chennai City', *M.Phil. Dissertation*, Madras University, Madras, October, 1999.

75. Ch. Aravinda and Renuka S., 'Women Entrepreneurs: An Exploratory Study', *SEDME* , Vol.28, No.3, pp.71- 81, Sep.2001.

76. Sumi Guha, *Entrepreneurship and Empowerment of Women Entrepreneurship and Education*, Rawat Publication, New Delhi, 2001.

77. Nirmala Karuna D'Cruz, *Constraints on Women Entrepreneurship Development in Kerala: An Analysis of Familial, Social, and Psychological Dimensions,* Centre for Development Studies, Thiruvananthapuram, 2003.

78. Economic and Social Commission for Asia and Pacific Study, 'Fewer Changes for Asian Women', *Documentation on Women's Concerns*, Oct/March, p. 32, 1991.

79. N.P. Singh, Sehgal. P, Tinani. M and Senguptha. R, 'Successful Women Entrepreneurs-their Identity, Expectation and Problems - An Exploratory Research Study', *Research Report Serial II*, New Delhi, /MDI Collaboration, 1986.

80. S. Jayasree, 'Entrepreneur's Access to Household Resources, Abstracts Survival and Sovereignty Challenges to Women's

Studies', VIII *National Conference of Women's Studies*, Bombay, May, 1998.

81. Krishnaveni Motha, 'Women Entrepreneurship in Rural Areas of India', *SEDME*, Vol.No.31, No.3, pp. 8-32, Sep. 2004.

82. Shah and Hina, *Fostering Women Entrepreneurs in India*, Mittal Publications, New Delhi, 1987.

83. V. Anna, Women Entrepreneurship in Industrial Manufacturing Sector of Kerala, *Ph.D. Thesis*, Cochin University of Science and Technology, Cochin, 1989.

84. S.K. Dharmaja, Bhatia B.S. and Saini J.S, *Women Entrepreneurs: Perceptions, Attitudes and Opinions-Entrepreneurship and Education*, Rawat Publications, New Delhi, 2001.

85. Radhika Sachdev, 'Where is the Queen Bee', *Documentation on Women's Concerns*, July/Sep, p.68, 1999.

86. R. Seenivasagalu, 'Women Entrepreneurs and Executives-A Comparative Study', *Ph.D. Thesis*, Madras University, Madras, March, 2001.

87. R. Mathialagan, 'Women Entrepreneurs in Tamil Nadu – A Socio-Economic Study of Selected Women Entrepreneurs at Chennai City', *Ph.D. Thesis*, Madras University, Madras, March, 2002.

88. Shoma A Chatterji, 'Under the Thumb', SIETI, *Documentation on Women's Concern*, April/June, p.135, 1999.

89. Nagendra P. Singh and Rita Sen Gupta, 'Potential Women Entrepreneurs, Their Profile, Vision and Motivation - An Exploratory Study', *Research Report Serial II, New* Delhi, NIESBUD, 1985.

90. Paramjeet Kaur Dhillon, *Women Entrepreneurs, Problems and Prospects*, Blaze Publishers & Distributors Pvt. Ltd., New Delhi, 1993.

91. Y. Lokeswara Choudary, 'Women Entrepreneurs - A Case Study of Vikram Sarabhai Industrial Estate in Chennai City', *M.Phil. Dissertation*, Madras University, Madras, October, 1999.

92. K.P. Saraswathi Amma and Sudarsanan Pillai. P, 'A Study on Women Entrepreneurs in Garment Making Industries in Kerala – A Profile', *Management Researcher* VI,VII, pp.45, Oct 2000-March 2001.

93. R. Mathialagan, 'Women Entrepreneurs in Tamil Nadu –A Socio-Economic Study of Selected Women Entrepreneurs at Chennai

City', *Ph.D. Thesis*, Madras University, Madras, March, 2002.

94. M.B. Chittawadagi, 'Women Entrepreneurship in Co-operative Banking Sector', *Southern Economist*, Vol.42, No.19, pp. 7-16, Feb.1, 2004.

95. Anil Kumar, 'Enterprise Location: Choice of Women Entrepreneurs', *SEDME,* Vol. No. 31, No.3, pp. 8-32, Sep., 2004.

96. P.K. Choudhury, Shashi Baijal and Asokan M., 'Banks and Women's Development: A Comparison of Approaches in India and the U.K', *SEDME*, Vol. XXIV No.2, pp. 77-87, June, 1997.

97. Savitri Ramamurthy, 'Women Entrepreneurs in Delhi', *The Economic Times*, p. 5, April 10, 1988.

98. Kerala Women's Commission, *Status of Women in Kerala,* Kerala Women's Commission, Thiruvananthapuram, 30th May, 2002.

99. C. Beena and Sushma. B, 'Women Entrepreneurs Managing Petty Business-A Study from Motivational Perspectives', *Southern Economics*, Vol. 42, No.2, pp.5-8, May 15, 2003.

100. P.V. Narasaiah and Ramakrishnaiah. K, 'DWCRA Programme in Cuddapah District: An Evaluation', *SEDME,* Vol. No.31, No.3 , pp. 8-17, Sep., 2004.

101.R. Seenivasagalu, 'Women Entrepreneurs and Executives-A Comparative Study', *Ph.D. Thesis*, Madras University, Madras, March, 2001.

102. Sulochana A. Nadkarni, 'Women, Entrepreneurship and Economic Development', *Paper of First National Conference on Women's Studies,* Bombay, April, 1981.

103. Aruna Prasad, Shashi Raja Gopal, Tara Appachoo and Narayan Prasad , 'A Review of the Schemes for the Development of Women in the Past Decade with Special Reference to Karnataka State'- *Second National Conference on Women's Studies*, Institute of Social Studies Trust, Trivandrum, April 9-12, 1984.

104. C.B. Gupta and Srinivasan N.P, *Entrepreneurship Development,* Sultan Chand and Sons, New Delhi, 1992, p.132.

105. Shanta Kohli Chandra, *Development of Women Entrepreneurship in India*, Mittal Publications, New Delhi 1991, p.70.

106. Tara S. Nair , 'Entrepreneurship Training for Women in the Indian Rural Sector: A Review of Approach and Strategies', *The Journal of Entrepreneurship,* Vol. 5 (1), pp.65-94, 1996.

107. K.P. Saraswathy Amma and Sudarsanan Pillai P, 'A Study

on Women Entrepreneurs in Garment Making Industries in Kerala – A Profile', *Management Researcher* VI, VII, pp.45, Oct 2000-March 2001.

108.S.K. Dharmaja, Bhatia B.S. and Saini J.S, *Women Entrepreneurs: Perceptions, Attitudes and Opinions-Entrepreneurship and Education,* Rawat Publications, New Delhi, 2001.

109.G. Anjaneya Swamy and Deepak Rajan, 'Women Entrepreneurship - Need for a Fresh Look', *Indian Economic Panorama,* Vol.13, No.3, pp.34-36, Oct. 2003.

110. D.P. Sosamma, 'Margine Money Assistance for Women May be Enlarged', Chennai, *Documentation on Women's Concerns,* p.70, April-June, 1999.

111.Kerala Women's Commission, *Status of Women in Kerala,* Kerala Women's Commission, Thiruvananthapuram, 30th May, 2002, pp. 185-233.

112.P.K. Choudhury, Shashi Baijal and Asokan M., 'Banks and Women's Development: A Comparison of Approaches in India and the U.K.', *SEDME,* Vol. XXIV, No.2, pp.77-87, June 1997.

113. M.B. Chittawadagi, 'Women Entrepreneurship in Co-operative Banking Sector', *Southern Economist,* Vol.42, No.19, pp. 7-16, Feb.1, 2004.

114.Y. Lokeswara Choudary, 'Women Entrepreneurs-A Case Study of Vikram Sarabhai Industrial Estate in Chennai City', *M.Phil. Dissertation,* Madras University, Madras, October,1999.

115.N.P Singh, Sehgal P, Tinani M and Senguptha R , 'Successful Women Entrepreneurs - their Identity, Expectation and Problems - An Exploratory Research Study', *Research Report Serial II,,* New Delhi, /MDI Collaboration , 1986.

116.Surti K. and Sarupriya D., 'Psychological Factors Affecting Women Entrepreneurs: Some Findings', *Indian Journal of Social Work,* 44(3), pp.287-295, 1983.

117.C.B. Gupta and Srinivasan N.P., *Entrepreneurship Development,* Sultan Chand and Sons, New Delhi, 1992, p.132.

118. Nirmala Karuna D'Cruz, *Constraints on Women Entrepreneurship Development in Kerala: An Analysis of Familial, Social, and Psychological Dimensions,* Centre for Development Studies, Thiruvananthapuram, 2003.

119.Papisetty Rama Mohana Rao, 'Problems of Women Micro Entrepreneurs in Chennai with Special Reference to Access to

Credit', *Ph.D. Thesis* , Madras University, Madras, January, 2004.

120. P.K. Choudhury, Shashi Baijal and Asokan M. Op. cit, pp.77-87.

121. V. Balu and Seenivasagalu R., *A Study on Innovation, Creativity and Women Entrepreneur, A Case Study*, Madras University, Madras, 1999.

122. R. Mathialagan, 'Women Entrepreneurs in Tamil Nadu – A Socio-Economic Study of Selected Women Entrepreneurs at Chennai City', *Ph.D. Thesis*, Madras University, Madras, March, 2002.

123. Mallika Das, 'Women Entrepreneurs from Southern India: An Explorative Study', *The Journal of Entrepreneurship,* Vol.8, (2), pp.147-160, July-December, 1999.

124. The Department of Economics and Statistics , 'Study on Women's Industrial Programme in Kerala', Government of Kerala, Thiruvananthapuram, 1984.

125.Hariram and Chitra Narayanan, 'Train a Woman and She is Better than a Man', *Documentation on Women's Concerns*, July-Sep, p.20, 1992.

126.Dhanalakshmi, Bhatia B.S. and Batra G.S., *Entrepreneurship and Small Business Management*, Deep and Deep Publications Pvt. Ltd., New Delhi, 2000, pp.101-115.

127.M.K, Savithri, 'Stress Management - A Comparative Study of Women Executives and Women Entrepreneurs', *Ph.D. Thesis,* University of Madras, Madras, July, 2002.

3

Schemes for Women
Entrepreneurship in India

In India, though women have played a key role in the society, the entrepreneurial ability of women has not been properly developed and efficiently elicited due to the lower status of women in the society. It is only from the Fifth Five Year Plan (1974-79) onwards that their role has been explicitly recognized with a marked shift in the approach to women issues from women welfare to women development. Since then, Government is more concerned about the overall economic development of women. The development of women entrepreneurship has become an important aspect of our plan priorities. Several policies and programmes are implemented for the development of women entrepreneurship in India.

Government has taken several measures to encourage women entrepreneurs to set up small scale and micro enterprise. The Small Industries Development Organisation (SIDO), the various State Small Industries Development Corporations (SSIDCs), the nationalised banks and even NGOs are conducting various programmes including Entrepreneurship Development Programmes (EDPs).

3.1 Entrepreneurship Development Programmes (EDPs)

The main objectives of EDPs are to identify people with entrepreneurial ability and motivate them through a structured training course so as to enable them to set up tiny and small scale units with the assistance available from various agencies. Under these programmes, intensive seminars and campaigns are conducted to identify, select, motivate and cater to the needs of potential women entrepreneurs, who may not have adequate educational background and skills. A training course for 30 participants for duration of four weeks is also organised. SIDO has introduced process/product oriented EDPs in areas like TV repairing, printed circuit boards, leather goods, screen printing etc.

3.2 Development Programmes of Central Social Welfare Board

The Central Social Welfare Board is running a number of programmes for the development of women and children. All these programmes are fully funded by the Department. Grant for setting up a production unit is also available under Socio-Economic Programme of Central Social Welfare Board.

3.2.1 Vocational Training for Women: Vocational Training Programme was started during the year 1975 to train women in the trades which are marketable and also to upgrade their skills in order to meet the demands of changing work environment. Main objective of training interventions is to enable and empower women to access remunerative employment opportunities, which will instill self-confidence and enhance their self-esteem. From the year 1997-98, funds for vocational training are being provided under NORAD assisted scheme on Training and Employment of Women. The main emphasis of the programme is training and skill up gradation of women for their employment and self-employment on a sustainable basis.

3.2.2 Socio-Economic Programme: The Socio-Economic Programme of the Central Social Welfare Board endeavours to provide employment opportunities on full or part time basis to destitute women, widows, deserted and the physically handicapped, to supplement their meager family income. Besides, women entrepreneurs are encouraged to exhibit and sell their products through Exhibition-cum-Melas organised by State Boards at District level. The Central Social Welfare has two different types of schemes of assistance under Socio-Economic Programme.

- **Agro-based Units:** The Board assists voluntary

organisatons for setting up agro-based units like dairy, poultry, piggery, goatery etc. for poor and needy women. However, for the past few years proposals for Agro-based Units are not being considered since another Programme of the Department of Women and Child Development, namely Support for Training and Employment of Women (STEP) is taking care of these sectors.

- **Production   Units:** Voluntary   organisations   are encouraged to set up production units, which can provide employment on full or part time basis to women. Project proposals are examined by District Industrial Centres, KVICs etc. who look into viability of the projects. A grant is provided by the Board to facilitate setting up a production unit by the grantee institution. The grant is finalised on a case-to-case basis subject to a limit of Rs.3 lakh.

3.3 Rural Industries Programme of SIDBI

This programme has been devised by Small Industries Development Bank of India (SIDBI) to promote rural enterprises through identifying potential entrepreneurs, motivating them and providing a package of assistance including technology and market linkages. The programme is to facilitate better commercial exploitation of local resources and employment generation in rural areas.

3.4 Prime Minister's Rozgar Yojana (PMRY)

The scheme was launched in 2nd October 1993 to create and provide sustainable self employment opportunities to one million educated unemployed youth in the country during the Eighth Plan period. This scheme is offered to any permanent resident (at least 3 years) unemployed youth between 18-35 years, having minimum educational qualification (VIII passed) Preference will be given to those who have passed ITI or undergone Government sponsored technical course for a minimum duration of 6 months. Their family income should be less than Rs. 40,000.

Maximum amount of loan granted under this scheme is Rs. 1 lakh for business sector, Rs. 2 lakh for manufacturing and other activities - loan has to be of composite nature. If two or more eligible persons join together in a partnership, project up to Rs. 10 lakh would be eligible for funding. Assistance shall be limited to individual admissibility. Subsidy will be limited to 15 per cent of the project cost subject to a ceiling of Rs. 7,500 per entrepreneur. Banks will be allowed to take margin money from the entrepreneur varying from 5 per cent to 16.25 per cent of the project cost so as to make the total of the subsidy and the margin money equal to 20 per cent of the project cost. No collateral contribution for projects up to Rs. 1 lakh. Exemption from collateral in case of partnership project will also be limited to Rs. 1 lakh per person participating in the project. Normal rate of interest shall be charged and repayment schedule may range between 3 and 7 years after an initial moratorium as may be prescribed. Preference will be given to weaker sections including women. The scheme envisages 22.5 per cent reservation for SC/ST and 27 per cent for other backward classes (OBCs). In case SC/ST/OBC candidates are not available, States/UTs Govt. will be competent to consider other categories of candidates under PMRY.

3.5 Micro Credit Scheme

Micro Credit programme was introduced in the Sixth Plan (1980-85) for the upliftment of rural women through increased access to formal banking services. Loans under this scheme are very small and are targeted to women borrowers. This scheme helps women to organise their own business and production units. For women self help group special schemes are available with public sector banks to start SSI units extending concessional rate of interest and low margin and longer repayment period.

3.6 Mahila Samakhya Project (MSP)

This project is for women's awakening spreads over 1030 villages and spans 10 districts of three Indian States-Karnataka, Uttar Pradesh, and Gujarat. The project was emanated from the Education Ministry of the Central Govt., under an Indo-Dutch agreement. The main goal of this project was the empowerment of women without causing any disturbance in their family and social lives. It not only focuses on women's problems but also deals with social and economic issues that concern the entire family. It helps women in rural areas to realize their rights, understand the strength of collectiveness and gradually empower themselves for a better life-socially, legally, physically and emotionally. In Uttar Pradesh this project was launched in 1989.

3.7 National Policy for the Empowerment of Women

This Policy was announced by the Government on 20th March, 2001. The main objective of this Policy is to bring about the advancement, development and empowerment of women through increased access to resources like micro credit, better resource allocation through Women's Component Plan, Gender Budget exercises and development of Gender Development Indices, to eliminate all forms of discrimination against women and to ensure their active participation in all spheres of life and activities.

3.8 Indira Mahila Yojana (IMY)

IMY launched in 1995, was recast, as 'Swayamsidha' in 2001 is a centrally sponsored integrated programme for the empowerment of women by generating awareness through the network of Self-Help Groups of women and helping them to achieve economic strength through micro-level income generation activities and facilitate easy convergence of various services including entrepreneurship of State and Central Governments at the block level.

3.9 Women's Component Plan (WCP)

The genesis of WCP was officially launched in the Ninth Plan where not less than 30 percent of funds/benefits are earmarked in all the women related sectors. The flow of funds/benefits was monitored through an effective mechanism of inter-sectoral review to ensure that adequate funds/benefits flow to women from all the related sectors for the development and advancement of women.

3.10 Swarna Jayanti Shahari Rozgar Yojana (SJSRY)

This programme was implemented in1997 to provide gainful employment to the urban unemployed /under employed through encouraging the setting up of self-employment ventures/provision of wage employment. The special scheme of Urban Self-Employment Programme (USEP), which is a component of SJSRY, provides assistance to the urban poor, especially women living below urban poverty line.

3.11 Technology Development & Utilisation Programme for Women (TDUPW)

In order to meet the specific needs of women and to enhance the contribution of women towards technology capability building, the "Technology Development & Utilisation Programme for Women (TDUPW)" has been formulated by the Department of Scientific and Industrial Research (DSIR). DSIR has a mandate to carry out the activities relating to indigenous technology promotion, development, utilisation and transfer. The objectives of the programme are:

- Promoting the adoption of new technologies by women.
- Awareness creation and training of women on technology related issues with regard to women.
- Promoting technological upgradation of tiny, small and medium enterprises run by women entrepreneurs.
- Showcasing of appropriate technologies and organising demonstration programmes for the benefit of women.

- Design and development of products, processes beneficial to women.

3.12 Swa-Shakti Project

Swa-Shakti Project (earlier known as Rural Women's Development and Empowerment Project) was sanctioned on 16 October 1998 as a Centrally-sponsored project for a period of five years. The objectives of the project are establishment of self-reliant women's Self-Help Groups (SHGs), sensitising and strengthening the institutional capacity of support agencies to proactively address women's needs, developing linkages between SHGs and credit-lending institutions, enhancing women's access to resources for better quality of life and increased control of women, particularly poor women, over income and spending, through their involvement in income-generation activities.

3.13 Trade Related Entrepreneurship Assistance and Development of Women (TREAD)

In order to alleviate the problems faced by women entrepreneurs, the Ministry of Small Scale Industries (SSI) in the Government of India has launched this scheme in 1998. The Office of the Development Commissioner (SSI) in the Ministry of SSI is responsible for the implementation of this scheme. The scheme envisages development of micro/tiny women enterprises in the country both in the urban and rural areas. The main objective of the scheme is to empower women through development of their entrepreneurial skills in non-farm activities by eliminating constraints faced by them in their sphere of trade.

3.14 Swarnajayanti Gram Swarozgar Yojana (SGSY)

SGSY has been launched in April 1999, in rural India by merging six self-employment programmes, viz. RDP, TRYSEM, DWCRA, SITRA, GKY and MWS for covering various aspects of self- employment such as organisation of poor into self-help groups, training, credit, technology, infrastructure and marketing. It is envisaged that 50 per cent of the Groups formed in each Block should be exclusively for women. Under this scheme women are encouraged in the practice of thrift and credit which enables them to become self-reliant. They provide assistance in the form of Revolving Fund, bank credit and subsidy and integrate women in the economy by providing increasing opportunities of self-employment.

3.15 Revised Scheme of TREAD

A revised scheme of TREAD was launched in May, 2004. The scheme is implemented by SIDO. The scheme envisages economic empowerment of women through trade related training, information and counselling, extension activities related to trades, products, services etc. The scheme provides for market development and financial loans through NGOs, which are also provided grants for capacity building. This assistance is to be provided for self-employment ventures by women for pursuing any kind of non-farm activity. In TREAD scheme, there is no monetary ceiling.

3.16 Scheme of Assistance to Women Co-operatives

The Scheme of Assistance to Women Co-operatives was launched during 1993-'94 for the economic betterment of women, by focusing special attention on their needs and provide assistance in the form of assured work and income by organising co-operative societies for undertaking economic activities in agro-based, commercial/ industrial sectors. During the Ninth Plan 850 women's co-operatives were benefited under this scheme.

3.17 Schemes of NABARD

NABARD has adopted multi-pronged strategies for addressing various constraints that come in the way of success of women entrepreneurs and has introduced women specific programmes with the objective of addressing the gender issues in credit dispensation and support services. These include:

3.17.1 Support and Linkage Programme: Support and linkage programme of National Bank of Agriculture and Rural Development (NABARD) was launched of to provide financial services from the formal banking system through SHGs. By March 2000, nearly two million rural poor families availed these facilities where 84 per cent of these groups are exclusive women's groups.

3.17.2 Credit-Linked Rural Entrepreneurial Development Programme: The credit-linked rural entrepreneurial development programme has been introduced to promote entrepreneurship, particularly among women.

3.17.3 Non-farm Sector Schemes: The NABARD's non-farm sector schemes help most of the rural trained women to become micro-entrepreneurs.

3.17.4 Assistance to Rural Women in Non-Farm Development (ARWIND): Under ARWIND, financial assistance is provided by NABARD to NGOs, Women Development Corporations, KVIC/ KVIB, Co-operative Societies, Trusts etc., for taking up various aspects of capacity building needs of women for promotion of women entrepreneurship. The assistance is provided for activities like training for skill development, skill upgradation, enterprise management skills, escort services, setting up of common facility centers/ common service centers, setting up of mother units, organising women, product design, quality control etc.

3.17.5 Swarojgar Credit Card (SCC): NABARD has formulated a special credit card scheme called Swarojgar Credit Card (SCC) which would take care of investment and working capital requirement of small borrowers, especially in the non-farm sector and service sector in rural areas. Entrepreneurs could borrow Rs. 25,000 under the scheme. NABARD also holds national exhibition to showcase products of best rural entrepreneurs.

3.17.6 Assistance for Marketing of Non-Farm Products

of Rural Women (MAHIMA): Recognising the importance of marketing as a crucial link for women entrepreneurs, NABARD supports various initiatives for promotion of marketing of products produced by rural women under its MAHIMA Scheme. The assistance is given for various aspects related to marketing like market survey, capacity building including training programmes on marketing, quality control, technology upgradation, design development, branding, labeling, preparation of catalogues, packaging design, publicity, common marketing facilities, setting up of showrooms, sales outlets, mobile vans, organisation/ participation in exhibition and melas, etc.

3.17.7 Development of Women Through Area Programme (DEWTA): NABARD has introduced a new programme, viz. DEWTA for women, on pilot basis, in four RRBs i.e. Aligarh, Rushikulya, Tungabhadra and Sri Anantha Regional Rural Banks to bring women to the mainstream of economic development. This is an area-based approach to address area-specific problems, issues and promoting women specific activities and clusters. The main objectives of the programme were:

- Employment creation by enhancing entrepreneurship among women and income generation through sustainable livelihoods for women.
- Facilitating setting up of micro enterprises by women and its development.
- Facilitating access to basic services. Its activities include training/ skill upgradation, credit, exposure to markets, other capacity building activities.

3.18 National Entrepreneurship Development Board (NEDB) Scheme

The main objective of the National Entrepreneurship Development Board (NEDB) Scheme is promotion of entrepreneurship for encouraging self-employment in small scale industries and small business. The other objectives include:

- To identify and remove entry barriers for potential entrepreneurs (first generation and new entrepreneurs) including study on entrepreneurship development.
- To focus on existing entrepreneurs in micro, tiny and small sector and identify and remove constraints to survivals, growth and continuously improve performance.
- To facilitate the consolidation, growth and diversification of existing entrepreneurial venture in all possible ways.
- To support skill upgradation and renewal of learning processes among practicing entrepreneurs and managers of micro, tiny, small and medium enterprises.
- To sensitise to support agencies in the area of entrepreneurship about the current requirement of growth.
- To act as catalyst to institutionalise entrepreneurship development by supporting and strengthening state level institutions for entrepreneurship development as most entrepreneurship related activities take place at the grass root level and removing various constraints to their effective functioning.
- To set up incubators by entrepreneurship development institutions and other organizations devoted to the promotion of entrepreneurship development.

3.19 Schemes of Consortium of Women Entrepreneurs of India (CWEI)

3.19.1 SHASHWAT is the rural wing of the Consortium of Women Entrepreneurs of India (Cwei) which was set up in 2001, with a view to act as the Common Facility Centre for the adoption and assimilation of appropriate technologies and training for income generation and self-employment through cluster approach. Another objective was to give a Common Brand name for cottage & SSE products for sale promotion and to conduct "Shashwat" bazaars - Model trade fairs for backward and forward to showcase products exclusively at India International Trade Fair (IITF), Pragati Maidan New

Delhi.

3.19.2 Cwei- Annual Event (IWEM&C):   International Women Entrepreneurs Meet & Conference (IWEM & C) was declared as one of the Cwei's annual events to highlight issues pertaining to marketing finance, training, product design and development and a host of other critical problems in order to bring the issues to the notice of policy makers, implementing agencies and women entrepreneurs themselves.

3.19.3 One to One Buyer Seller Meet: Cwei organises one to one Buyer Seller Meet. This project has been undertaken to increase exports of identified products of women entrepreneurs of India to selected countries.

3.19.4 Online Web Portal: Cwei has also launched Online Web Portal which is the easiest means for women entrepreneurs to conduct business communications, management, etc. through electronic media i.e. buying, selling marketing, accounting and other services.

The other programmes of Cwei include skill development workshop, Training cum Demonstration Programme, Design and Technical Development etc. Cwei assists in forming new alliances between producers, entrepreneurs, and buyers including establishment of effective linkages for up-gradation of skills, technical know how and innovations in designing of products. Cwei facilitates exchange of entrepreneurs for enhancing skills, design and product development & open new market opportunities between the two countries.

Cwei provides Extensive Training Programmes in different province of India Under 'SHASHWAT' Swa Rojgar Jagrukta Abhiyan, Delhi.Cwei conducts an Awareness Generation Camp to encourage women to take initiative in identifying their skills and adopting them for self employment and thus to be independent. Cwei conducts training programmes on fashion designing with NIFT and also assists in upgrading traditionally skills with NRDC. NIFT outreach programme for self-employment of women.

3.20 HUL-Shakti project of Hindustan Unilever Limited

The Rural Managers' Association of Xavier Institute of Management, Bhubaneswar (RMAX) and the biggest FMCG Company in India, Hindustan Unilever Limited started a new project, HUL-Shakti project for promoting women entrepreneurs in Orissa, by identifying 20 to 50 year old women in the villages for promoting HUL's customised products in rural areas. HUL-Shakti project provides an excellent opportunity for women of rural India. HUL provides support services like doorstep delivery of the products and training to market them successfully.

3.21 Centre for Entrepreneurship Development

Canara Bank has established the Centre for Entrepreneurship Development (CED) for Women at the bank's Corporate Office in Bangalore in 1988 to assist potential women entrepreneurs in selecting income generating activities and start ventures of their own and subsequently nine such CEDs were opened at various state capitals. The bank has also opened an exclusive branch for women—the Mahila banking division—the first of its kind in the banking industry.

3.22 Financial Institutions

Finance is the lifeblood of any industry. It is required continuously through out the life of the business. Financial institutions provide funds to entrepreneurs for meeting their fixed and working capital requirements. Credit is provided by different agencies including banks. In India, for the past several years, financial institutions are playing pivotal role in giving financial assistance and consultancy services to entrepreneurs for the setting up of new ventures and for modernisation, diversification and expansion of their existing industrial units.

All-India Development Banks (AIDBs)viz. IDBI, IFCI, ICICI (the erstwhile DFI), IIBI, IDFC and SIDBI, Specialised Financial Institutions (SFIs) viz. Exim Bank and NABARD,

Investment Institutions viz. LIC, GIC, NIC, NIA, OIC, UII and UTI and Regional/State-level Institutions viz. NEDFI, SIDCs and SFCs. etc   assist small scale entrepreneurs in India in different forms, viz. IDBI's loans to and investments in shares and bonds of other financial institutions, term loans by LIC to/special deposits of UTI (erstwhile) with IDBI, IFCI and ICICI, and IDBI/SIDBI's refinance to SFCs/SIDCs, seed capital/equity type assistance and lines of credit. Financial institutions and banks have also set up special cells to assist women entrepreneurs. Co-operatives and SHGs are also playing a major role in the credit market.

3.22.1 Small Industries Development Bank of India (SIDBI): Small Industries Development Bank of India (SIDBI) was established in April 1990 by an Act of Parliament, as an apex institution for promotion, finance, and development of small scale industries and for co-coordinating the functions of other institutions engaged in similar activities. It provides direct and indirect assistances to small scale sector. Its direct assistance schemes are Project Finance Scheme, Equipment Finance Scheme, Marketing scheme, Vendor Development Scheme, Infrastructural Development Scheme, ISO Certification, Technology Development & Modernisation Fund, Venture Capital Scheme, Assistance for Leasing to NBFCs, SFCs, SIDCs and Resource Support to Institutions involved in the development and financing of small scale sector. It also provides refinance facilities to small scale sector by primary lending institutions, viz. SFCs, SIDCs and banks. The banks' lending operations are supplemented with developmental activities so as to facilitate the entry of new entrepreneurs and the strengthening of the SSI sector.

3.22.2 Commercial Banks: Small-scale sector has been included in the priority sector for providing liberal and timely financial assistance through the commercial banks. Commercial banks cater to the working capital requirements of small-scale industries through their countrywide network of branches. Besides the short-term assistance, term loans and other assistances are also provided by these banks. Specialised branches are opened in selected industrial estates and cities to exclusively cater to the requirements of the small-scale entrepreneurs. PMRY loan is granted through commercial banks.

3.22.3 Regional Rural Banks: Regional rural banks (RRBs) has been set up to improve the efficacy of rural credit delivery mechanism in India. It promotes agriculture, trade, commerce and industry in rural areas and thereby improves the rural economy. They provide credit facilities in the rural areas particularly to artisans, farmers and small entrepreneurs. With joint share holding by Central Government, the concerned State Government and the sponsoring bank, an effort was made to integrate commercial banking within the broad policy thrust towards social banking keeping in view the local peculiarities.

3.22.4 Co-operative Banks: Cooperative banks play a significant role in providing various assistances to agriculture, agro-based industries, small-scale and tiny industries for encouraging self employment .These banks provide working capital funds to small entrepreneurs. The Primary Agriculture Co-operative Society (PACS) finances the agriculture and agriculture related industry. The Primary Co-operative Banks (PCBs) meet the working capital needs of cottage and tiny industries.

3.22.5 National Bank for Agriculture and Rural Development (NABARD): The main objective of NABARD is to provide assistance to agriculture and agriculture related activities. The bank also conducts promotional programmes for rural development such as Rural Entrepreneurship Development Programme (REDP), training cum production programmes and action plan for rural industrialisation.

3.22.6 North Eastern Development Finance Corporation Ltd.: North Eastern Development Finance Corporation Ltd. (NEDFI), promoted by All-India Financial Institution and SBI, was incorporated in August 1995 under the Companies Act, 1956 with the objective of providing long-term solutions to the industrial financing needs of the North-Eastern Region as also to guide entrepreneurs in identifying viable projects, equip them with requisite skills and technical capabilities. NEDFI hitherto focussed on projects in the eight States of North-Eastern Region viz. Arunachal Pradesh, Assam, Manipur, Meghalaya, Mizoram, Nagaland, Tripura and Sikkim. NEDFI deals mainly with first generation entrepreneurs, small-scale industries, new technologies and start-up projects. Besides offering financial products like Working Capital Loan, Composite Loans, North-East Equity Fund and Micro-Finance, NEDFI also provides marketing assistance in the North-Eastern Region and helps in the preparation of techno-economic feasibility studies. NEDFI also acts as a nodal agency for disbursement of Central capital investment subsidy, transport subsidy and working capital interest subsidy for the North-Eastern States. Besides, NEDFI works on State-specific programmes for all the eight States based on the resources available locally. It identifies thrust areas for the constituent States and conducts industry/sector-specific studies relevant to the Region.

3.22.7 State Financial Corporations: The State Financial Corporations (SFCs) are State-level financial institutions and play a crucial role in the development of small and medium enterprises in their respective States in tandem with national priorities. Of the 18 SFCs in the country, 17 were set up under the SFCs Act, 1951. Tamil Nadu Industrial Investment Corporation Ltd., which was originally established as Madras Industrial Investment Corporation in 1949 under the Companies Act, 1913, also functions as a SFC. The SFCs provide financial assistance by way of term loans, direct subscription to equity/debentures, guarantees, discounting of bills of exchange and seed/special capital. Besides, the SFCs operate a number of schemes of refinance and equity type assistance on behalf of SIDBI, in addition to special schemes for artisans and special target groups such as SC/ST, women, ex-servicemen and physically handicapped.

3.22.8 Industrial Bank of India (IDBI): IDBI was established on July1, 1964 as a wholly owned subsidiary of RBI. It is the principal financial institution for co-coordinating, in conformity with the national priorities the activities of the institutions engaged in financing, promoting or developing industry. The various schemes of IDBI are Project Finance, Soft Loan, Technical Development Fund, Refinance of Industrial Loans, Bills Discounting, Seed Capital Assistance, Subscription to shares/ bonds of financial institutions, Concessional Assistance Scheme for manufacture and installation of Renewable Energy System.

3.22.9 Industrial Finance Corporation of India (IFCI): IFCI is the first development bank, which was established on July 1, 1948 under a special statute with the aim of providing medium and long-term loans to industrial concerns in India.

3.22.10 Industrial Credit and Investment Corporation of India Limited (ICICI): ICICI was set up in 1955 to encourage and assist industrial development in India. Its objectives are assistance in the creation, expansion and modernisation of industrial enterprises, encouraging and promoting the participation of capital in such enterprises and encouraging and promoting industrial development and the expansion of capital markets.

3.22.11 Industrial Investment Corporation (IIC): It provides Soft Loan/Seed Capital Assistance to viable projects in the small- handicap of promoters or because of certain location disadvantages. The assistance under the scheme will be for meeting the gap between normally scale sector, which have difficulties of being implemented because of financial expected level of promoters' contribution envisaged by the corporation and actual amount that the promoters could bring in on their own. It also provides financial assistance to purchase generators, vehicles, fishing Trawler etc.

3.23 Schemes of SIDBI

The SIDBI has two schemes for women entrepreneurs, viz.

3.23.1 Mahila Udyam Nidhi Scheme (MUN): This scheme is offered to Women entrepreneurs for setting up new projects in tiny / small scale sector and rehabilitation of viable sick SSI units. Existing tiny and small scale industrial units and service enterprises undertaking expansion, modernisation, technology upgradation and diversification are also eligible. The scheme is operated through SFCs/Twin function SIDCs/ Scheduled Commercial Banks/ Scheduled Urban Co-operative Banks. The main purpose of this loan is to meet the gap in equity. The cost of the project shall not exceed Rs. 10 lakh. Soft loan limit is 25 per cent of the cost of project subject to a maximum of Rs. 2.5 lakh per project. Service Charges @ one per cent p.a. is charged on soft loan. Minimum promoters' contribution is 10 per cent and borrowers are allowed to retain central or state investment subsidy to meet working capital requirements.

3.23.2 Mahila Vikas Nidhi Scheme: SIDBI operationalises this programme by assisting accredited NGOs (NGOs that have been in existence for at least five years, registered with properly constituted bye-laws, memorandum and articles of association, governing body, broad-based management and properly maintained accounts and having good track record) to create training and marketing infrastructure especially for rural women. MVN is SIDBI's specially designed Fund for economic development of women, especially the rural poor, by providing them avenues for training and employment opportunities. A judicious mix of loan and grant is extended to accredited NGOs for creation of training and other infrastructural facilities. The basic activity involves setting up of Training-cum-Production Centres (TPCs) by the assisted NGOs to ensure that women are provided with training and employment opportunities. In addition, activities like vocational training, strengthening of marketing set up for the products of the beneficiary group, arrangements for supply of improved inputs, production and technology improvement are also covered under the MVN scheme. Assistance is given mainly towards capital expenditure and support of a recurring nature is discouraged.

3.23.3 Informal Channel for Credit Needs on Soft Terms: The SIDBI has also taken initiative to set up an informal channel for credit needs on soft terms giving special emphasis to women.

3.23.4 Training for Credit Utilisation and Credit Delivery: SIDBI also provides training for credit utilisation and credit delivery skills for the executives of voluntary organisations working for women. SIDBI has introduced several other schemes such as National Equity Fund, Micro Credit Scheme, and Entrepreneurship Development Programmes etc.

3.24 Women Enterprise Development Scheme (WEDS) of North Eastern Financial Institution

NEDFi, as a financial institution has been working for the economic upliftment of the women in the north-eastern region by providing them training and financial assistance under Micro Finance Scheme (MF), North East Equity Fund Scheme (NEEF), Scheme for North East Handloom and Handicrafts (SNEHH), Jute Enterprises Development Scheme (JEDS) etc. NEDFi offers a special scheme exclusively for women entrepreneurs at liberal terms and conditions wherein financial assistance would be provided for any viable income generating activity to help the women for taking up business ventures and will lead to economic development of the region. Existing business ventures will also be eligible under the scheme for expansion, modernization and diversification.

Skilled women entrepreneurs in the age group of 18 to 50 years can take loan for any viable income generating activity including small business trade. Soft loan is provided to the extent of 25 per cent and remaining 60 per cent as Term loan. Project cost (including working capital) should not exceed Rs.5 lakh. Minimum Promoter's Contribution shall be 15 per cent. First charge is created on assets financed by the

Corporation. Eligible units will be covered under CGFTSI (Credit Guarantee Fund Trust for Small Industries). For Soft loan, service charge @ one per cent is levied. For Term loan interest depends on PLR. Repayment period is 3 to 7 years.

3.25 Schemes of State Bank of India

3.25.1 Entrepreneur Scheme: Under this scheme, the bank provides assistance to technically qualified, trained and experienced women entrepreneurs to set up new viable industrial projects. This loan scheme provides assistance to technocrats, including those unable to meet the normal margin requirement under the liberalised scheme, to set up viable industrial projects. The applicant must hold a degree/diploma in Engineering/Technology or a degree in Business/Industrial Management/CA/Cost Accountancy with adequate experience. A craftsman with adequate experience is also eligible. The amount of loan is limited to the project cost. The bank gives assistance by way of term loans, working capital and equity funds to meet margin requirements. The bank is quite flexible in terms of security and insurance, depending upon the merits of the application. It charges a low rate of interest and repayment can be made over a period of five to seven years.

3.25.2 Liberalised Scheme: Under the Liberalised Scheme for small-scale industries, entrepreneurs are eligible to get need-based credit for productive purposes. Comprehensive credit facilities for acquisition of fixed assets, working capital, bills facility, etc. are available under the scheme.

3.25.3 Small Business Finance: This scheme aims at creating self-employment opportunities in small business ventures. It is beneficial to a larger section of people with lower investment needs. Credit is offered on liberal terms to priority sectors like retail traders, professional/self-employed, business enterprises and transport operators.

3.25.4 Scheme for Professionals and Self-Employed: Financial assistance under this scheme is offered to women who are doctors, chartered accountants, cost accountants, lawyers, solicitors, management consultants, journalists and with other qualifications.

3.25.5 Loans to Business Enterprises: Loans are given to women who wish to set up business enterprises like restaurants and Xerox centres and computer centres.

3.25.6 The Stree Sakthi Package: The Stree Sakthi Package offered by the SBI and its subsidiaries gives 0.5 per cent concession on interest rates and reduction in margin money by 5 per cent. The proposals are proposed with in 30 days. And the stake of the women entrepreneurs is nil for loans up to Rs.25 000. The same applies for loans up to Rs.200000 to repair fixed assets and working capital. Equity assistance is also provided in rare cases.

The other Schemes of SBI include credit facilities to women entrepreneurs under various Central and State Government-sponsored poverty alleviation and self-employment schemes like Prime Minister's Rozgar Yojana and the Swarnajayanti Gram Swarozgar Yojana (SGSY), encouragement of women to form Self-Help Groups under the SGSY scheme etc. Each Self-Help Group is eligible for a maximum subsidy of Rs. 1.25 lakh. Loans up to Rs. 25,000 are sanctioned within 15 days of the submission of the applications with all the required particulars. Loans for higher amounts are sanctioned within eight to nine weeks. No collateral security is necessary for loans up to Rs. 5 lakh in the case of advances to Small-Scale Sectors.

3.26 Schemes of Punjab National Bank

Punjab National Bank provides two schemes, viz. Mahila Udyam Nidhi Scheme and Mahila Sashaktikaran Abhiyan exclusively to women for their empowerment. Besides these schemes, the bank provides Priority Sector Schemes to women entrepreneurs, viz. credit assistance to women entrepreneurs in tiny and SSI sector, credit Assistance to women beneficiaries in other Priority Sector Schemes, credit facilities to women entrepreneurs under various Govt. sponsored schemes like

Prime Minister's Rozgar Yojana(PMRY), Swarnjayanti Gram Swarozgar Yojana (SGSY), Swarnjayanti Shahari Rozgar Yojana (SJSRY), Differential Rate of Interest Scheme (DRI),Micro credit to Self-Help Groups(SHGs) etc. Women borrowers are given special relaxations in interest rates, margins and upfront fees in all these schemes (except DRI).

3.27 Schemes of Canara Bank

Canara Bank offers various schemes to finance women entrepreneurs like

- **Stree Shakti Package:** This package is offered to women to put up small-scale industry.
- **Mahila Udyam Nidhi Scheme:** This scheme is offered by the bank to the tiny and small scale industry with the support of various State Governments and banks.
- **Annapurna Scheme:** This scheme has been introduced to provide finance to women for the establishment of food catering units.
- **Priyadarshini Scheme:** This loan is offered to women entrepreneurs. Maximum loan granted under this scheme is Rs. 25,000.
- **Can Mahila:** Loans are granted up to Rs. 50,000 to women under this scheme.
- **Artisan Credit Cards and Laghu Udyami Credit Cards:** This is a loan to meet the financial need of women. It can be used to buy house hold articles, gold, jewellery, computers etc. Women between the age 18 to 55 can avail this loan. They can be house wife. working or self-employed. The present rate of interest is 11.5 per cent .For salaried and self employed the loan limit is Rs. 50,000 and for non-workers with an annual family income it is Rs. 25,000 and Rs. 50,000 for women with a family income of Rs. 1.5 lakh.

3.28 Schemes of Dena Bank

This bank has special schemes to finance women

entrepreneurs. Some incentives offered are five per cent concession in the interest rate, no processing fee, easy payment options and no penalty for repayment. The loan amount up to Rs. 5 lakh is offered to women entrepreneurs who are professionals. The loan is also extended to artists, small and medium cottage industries run by women.

3.29 Scheme of Bank of India

3.29.1 Priyadarshini Yojana: This facility is offered to women for setting up of small, village and cottage industries. The loan covers the payment for machinery. There is a one per cent cut in the interest rate for loans above Rs. 2 lakh.

3.30 Scheme of Union Bank of India

3.30.1 Viklang Mahila Vikas Yojana: This is a special scheme for handicapped women for starting their own vocations. Physically handicapped women are identified and after providing vocational training according to their aptitude financial assistance of Rs. 25,000 is offered to start the new vocation.

3.31 Schemes of Central Bank of India

3.31.1 Kalyani: This is a scheme launched to benefit the women entrepreneurs and to the requirements of women professionals for economic pursuits in industry, agricultural and allied activities, business or profession. Women entrepreneurs could avail financial assistance for pursuing vocations of their choice, viz. small businesses (setting up a small lunch/canteen, mobile restaurant, circulating library etc.), professional and self employed(doctors, chartered accountants, engineers or trained in art or craft etc.), retail trade, village and cottage/tiny industries(manufacturing, processing, preservation and services such as handloom, weaving handicraft, food-processing, garment making etc in village and small towns with a population not exceeding Rs. 50,000 utilising locally available resources/ skills), small scale industries(unit engaged in manufacture, processing or preservation of goods), agriculture and allied activities(raising of crops, floriculture, fisheries, bee-keeping, nursery, sericulture etc. and also trading in agricultural inputs), and Government sponsored programmes, where capital subsidies are available.

3.32 Scheme of Orient Bank of Commerce

3.32.1 Orient Mahila Vikas Yojana: This special scheme is offered for the benefit of woman entrepreneurs. The loan amount is offered between two and 10 lakh with a two per cent concession in interest. Loans above Rs.10 lakh are also offered at one per cent concession. Enterprises consisting of all units managed by women and have a share of 51 per cent are eligible for this loan. In case of term loans, the repayment period is up to seven years with a maximum grace period of 12 months depending on the nature of the activity.

4

Government Agencies Promoting Women Entrepreneurship in India

The development of entrepreneurship among women requires Government support and the elaboration and implementation of targeted policies and programmes enabling women to enter the private sector with greater confidence, develop their businesses and provide equal opportunities for entering competitive markets in and outside the country. The role of various institutions set up specifically for the promotion and fostering of entrepreneurship in SME sector is quite unique. The Government of India has created Ministry of Small Scale Industries and Agro and Rural Industries (SSI&ARI) in October 1999 as the nodal Ministry for formulation of policy and co-ordination of Central assistance relating to promotion and development of the small-scale industries in India.

The Ministry of Small Scale Industries and Agro and Rural Industries was bifurcated into two separate Ministries, namely, Ministry of Small Scale Industries and Ministry of Agro and Rural Industries in September, 2001. The Central Government has set up a number of organisations for the promotion of small scale industries in order to meet the requirements of the rapidly developing entrepreneurship in the SME sector. Through theses institutions, the Government of India provides adequate credit, funds for technology up gradation and modernisation, adequate infrastructure facilities, modern testing facilities and quality certification, modern management practices and skill up gradation through advanced training facilities; marketing assistance etc., at par with the large industries sector.

The policy measures taken by the Government include credit, marketing, technology, entrepreneurship development or fiscal, financial or infrastructural support. In recent years, the Government policies have stressed the increasing role of Industry Associations in the setting up of common facilities and other ventures in the area of technology, marketing and other support services. Industry Associations also impart institutional support to the small-scale sector. There has been several industrial policy resolutions over the years specifically articulated and clearly spelt for encouraging entrepreneurship.

The identification, training and development of a large number of local entrepreneurs are strategic to the development of entrepreneurship in rural and backward areas. Training is provided for developing their entrepreneurial skills such as technical, managerial, financial, communication crisis management, leadership etc. Successful SMEs do not come up into being without proper technical assistance. A positive encouragement on the part of Government agencies is required for the development and growth of entrepreneurship in the private sector. The success of entrepreneurship mainly depends on the well established institutional set-up.

Responding to the increasing trend of women opting for entrepreneurship, many organisations have come up with the idea of special training for women interested in setting up their own enterprises. The Government has laid special emphasis on the need for conducting special entrepreneurial training programmes for women to enable them to start their own ventures. For women various development programmes have been implemented by the Government. But the efforts to percolate information by the institutions and accessing them to women entrepreneurs is missing which is further aggravated by women's lack of initiative to seek out information to help themselves.

The policies and programmes of Government agencies should reach the ultimate consumers properly so as to ensure their success. But, these policies and programmes have not been able to facilitate the growth of women entrepreneurship to the expected level due to various reasons, viz. bureaucratic control, rigid procedures, limitations on the part of women themselves, Most of the women both in absolute and in relative terms have not reached the critical mass to make an impact on the system.

More than 3,000 organisations are today promoting entrepreneurship in India through a variety of strategies. Following are the major Government agencies/organisations that assist entrepreneurs in the SME sector in India which are functioning at the national level.

4.1 National Level Agencies

4.1.1 Ministry of SSI: The Ministry of SSI is the nodal agency which designs policies, programmes, projects and schemes in consultation with its organisations and various stakeholders and monitors their implementation with a view to assist the promotion and growth of small-scale industries. The Ministry also performs the function of policy advocacy on behalf of the SSI sector with other Ministries/ Departments of the Central Government and the State and Union Territories. The policies and various programmes/projects/schemes for providing infrastructure and support services to small enterprises is implemented through its attached office, namely the Small Industry Development Organisation (SIDO) and the National Small Industries Corporation (NSIC) Ltd., a public sector undertaking under the Ministry.

4.1.2 Small-Scale Industries Board: The SSI Board is the apex non-statutory advisory body constituted by the Government of India to render advice on all issues pertaining to the SSI sector. The SSI Board provides to its members a forum for interaction to facilitate co-operation and inter-institutional linkages and to render advice to the Government on various policy matters, for the development of the sector.

4.1.3 Small Industry Development Organisation (SIDO): SIDO, established in 1954, is an apex body for formulating, coordinating, implementing and monitoring policies and programmes for the promotion and development of the small-scale industries in the country. The Development Commissioner (SSI) heads it.   The SIDO provides a comprehensive range of common facilities, technology support services, marketing assistance, etc., through its network of 30 Small Industries Service Institutes (SISIs), 28 Branch SISIs, 7 Field Testing Stations (FTS), 4 Regional Testing Centres, 2 Small Entrepreneur Promotion and Training Institutes (SEPTI) and 1 Hand Tool Design Development and Training Centre.

4.1.4 Small Industries Service Institutes (SISIs): The SISIs provide services such as technical consultancy, training, testing, marketing, economic information service including sub contract change, common facility service and advisory service. The SISIs also perform job works and provide common facility services to the small / tiny units through workshops set up in these institutes. Out of the 58 SISIs / Br. SISIs, 15 SISIs/Br. SISIs are in the backward and hilly areas of the country.

4.1.5 Product-cum-Process Development Centres (PPDCs): Six PPDCs have been set up at Firozabad for glass industry, Kannauj for essential oils, Meerut for sports goods and leisure time equipments, Agra for foundry and forgings, Ramnagar for electronic industries and Mumbai for electrical measuring instruments. They provide the following services:

- Product design and innovation.
- R&D support.
- Technical support.
- Manpower development and training.
- Development of new processes and upgrade the existing level of technology.

4.1.6 Regional Training Centres (RTCs): RTCs have been set up in four metropolitan cities, viz. New Delhi, Mumbai, Calcutta and Chennai for providing technical consultancy and testing facilities. RTCs also have eight field testing stations for providing testing services to SSI units.

RTCs are accredited to Bureau of International Standards (BIS), NTPC, RITES, Pollution Control Board and NABL. These Centres provide performance testing, type testing, acceptance testing, calibration services and development of processes for various products.

4.1.7 Central Footwear Training Institutes (CFTIs): CFTIs provide training facilities and design development facilities for the footwear and leather industry. Their branches are situated at Agra, Chennai, Mumbai and Calcutta. The CFTIs in Agra and Chennai are autonomous organisations, a Government of India Society under the purview of Small Industries Development Organisation, Ministry of Industry.

4.1.8 National Small Industries Corporation (NSIC) Ltd.: NSIC, an ISO 9001-2000 Government organisation was established in 1955 by the Government of India to promote, aid and foster the growth of small-scale industries in the country through a blend of promotional and commercial activities.

4.1.8 National Institutes for Entrepreneurship Development: The Ministry has established three National Institutes, viz. the National Institute of Small Industry Extension Training (NISIET) at Hyderabad, the National Institute of Entrepreneurship and Small Business Development (NIESBUD) at New Delhi and the Indian Institute of Entrepreneurship (IIE) at Guwahati as autonomous bodies for entrepreneurship development and training. These Institutes are responsible for development of training models and undertaking of research and training for entrepreneurship development in the SSI sector.

4.1.9 National Institute of Small Industry Extension Training (NISIET): NISIET is an autonomous body under the administrative control of office of the DC (SSI) which was set up as an apex institute in 1960 by the Government of India with the charter of assisting in the promotion, development, and modernisation of small and medium enterprises (SMEs) in the country, mainly by creating a pro-business environment that would enable SMEs to progress towards success and prosperity. As a global organisation, NISIET plays a stellar role in positioning the SMEs on the growth trajectory of the Indian SME sector and developing countries around the world in promoting self-employment and enterprise development. The institute provides consultancy, training, research, and education for retaining the competitive edge of SMEs in ever-changing markets. NISIET trains entrepreneurs, managers and various functionaries of the Government through its various training programmes. NISET also undertakes research and consultancy activities for small -scale industries. The institute conducts national and international training programmes every year.

4.1.10 National Institute for Entrepreneurship and Small Business Development (NIESBUD): NIESBUD is an apex body for coordinating entrepreneurship and small business development activities in India. It is an autonomous body under the administrative control of the office of the DC (SSI) and is a part of SIDO. It coordinates and oversees the activities of various agencies engaged in entrepreneurship development. Its activities include conducting training programmes, preparing model syllabi for training programmes, conducting seminars and developing teaching aids.

4.2 State Level Agencies

4.2.1 Directorate of Industries: The Directorate of Industries is the executive agency for the promotion and development of the village and small industries sector. It acts under the overall guidance of SIDO. Its functions are of both regulatory and developmental in nature. The Directorate of Industries has a network of District Industrial Centres (DIC) at the district level, industrial officers at the sub-divisional level and extension officers at the block level functioning under its control.

4.2.2 District Industries Centre (DIC): DICs play a vital role in promoting industries at the District level. DICs provide necessary project assistance for the prospective entrepreneurs. The services being rendered by the District Industries Centres include, identification of prospective entrepreneurs to take up viable projects, issue of SSI registration certificates, maintenance of SSI database, recommendation of technical feasibility reports to various financial institutions, allotment of industrial land in industrial development areas, development plots, industrial estates, mini industrial estates etc. arrangement of entrepreneurship development training, recommendation of various incentives as per the industrial policy of the State Government, implementation and monitoring of Prime Minister's Rozgar Yojana, registering of new cooperative societies and to extend financial assistance to the existing ones, assistance for the revival of sick SSI units, conducting seminars, technology clinics, entrepreneurs development programmes for prospective entrepreneurs and organise various exhibitions, fairs etc. implementation of schemes, which are beneficial for the weaker section as well as for women.

4.2.3 State Small Industries Development Corporations (SSIDCs): The SSIDCs were established under the Companies Act, 1956 as State Government undertakings with the specific objective of promoting and developing small, tiny and village industries in the States/Union Territories, which, in turn, stimulate self-employment opportunities. The important functions/activities of SSIDCs include procurement and distribution of raw materials, supply of machinery on hire-purchase basis, assistance to SSI units for marketing their products, construction/upgradation of basic infrastructure facilities in industrial estates/sheds, extending seed capital assistance on behalf of the respective State Governments, organising training programmes for unemployed youth, providing managerial assistance to production units and management of States' Emporia for providing sales window for handlooms, handicrafts and SSI items.

4.2.4 State Industrial Development Corporation/State Industrial Investment Corporation (SIDC/SIIC): The SIDCs were established under the Companies Act, 1956, as wholly-owned undertakings of the respective State Governments with the specific objective of promoting and developing medium and large-scale industries in their respective States/Union Territories. There are 28 SIDCs in the country. These institutions act as catalysts to industrial growth. The SIDCs extend financial assistance in the form of rupee loans, underwriting and direct subscription to shares/debentures, guarantees, inter-corporate deposits, and also open letters of credit on behalf of their borrowers. The SIDCs also undertake a range of promotional activities, including preparation of feasibility reports, conducting industrial potential surveys, entrepreneurship development programmes and developing industrial areas/estates. The SIDCs, as nodal agencies of State Governments, also manage and operate State incentive schemes. Further, some SIDCs act as nodal agencies for NRI investment and Foreign Direct Investment (FDI) in their respective States.

4.3 Other Agencies

4.3.1 Khadi and Village Industries Commission (KVIC): VIC, established in 1957 as a statutory body under an Act of Parliament, is entrusted with the responsibility of planning, promoting, organising and implementing programmes for the development of khadi and village industries in rural areas in co-ordination with other agencies engaged in rural development in the country.

4.3.2 Technical Consultancy Organisations (TCOs): TCOs were promoted by all-India financial institutions in various States in collaboration with State-level financial /development institutions and commercial banks during the seventies and eighties to cater to the consultancy needs of the small and medium enterprises and new entrepreneurs. At present, there are 18 TCOs operating in various States with some of them operating in more than one State. TCOs provide various types of consultancy services, which include preparation of feasibility studies and project reports/ profiles, identification of potential entrepreneurs, technical and management assistance to new entrepreneurs, product-specific market research/surveys, project supervision, energy audit and energy conservation assignments, consultancy assignments on turn-key basis, export consultancy for export-oriented projects, management consultancy services, especially for diagnostic study of sick units or improvement in the existing units and rehabilitation programmes, entrepreneurship development programmes/skill upgradation programmes and merchant banking services.

4.3.3 Entrepreneurship Development Institute of India (EDII): EDII is an autonomous body situated in Ahmedabad which was sponsored jointly by leading financial institutions in India and Government of Gujarat. Its main objectives are to augment the supply of trained entrepreneurs, to promote micro enterprises at the rural level and to inculcate the spirit of entrepreneurship amongst youth. EDII conducts training programmes on entrepreneurship education, micro finance and micro enterprise development. It designs training programmes through innovative training techniques and updated information. It also conducts trainers meet and chief executives meet to facilitate sharing of information and experience.

4.3.4 National Science and Technology Entrepreneurship Development Board (NSTEDB): The NSTEDB was established in 1982 by the Government of India under the aegis of Department of Science & Technology, is an institutional mechanism to help promote knowledge driven and technology intensive enterprises. The Board, having representations from socio-economic and scientific Ministries/Departments, aims to convert "job-seekers" into "job-generators" through Science & Technology (S&T) interventions. It is a National Resource Institution exclusively for entrepreneurship development to promote knowledge driven and technology intensive enterprises. The Board, has representations from socio-economic and scientific Ministries/Departments.

The main objectives of NSTEDB are:

- To promote and develop high-end entrepreneurship for S&T manpower as well as self-employment by utilising S&T infrastructure and by using S&T methods.
- To facilitate and conduct various informational services relating to promotion of entrepreneurship.
- To network agencies of the support system, academic institutions and Research & Development (R&D) organisations to foster entrepreneurship and self-employing/using S&T with special focus on backward areas as well.
- To act as a policy advisory body with regard to entrepreneurship.

4.3.5 National Commission on Enterprises in the Unorganised/Informal Sector: The National Commission on Enterprises in the Unorganised/Informal Sector was constituted in September, 2004. The Commission recommends measures considered necessary for bringing about improvement in the productivity of the informal sector enterprises, generation of large scale employment opportunities on a sustainable basis, particularly in the rural areas, enhancing the competitiveness of the sector in the emerging global environment, linkage of the sector with institutional framework in areas such as credit, raw material, infrastructure, technology up gradation, marketing and formulation of suitable arrangements for skill development.

4.3.6 National Research and Development Centre (NRDC): NRDC and 40 National Laboratories provide new technology to small-scale sector through SIDO and extension facilities through SISIs and their branches.

4.3.7 National Centre for HACCP Certification (NCHC): NCHC was set up to ensure that internationally traded products are safe and free from adulteration. The fundamental criterion for international trade is food quality. Foods should be safe and free from adulteration. Governments have designed and enacted standards and regulations that ensure consumer safety and prevent malpractices in the production and sale of foods. Many importing countries have established food control agencies to ensure that all imported foods comply with those produced domestically. All exporting nations have food control agencies to ensure that export products comply with the statutory requirements of the importing countries.

4.3.8 National Horticulture Board (NHB): NHB was set up by the Government of India in 1984 as an autonomous society under the Societies Registration Act 1860 with an objective to promote integrated development of horticulture in the country by co-ordinating, stimulating, sustaining production and processing of fruits and vegetables establishment of sound infrastructure and focus on post-harvest management to reduce losses. The subsidy is released to the leading participating leading financial institution on the completion of project approved by the Government.

4.3.9 National Productivity Council (NPC): NPC aims at combining its promotional mission with a totally professional approach to provide world class services needed by Indian industry to become internationally competitive in a global economy. NPC aims at propagating productivity as an evolving concept, which includes attention to special issues, and concerns relating to quality, environment, energy, integrated rural and community development, women workers etc. Productivity shall increasingly be viewed in this context and not in the conventional sense of mere production increases with constant resources. NPC's thrust is on providing modern and high quality productivity-related services to sectors not adequately addressed by others, especially the small-scale industry and informal sector. NPC is also a change agent, aiming to assist the Central and State Governments, local bodies and other organisations in improving the quality and efficiency of public services. NPC does not seek to supplant the private sector consultancy organisations or specialised bodies, though it would compete with them to the extent that it helps keep its professional skills upgraded and maintain its market credibility.

4.3.10 Rural Development and Self- Employment Training (RUDSET) Institute: RUDSET Institute conducts specific custom-made programmes for women empowerment, viz. programmes for SHG leaders on SHG formation and management, programmes for SHG members on entrepreneurship development and skill development.

4.3.11 Directorate of Handloom and Textiles: Government participates in factory type handloom co-operative societies, revitalises factory type handloom co-operative societies and assists silk weaving subsidy for hank yarn. Assistance is also given for exporting of handloom goods, schemes for handloom and power loom co-operative societies, under the financial assistance of National Co-operative Development Corporation.

4.3.12 Central Institute for Research and Training in Employment Service (CIRTES): Recognising the need for conducting incessant research and regular training to the employment service personnel, CIRTES was established in October, 1964 under the aegis of Directorate General of Employment & Training (DGE&T), Ministry of Labour, and Government of India. Later, in 1970 and in 1987, the Institute was expanded with the added responsibilities of developing career literature and to provide guidance for the promotion of self-employment.

4.3.13 Directorate General of Employment and Training (DGE&T): DGE&T was set up in July 1945 for the purpose of resettling demobilised defense service personnel and discharged war workers in civil life, in pursuance of the recommendations of the Training and Employment Service Committee (Shiva Rao Committee set up in 1952). The day-to-day administrative control of the Employment Exchanges and Industrial Training Institutes (ITIs) was transferred to the State Governments /Union Territory Administrations with effect from 01.11.1956 on cost sharing basis between Centre and States.

4.3.14 Central Institute for Research and Training in Employment Service (CIRTES): CIRTES was established in October, 1964 under the aegis of Directorate General of Employment & Training (DGE&T), Ministry of Labour, and Government of India for a systematic approach in dealing with the matters relating to formulation of policies and procedures, standards, staff training and evaluation of employment exchanges. This necessitated systematic research, development of tools and techniques and training of the personnel. Recognising this need for conducting incessant research and regular training to the employment service personnel, Later, in 1970 and in 1987, the Institute was expanded with the added responsibilities of developing career literature and to provide guidance for the promotion of self-employment.

4.3.15 Information and Facilitation Counter (IFC): The IFC in the office of DC (SSI) disseminates updated information for the benefit of the services and activities of the DC (SSI) and related institutions in the area of small scale industry promotion and development. The Information Counter is computerised and supplemented by hard copies of information such as brochures, pamphlets, books, etc. The services made available are (i) counselling and information on how to set up a SSI unit, (ii) supply of technical information, project reports and details of various programmes, guidance on policies concerning small enterprises and schemes of various State Governments, (iv) information on the registration scheme and supply of registration forms, (v) information on the IDR Act and the Notifications on definition, etc. issued under the Act. (vi) educates on credit policies of the Government, (vii) supply of statistics related to the small scale industries, (viii) technical and marketing information concerning small scale industries, (ix) list of Items reserved for exclusive manufacture in the SSI sector.

4.3.16 Bureau of Indian Standards (BIS): The BIS, the national standards body of India, was established in the year 1947 under the name Indian Standards Institution (ISI). The ISI was set up as a registered society, under a Government of India resolution to induct the culture of standardisation and quality in the Indian industry. For building the climate of quality culture and consciousness and greater participation of consumers in formulation and implementation of National Standards, the Bureau of Indian Standards Act was passed in 1986 and on 1 April 1987, the newly formed BIS took over the staff, assets, liabilities and functions of the erstwhile ISI.

4.3.17 Small Enterprise Information & Resource Centre Network (SENET): SENET was launched by the Office of the DC(SSI) in April, 1997to pioneer, create and promote databases and information, to facilitate networking amongst the information seekers, of the small scale sector, including the central/state Governments, Government agencies engaged directly or indirectly in the promotion and development of the SSI sector, national and state level industry associations, NGOs, to establish linkages with existing databases and the entrepreneur, for development and promotion of the small scale sector, to carry out office automation in the office of the DC(SSI) for bringing out transparency in the functioning of the office, to create a website for hosting data available within the organisation, to host alliance databases in order to serve as a one-stop-shop for information seekers, industry associations and also individual industries.

4.3.18 Export Guidance Cell: Export Guidance Cell provides information on existing export activities to the entrepreneurs and necessary assistance on procedural matters for export. In order to render service effectively, providing Computers with Internet and Portal connectivity have strengthened the Export Guidance Cells. The globalization has accelerated the process of opening up of economy and competition in the market. Difficulties in marketing of SSI products have always been a major problem for small-scale manufacturers .The SSIs should have access to the export potential for expanding the marketing network. Towards this initiative, the Government has formed Export Guidance Cell in all the District Industries Centres.

4.3.19 Indian Investment Centre: The Indian Investment Centre, a Government of India organisation is the single window agency which provides authentic information or any assistance that may be required for investments, technical collaborations and joint ventures at free of charge. It provides information and assistance to Indian entrepreneurs for setting up joint ventures in other countries. It provides information and assistance to foreign entrepreneurs in locating suitable Indian parties for collaboration in the establishment of projects abroad including third country projects.

4.3.20 Entrepreneurship and Business Development Centres (EBDCs): EBDCs have been established in selected Universities and Colleges, Regional Engineering Colleges and other Institutions/Organisations under the NEDB Scheme to motivate students to take up entrepreneurship as a career option with the objective to promote self-employment through creation of small, micro and tiny enterprises in the country which would not only provide self-employment opportunities but are also expected to create additional job opportunities in these enterprises.

4.3.21 Resource Development International Ltd. (RDI): RDI India is engaged in the process of human capital actualisation through management education, consultancy and training and development initiatives. RDI provides education from credible Universities to help a corporate build and also helps to develop a work culture and learning environment. The core services include education, training development, organisational development, human resource consulting, personal empowerment programmes, recruitment and staffing etc.

4.3.22 Federation of Association of Small Scale Industries (FASSI): FASSI was established in 1959 to promote the development of SSI, co-operate with industries and other institutions. It undertakes consultancy and research studies and has established trade centers and test centers. It offers services like organising meetings/ conferences, analysis and interpretation of policies and taking up members' difficulties to the Government for redressal of their complaints.

4.3.23 Confederation of Indian Industry (CII): The CII provides advisory and consultative services and disseminates information to the Government and industry. It also organises industry exhibitions, trade fairs and the India Engineering Trade Fair. CII also plays an important role in promoting international industrial co-operation.

4.3.24 Federation of Indian Chamber of Commerce of India (FICCI): FICCI provides a platform for discussing various industry related issues. It is the rallying point for free enterprises in India. It has empowered Indian businesses, in the changing times, to shore up their competitiveness and enhance their global reach. It has an expanding direct membership of enterprises drawn from large, medium, small and tiny segments of manufacturing, distributive trade and services It has a network of around 400 chamber of commerce across the country. FICCI maintains the lead as the proactive business solution provider through research, interactions at the highest political level and global networking. It also maintains synergic relationships with the central and state Governments. FICCI is the nodal agencies for several agencies, like International Chamber Of Commerce, Confederation of Asia-Pacific Chamber of Commerce and Industry, which provides a platform for promoting international trade and investment.

4.3.25 Associated Chamber of Commerce and Industries in India (ASSOCHAM): ASSOCHAM represents the cross-section of business industry, services and professions located all over the country. Its main thrust is on "Infrastructure for accelerating economic growth".

4.3.26 Indian Merchants' Chamber: IMC's goal is to create cutting-edge communication systems; create and project the Indian business image in the correct perspective, nationally and globally. It also has a Women's and Young Entrepreneurs' Wing.

4.3.27 All India Association of Industries (AIAI): AIAI is an apex industry association established in the year 1956 by a team of dedicated businesses persons with the primary task of fostering sustained industrial development in the country. It provides an effective platform to address the issues relating to trade and industry to the Government both at Central and State levels. It also helps the Indian industries in meeting the challenge of liberalisation and globalisation by providing a vital link to explore the world of new opportunities. AIAI has set up Women Entrepreneur Council for assisting women entrepreneurs.

4.3.28 World Association of Small and Medium Enterprises (WASME): WASME is a NGO governed by representatives from financial institutions, chamber of commerce, banks, department of small industries of various Governments etc. Its main aim is to bring about business co-operation among developing countries. Some of their functions include disseminating policies, strategies and support systems for promotion of SMEs in member countries, providing marketing opportunities, identification of training facilities for entrepreneurs, managers etc. Moreover, WASME also organises workshops and seminars, undertake consultancy works and act as a clearing-house of information relating to SMEs.

5

Women-specific Indian and International Agencies Promoting Women Entrepreneurship

5.1 Indian Agencies

5.1.1 Central Social Welfare Board (CSWB): CSWB is a charitable company registered under the Companies Act, 1956 assisting both in promoting voluntary action and implementing programmes fully funded by the Department. It was established in August 1953, to bring the neglected, weak, handicapped and backward sections of society into the national mainstream. As a follow up, the State Social Welfare Advisory Boards were set up with the task of implementing and monitoring of different programmes of the CSWB.

It is the pioneering national level organisation in the field of development and empowerment of women in the country. The CSWB was also envisaged as an interface between the Government and the voluntary sector for social development in the country. It has made a signal contribution in encouraging, assisting and promoting the growth of nearly twenty five thousand voluntary organisations for reaching the neglected women and children of the country.

5.1.2 Rashtriya Mahila Kosh (RMK): RMK is constituted by the Government in 1993, with the objective of meeting the credit needs of poor, asset less women, especially in the informal sector. It also offers support to develop and stabilise Self-Help Groups. RMK has taken several promotional measures to promote micro- financing, thrift, credit, formation and stabilisation of SHGs and also enterprise development for poor women.

5.1.3 Women's Wing of National Alliance of Young Entrepreneurs (NAYE): Women's Wing of NAYE was set up in 1975 for the promotion and development of women entrepreneurship. It assists women entrepreneurs in getting better access to capital, infrastructure and markets, development of management and production capabilities, identifying investment opportunities, attending to problems by taking up individual cases with appropriate authorities, sponsoring delegations, participation in trade fairs, exhibitions, buyer-seller meets, specialised conferences etc. organising seminars, workshops and training programmes for giving them wider exposure to available facilities and developing their entrepreneurial capabilities.

5.1.4 Department of Women and Child Development (DWCD): DWCD is the separate nodal agency set up by the Government of India in 1985 for development of women. The department formulates policies and programmes, enacts/amends legislations affecting women and coordinates the efforts of both Governmental and NGOs working for the development of women. The programmes include employment and income generation welfare and support services and gender sensitization and awareness generation programmes.

5.1.5 Women Entrepreneurship of Maharashtra (WIMA): WIMA was set up in 1985 with its head office in Pune. The main objective is to provide a forum for members and to help them sell their products. WIMA also provides training to its members. It has established industrial estates in New Bombay and Hadapsar.

5.1.6 Women Development Corporation (WDC): WDCs were set up in 1986 to give the necessary thrust to development of women in the states. The main objective is to create sustained income generating activities for women to provide better employment avenues for women so as to make them economically independent and self-reliant. WDCs identify women entrepreneurs, prepare a shelf of viable projects, provide technical services, to facilitate to avail credit from banks and other financial institutions, provide training and promote women's co-operative and other organisations.

5.1.7 National Commission for Women: The National Commission for Women, a statutory body, set up under the National Commission for Women Act, 1990 safeguards the rights and interests of women. The Commission continued to pursue its mandated activities, namely review of laws, interventions into specific individual complaints of atrocities and remedial action to safeguard the interests of women, whatever appropriate and feasible. The Commission has accorded highest priority to securing speedy justice to women. The Commission has been instrumental in introducing fresh ideas, innovative model, training, packages, and model for speedy justice etc.

5.1.8 Development of Women and Children in Urban Area (DWCUA): DWCUA was introduced in 1997 to organise women in socio-economic self-employment activity groups with the dual objective of providing self-employment opportunities and social strength to them. This is to be achieved through technology services, which may enable them to take up income generating activities. It provides assistance to groups of urban poor women for setting up gainful self-employment ventures. The Revolving Fund given to these groups is meant for the purposes like purchase of raw materials and marketing, infra structure support, one-time expenses on child care activity etc.

5.1.9 Women's Occupational Training Directorate: There are 10 Regional Vocational Training Institutes (RUTIs) in different parts of the country, besides a National Vocational Training Institute (NVTI) at NOIDA which organise regular skill training courses at basic, advanced and post advanced levels. By the end of the Ninth Plan there were 4, 499 Industrial Training Institutes.

5.1.10 Self-Help Groups (SHGs): SHGs are basically an association of women constituted mainly for the purpose of uplifting the women belong to the Below Poverty Line (BPL) categories to the Above Poverty Line (APL) category. Identified poor women from each family will be formed in to a group consisting of 10-15 members. Major activities of the group are income generation programmes, informal banking, credit unions health, nutritional programmes etc. The SHGs formed under each development block will be later converted into SGSY units. SHGs disburse micro credit to the members and facilitate them to enter into entrepreneurial activities.

5.1.11 National Resource Centre for women (NRCW): The NRCW is an autonomous body, which was set up to orient and sensitise policy planners towards women's issues, facilitating leadership training and creating a national data base in the field of women's development. The Department monitors the implementation of 27 beneficiary oriented schemes for women implemented by different central departments.

5.1.12 Consortium of Women Entrepreneurs of India (CWEI): CWEI is a registered civil society, a voluntary organisation that works for the economic empowerment of women in the country and world over. It gives manpower training, undertake product development activities and also act as an intermediary between Indian entrepreneurs and overseas agencies for marketing and exports. The most effective function of all these associations is their lobbying for the cause of the SSIs. It acts as a springboard for entrepreneurship, provides all escort services leading to higher productivity, competitive prices and stringent quality control for export, facilitates technology transfer, improves access to natural resources, product and design development, explore marketing linkages within and outside the country through various Haats, Buyer Seller Meets, Exhibitions and Fairs in India and abroad, disseminates timely information on policies and programs, implements and monitors govt. schemes and programs for sustainable growth of enterprises. This consortium consisting of NGO's, voluntary organisations and self-help groups, both from rural and urban areas, helps the women entrepreneurs in finding innovative techniques of production, marketing and finance.

5.1.13 Acme Centre of Management Excellence (ACME): ACME is an institute set up in New Delhi by Alternate Energy, Cold Chain Management and Environment. It provides women from business families and those who wish to venture in to the world of business, an opportunity to learn about business. The first management course for wives of businessmen which aims at developing the considerable latent talent within business families has been launched by ACME in 2000. It provides a one-year, full-time post-graduate diploma programme in business management with special focus on international business. It gives strong emphasis to teaching about the international business environment, international marketing management, research in management, international marketing logistics, international financial management, legal aspects of international business, and management information systems.

5.1.14 Mahila Vikas Samabaya Nigam (MVSN): The Mahila Vikas Samabaya Nigam (MVSN) is the nodal agency at State level for empowerment of women in Orissa. It has 217 affiliated societies out of which 54 are Women Co-operative Societies and the remaining 163 are registered under the Societies Registration Act, 1860. As a State nodal agency, the Nigam undertakes activities in three categories namely, economic programmes, social sensitisation programmes and allied infrastructural activities. The Mahila Vikas Samabaya Nigam undertakes various training programme for woman for capacity building as well as for persons with disabilities in order to enable them to take up different income generating activities. The expenditure on account of such training is met from the training grant received from the State Government. The types of training programmes conducted are Entrepreneurship Development Programme, Managerial Development Programme, and Leadership Development Programme, Training on Marketing and Sales promotion, Business Orientation Programme for persons with disabilities and other special training programmes for women. Besides, trade based technical training programmes are also conducted mostly in non-traditional sector, such as, woolen carpet weaving, fancy leather, raxin bags, gems and American diamond cutting, polishing and other activities.

5.2 International Agencies

5.2.1 Southeast Asian Nations (ASEAN) Committee on Women (ACW): ACW has developed an operational work plan for protecting and empowering ASEAN's women and in reducing their vulnerability to exploitation through increased participation in the productive workforce. It encourages their entrepreneurship and employability, leadership and regional awareness.

5.2.2 United Nations Development Fund for Women (UNIFEM): UNIFEM is the women's Fund at the United Nations. It provides financial and technical assistance to innovative programmes and strategies to foster women's empowerment and gender equality. In India, the Fund enables women entrepreneurs from Bangladesh, India, Nepal, and Pakistan to participate in the India International Trade Fair (IITF). UNIFEM has been supporting annually since 1996.

5.2.3 South Asian Women Entrepreneurs (SAWE): SAWE is a forum developed by the UNIFEM. It has made special efforts to include women artisan producers and entrepreneurs in the IITF. It supported the initiative to bring women entrepreneurs together on common platform to explore new marketing linkages and exchange of technology within and outside the country. Through experts, UNIFEM provides technical inputs, business counselling, Information and Communication Technology training and design support for increased export orders. It also helps to enhance their capacity, market linkages, formation of business alliances and improved awareness on possibilities of e-commerce. It aims at strengthening the regional network of women entrepreneurs through enabling their access to global markets, in partnership with Governments and NGOs. UNIFEM promotes exchange of information on marketing, technology exchange and trade development among women entrepreneurs from South Asia and other parts of the world.

5.2.4 South Asian Network of Women Artisans and Primary Producer Groups (ARTRAC): ARTRAC works to bring grassroots artisans and their associations closer to domestic and international markets through the use of ICT, product design support and business management training.

6

Women Development in India's Five Year Plans

A deep concern over the rights and status of women was made by the Government of India only in 1971 by appointing a Committee on the status of women (CWSI). Since then there has been a marked shift in the paradigm regarding women as critical groups for development as against targets of welfare policies in social sector. The empowerment of women has been recognised as the central issue in determining the status of women. Bringing women into the main stream of development has been a major concern for the Government of India. The Government laid special thrust on women's employment with the objective of making women self- reliant and economically independent. For this purpose, several women- specific and women- related policies were enunciated by the Government of India in all Plan documents.

6.1 First Five Year Plan (1951-1956)

The First Plan was the first attempt to lift the stagnant Indian economy from its morass. It did not introduce fresh schemes and was an attempt to synchronise and co-ordinate the post-war development programmes and the industrial sector was completely neglected. Women development programmes during the First Plan period were mainly welfare oriented. In the First Plan, it was held that 'women have the same opportunities as men for taking all kind of work, and this presupposes that they get equal facilities, so that their entity into the profession and public services is in no way prejudiced.

The Central Social Welfare Board set up in 1953 acted as an Apex Body at national level to promote voluntary action at various levels, especially at the grassroots, to take up welfare-related activities for women and children. The Central Social Welfare Board and the State Social Welfare Board implemented various women and children welfare programmes through Voluntary Organisations.

6.2 Second Five Year Plan (1956-1961)

The Second Plan had the broad objective of the establishment of a socialist pattern of society in a welfare state and continued to reflect the very same welfare approach, besides giving priority to women's education, and launching measures to improve maternal and child health services. During the Second Plan period, women were organised into Mahila Mandals in rural areas for facilitating convergence of health, nutrition and welfare measures.

6.3 Third Five Year Plan (1961-1966)

The Third Plan accorded high priority to women's education, immunisation of pre-school children and supplementary diet for children and expectant and nursing mothers.

6.4 Fourth Five Year Plan (1969-74)

Fourth Plan also accorded high priority to women's education, immunisation of pre-school children and supplementary diet for children and expectant and nursing mothers. Family and Child Welfare Centres were established to serve women and children and the families in the block. It would provide facilities for training women. Aided Centres were set up by Local Mahila Mandals with the help of the village panchayats. Provision for condensed courses for women, establishment of socio-economic units for training and employment and assistance to voluntary organizations and Mahila Mandals for carrying out various activities were made.

6.5 Fifth Five Year Plan (1974-79)

In the Fifth Plan, there was a shift in approach to women

issues from welfare orientation to a developmental approach with the objective of removal of poverty and attainment of self-reliance.

6.6 Sixth Five Year Plan (1980-1985)

The Sixth Plan adopted a multi-disciplinary approach with a special thrust on the three core sectors of health, education and employment. During the Sixth Plan, a variety of programmes were taken up under different sectors of development to ameliorate the working conditions of women and to raise their economic and social status. A significant step in this direction was to identify/promote the 'Beneficiary-Oriented Schemes' (BOS) in various developmental sectors which extended direct benefits to women. The thrust on generation of both skilled and unskilled employment through proper education and vocational training continued.

Three regional vocational training centres, one each at Bangalore, Bombay and Trivandrum, and a National Vocational Training Institute at New Delhi, with a total annual intake capacity of 600 women trainees, were set up by the Directorate General of Employment and Training (DGE&T). Apart from these, 144 Industrial Training Institutes (ITIs) exclusively meant for women were functioning in different States by the end of the Sixth Plan. The intake capacity in these institutions is 11,200 per annum.

In the Rural Development Sector, The Integrated Rural Development Programme has been extended to all the 5092 development blocks in the country during the Sixth Plan. This programme accorded priority to women heads of households. On the whole, women comprised 7 per cent of the beneficiaries covered under the IRDP during the Sixth Plan. A decision was also taken that a minimum of one-third of the beneficiaries under TRYSEM would be women and thereby, about 3.27 lakh women constituting 34.8 per cent of the total number of beneficiaries were trained.

A poverty alleviation scheme, viz. Micro Credit Scheme

was introduced to uplift rural women through rural credit.

A new scheme, namely, "Development of Women and Children in Rural Areas" (DWCRA) was started in 1982-83 as a pilot project in 50 blocks of the country. Women who were not in a position to take advantage of schemes under the IRD Programme were organised into homogeneous groups of 15 to 20. Each such group was provided training in a chosen economic activity along with necessary infrastructure. Such activities included weaving, fish vending, broom and rope making, brick making and pickle making. Training was also given in candle making and in baking. The scheme has proved quite popular. Over 1900 groups were formed and trained, benefiting about 30,000 women during the two-year period, 1983-85.

The scheme of Krishi Vigyan Kendras introduced for bridging the gap between the farmer's knowledge and available technology also covered women. Eight home science colleges for women under the scheme "Science and Technology for Women" were set up. New programmes which had a bearing on the overall economic development of women and reduction in their drudgery have been identified, comprising improved agricultural implements for farming in hill areas, better methods of sheep-rearing and wool-spinning devices for women.

Added impetus was given to the training of women in instrumentation technology for repair and maintenance of electronic equipments in offices and hospitals. In certain areas of West Bengal, tribal women were trained in making blocks from stone chips, in bamboo craft and rope making. With a view to training women in identification of herbs of medicinal value and cultivation and preparation of standardised medicinal formulations experiments were conducted on vegetable gardening in courtyards and on rooftops. A number of technology demonstration-cum-training centres at selected focal points all over the country were set up by National Research Development Corporation (NRDC) to provide expertise and resources to women entrepreneurs in respect of new technologies relevant to their daily needs and economic enterprises.

Low-cost industrial technologies were also developed, relating to food products, post-harvest operation, domestic aids for pure drinking water, educational toys, low-cost latrines and improved chullahs. A number of projects on agro-waste compaction, machines for converting agricultural waste into fuel and other technologies relating to food, chemicals, drugs and pharmaceuticals, energy and fuel, building materials, were taken up by NRDC. A compendium on appropriate technologies for women developed by NRDC was also published.

A number of schemes were taken up in the social welfare sector to benefit destitute and needy women. Nearly 3000 women were given training in skills in modern industries and provided employment under the scheme "Employment and Income-Generating. Training-cum-Production Centres for Women". Condensed courses of education and vocational training courses were organised by a number of voluntary organizations.

For creating increasing awareness of the role of women in development and the need for improvement of their status, various media units under the Ministry of Information and Broadcasting presented appealing programmes on social and economic problems and other related issues faced by women.

6.7 Seventh Five Year Plan (1985-1990)

Efforts would be made to extend facilities for income generating activities and to enable women to participate actively in socio-economic development.

In the field of science and technology, stress would be laid on evolving devices to reduce the drudgery of women, so that the time saved is utilised for developmental activities. Training and retraining would be ensured for many science and technology related programmes. The beneficiary-oriented programmes in the various sectors of development would be suitably modified or re-oriented so that the due share of benefits from such programmes is availed of by them.

Collation and analysis of information and relevant data on the development programmes for women will be undertaken in an effective manner.

Integrated Rural Development Programme (IRDP), National Rural Employment Programme (NREP), Training of Rural Youth in Self-Employment (TRYSEM) and other such programmes would have a component of functional literacy for women beneficiaries.

Special attention would be given to agriculture and allied sectors for improving existing skills of women and imparting to them new skills under the programmes of farmers' training, exchange of farmers, training in horticulture, fisheries, poultry, dairy development, fodder production, post-harvest technology, application of pesticides, budding and grafting, social forestry etc.

6.7.1 Rural Development: Efforts have been made under the Integrated Rural Development Programme to select households headed by women beneficiaries and importance would be given to achieve a larger coverage of women. Households headed by women would account for at least 20 per cent of the coverage. The scheme of DWCRA would be strengthened and modified in order to ensure that the benefits reach the target groups. The National Rural Employment Programme (NREP) and Rural Landless Employment Guarantee Scheme (RLEGP) would generate additional employment in rural areas during the lean season. Stress would be laid on giving adequate employment to women beneficiaries under these schemes. Under the programme of TRYSEM, 40 youths in the age-group 18-35 years per development block are identified and provided training in avocations which may enable them to set up self-employment ventures. About one third of the beneficiaries under this programme are expected to be women.

6.7.2 Industry: Public sector undertakings would be persuaded to sponsor ancillary industries in collaboration with State level agencies dealing with development programmes for women to provide increased employment opportunities around them. Attempts would also be made to identify and target the women beneficiaries under Entrepreneurial Development Programme (EDP) and Industrial Estates.

6.7.3 Village and Small-Scale Industries: The schemes for the introduction of new technologies and the induction of expertise through upgradation of training would be further expanded. The scope of the specific training programmes for women entrepreneurs will be widened in order to fully familiarise them with the technical know-how needed for setting up enterprises. The number of such women entrepreneurs would also be increased. Rural technology institutions, and mobile technology and training units would be considerably expanded. These organisations would regularly conduct special training courses for women at various levels. The training would be oriented, wherever possible, to schemes like IRDP, TRYSEM, etc. Taking up special programmes for women by agencies like process-cum-product development centres (PPDCs), training centres and small industries service institutes (SISI) would be examined.

A massive programme for training of artisans, managers, supervisors and entrepreneurs would have to be taken up to expand efficient production and for promotion of skilled employment. Women's participation in these schemes will be increased substantially. Besides, the district industries centres (DICs) will play a special role in the identification of groups of women artisans/workers for disseminating information relating to avocations to be taken up and the nature of support that could be extended by governmental agencies. Efforts would be made to set up mini-industrial estates exclusively for women on a much larger scale. Special facilities like sheds and plots at subsidised rates to units exclusively run by women and/or employing female labour will be given.

The National Small Industries Corporation and other apex organisations would extend support for marketing, product design and financial support for raw material procurement. Concessional financial requirements will also be considered for meeting fully the working capital requirements and for providing margin money for seed capital. The distinct and unique role assigned to the handloom sector will be preserved and several measures would be initiated both for consolidation and expansion of this sector. Under the programme of training of workers and entrepreneurs, women beneficiaries will be given importance. Women are expected to obtain sizeable employment under this sector. Coir making, sericulture and small scale industries are some such sectors which offer great potential.

6.7.4 Khadi and Village Industries: The employment coverage under khadi and village industries is likely to increase from the present 3.80 million persons to 5.86 million persons. A considerable proportion of this additional employment will come to women. Efforts would be made towards creation and promotion of equal employment opportunities for men and women. Special agencies will be set up for extending credit facilities for self-employment and home-based workers.

6.7.5 Science and Technology: Programme on "Science and Technology for Women" would be further strengthened to identify, formulate sponsor and implement research and development, demonstration and extension programmes, with special emphasis on providing opportunities for gainful employment/self- employment to women specially to those in rural areas.

The training programmes at different levels such as those for unemployed graduates, school drop-outs and housewives will be strengthened and expanded, for improving the trainees' skills. Besides, skill manuals and training aids in areas of agriculture, animal husbandry and other new occupations would be prepared to provide opportunities of independent employment and income for women. Assistance of voluntary organisations would be sought for taking need based technologies to the target groups and in obtaining feedback regarding the acceptance of the programme and in the identification of factors that influence the transfer of technologies. Under the concept of Vigyan Kendras, the possibility of setting up rural banks for lending improved agricultural tools would be explored and new groups would be identified, preferably those in which scientists and technologists are actively involved for taking up developmental programmes for women at the grass root level.

Special training programmes would continue to be sponsored for women in polytechnics and other institutions of technical education in areas such as repair and maintenance of radios, television and other electronic hardware or consumer durables, manufacture of PVC goods, lacquer work, fibre reinforced plastics etc. Involvement of women voluntary agencies and home science colleges would be ensured.

6.7.6 Social Welfare: The programmes for women under the social welfare sector are meant to supplement the services available to women under other developmental sectors. Further strengthening is envisaged of the on-going schemes which have been found useful in skill formation and creation of gainful employment among women. Very close linkages with specialised agencies such as ICAR, ICMR, DST, Rural Development, Industry and Education are called for.

To set up a variety of income generating units under the "Socio-Economic Programme" for the benefit of needy women, the Central Social Welfare Board would continue to extend grants-in-aid to voluntary organisations. Efforts would be made to improve the programme by introducing better technical and marketing support. The scheme of assistance to public undertakings/corporations and autonomous organisations for supporting projects aimed at income generation and employment among women from weaker sections on a sustained basis with the help of Norwegian

Agency for International Development (NORAD) would be further expanded, with focus on diversified occupations and inculcating new skills required by the job market. Grants would also be given for organising condensed educational and vocational training courses for adult women so as to improve their employment prospects. Short-duration training courses (not exceeding one year) in non-traditional trades would be expanded for rehabilitating women in distress and their dependent children.

A new scheme, namely, Women's Development Corporations, would be taken up for promoting employment-generating activities by supporting schemes for women's groups and women from poorer sections of society. These corporations would identify potential areas of employment and assist beneficiaries in project formulation, raising the requisite finances and marketing of their products. A Women's Development Planning and Monitoring Cell will be set up for collection of data and monitoring of Plan programmes. Provision has also been made for a few innovative schemes/projects which, if found successful, would be replicated.

6.7.7 Voluntary Organisations: The efforts by voluntary agencies have to be stimulated to extend their programmes to rural, hilly and backward areas. They would be encouraged to create public opinion against social evils like child marriage, dowry, illiteracy and atrocities on women. Sustained effort would be made for increasing the age at marriage of girls and for improving the adverse sex ratio. There is lack of awareness about the existing social legislation to protect the interests of women. Voluntary agencies would be supported to undertake educational work and bring in awareness among women regarding their rights and privileges. They would also be associated in extension activities.

A proper monitoring mechanism will be developed to ensure optimal utilisation of facilities meant for women under different sectors and to minimise leakages. The special cells which are being set up in the Ministries for this purpose will be strengthened in order to ensure proper monitoring and coordination of different schemes. Steps will be taken to strengthen the machinery for monitoring progress of various schemes at State and district levels.

6.8 Eighth Five Year Plan (1992-1997)

The Eighth Plan with human development as its major focus played a very important role in the development of women. It promised to ensure that benefits of development from different sectors do not by-pass women, implement special programmes to complement the general development programmes and to monitor the flow of benefits to women from other development sectors and enable women to function as equal partners and participants in the development process. A shift was made from development to empowerment of women.

The constitutional amendment was made for at least 30 per cent representation in all elected local self- government bodies such as Panchayati Raj Institutions and Municipalities. National Commission for Women at the Centre and State Commissions for Women at the State level were established. Mahila Samrudhi Yojana (MSY) was launched for sensitising women at grass root level. The Eighth Plan laid special thrust on employment, including women's employment with the objective of making women self- reliant and economically independent.

6.9 Ninth Five Year Plan (1997-2002)

In the Ninth Plan the key elements of the strategy for development of women in the Concrete efforts were made to improve the skills of women by way of providing vocational training in various fields and to enhance their capabilities to earn more. Additional productive opportunities were created for women through Women Self Help Groups and Associations. 'Empowerment of Women' became one of the nine primary objectives of the Ninth Plan. To this effect, the Approach of the Plan was to create an enabling environment where women could freely exercise their rights both within and outside home, as equal partners along with men. The Plan attempted 'convergence of existing services' available in both women-specific and women-related sectors. To this effect, it directed both the centre and the states to adopt a special strategy of 'Women's Component Plan' (WCP) through which not less than 30 per cent of funds/benefits flow to women from all the general development sectors.

It also suggested that a special vigil be kept on the flow of the earmarked funds/benefits through an effective mechanism to ensure that the proposed strategy brings forth a holistic approach towards empowering women. To ensure that other general develop-mental sectors do not by-pass women and benefits from these sectors continue to flow to them, a special mechanism of monitoring the 27 BOS for women was put into action in 1986, at the instance of the Prime Minister's Office (PMO). The same continues to be an effective instrument till today. Sector/scheme-wise achievements under women-specific and women-related sectors of health, nutrition, education, labour, rural development, urban development, science and technology and women and child development

6.10 Tenth Five Year Plan (2002-2007)

The following measurable/monitor able goals set in the Tenth Plan, having a direct bearing on the empowerment of women. Special programme for participation of women in agriculture is being launched. Development of special education zone for women and creating Help Centres to provide counseling and support to victims of domestic violence are other new schemes being introduced. Steps would be taken for providing gainful employment to the additional labour force. The process of organising women into Self-Help Groups will be encouraged to act as the agents of social change, development and empowerment of women. National

Institute for Entrepreneurship and Small Business Development organised Entrepreneurship programmes for women.

The integrated approach adopted by the two ongoing programmes of women's empowerment, viz. Swa-Shakti and Swayamsidha be further strengthened and expanded. Mobilisation of poor women into SHGs through convergence of services, offering them a wide range of economic and social options along with necessary support services to enhance their joint capabilities. To this effect, the available programmes for women are converged into block level action plans of Swayamsidha. Special training programmes in the latest technology, keeping in view the role of women as producers, will be expanded to assist rural women in meeting the market demands with the rise in the phenomenon of feminisation of agriculture, will be attended to as a concern at the policy level.

To increase the share of women in factories and industrial establishments, efforts will be made to encourage women to equip themselves with necessary professional/vocational skills and compete with men to make an entry into newer areas.

The on-going training-cum-employment-cum-income generation programmes viz. RMK, SGSY, SJSRY, PMRY, STEP, and NORAD etc be further expanded to create more employment-cum-income generation opportunities and to cover as many women as possible living below the poverty line giving priority to female-headed households and women living in extreme/abject poverty.

The programme of Swayamsidha is further expanded to 2000 additional blocks during the Tenth Plan.

The micro-credit programme of RMK is closely tied up with SHGs formed under Swayamsidha for financing various employments –cum-income-generation activities.

Necessary training programmes be introduced to retain/upgrade the skills of the displaced women to take up jobs in the new and emerging areas of employment.

Formulating of appropriate policies and programmes to

generate opportunities for wage/self-employment in traditional sectors like Khadi and Village industries, Handicrafts, Handlooms, Sericulture, Small Scale and Cottage industries.

Special attention will be given to women in the informal sector to ensure both minimum and equal wages for women on par with men.

Design suitable strategies to enhance the capacity of women and to empower them to cope with the negative economic and social impact of the globalisation process.

A minimum of 30 per cent reservation will be made for women in services in the public sector.

To increase the representation of women in services, coaching facilities, encouraging women to compete along with men in the competitive examinations and providing support services for working women to ensure mobility in the employment market.

The Tenth Plan recognises the need for a comprehensive Credit Policy to increase women's access to credit either the establishment of new micro-credit mechanisms or micro – financial institutions or strengthening existing ones. All States/UTs with Women's Development Corporations to be equipped to provide both forward and backward linkages of credit and marketing facilities to women entrepreneurs, besides being active catalysts for empowering women economically. Efforts be made to set up an exclusive Development Bank for Women entrepreneurs in the small scale and tiny sectors.

6.11 Eleventh Five Year Plan (2007-2012)

The government is planning to ensure that at least 33 per cent of all direct and indirect benefits of all schemes flow to women and girl children. A focus on pilot schemes would be made for Muslim women and SC/ST children .The Planning Commission wants the Government to lay emphasis on economic and social empowerment, besides enabling political environment, strengthening mechanisms for effective implementation of women related laws and augmenting delivery mechanisms.

The plan body has also suggested that focus be given on Integrated Child Protection scheme and the Scheme for Relief and Rehabilitation of Victims of Social Assault. The Government hopes to make a serious dent on poverty, malnutrition, school dropout rates and infant mortality and female health. Aware that success of its plans depends on correctly targeting women, Government plans a special focus on this key segment of population. Both Centre and states will frame policies to realise "monitorable targets" with stress on objectives like raising the sex ratio for age group 0-6 to 935 by 2011-'12 and to 950 by 2016-17.

It has been decided to set up a Working Group on Micro & Small enterprises (MSE) sector, consisting of the traditionally defined small scale industries and small scale service and business entities, on the one hand and khadi, village and coir industries, on the other to review the existing coverage of developmental schemes and programmes for SC, ST, Minorities and Women engaged in the sector and to suggest specific measures for their upliftment and promotion.

Women Development Programme to be strengthened and reactivated to create awareness among women for their social empowerment. Women support groups to be formed. SHGs will be strengthened and linkages with financial institutions facilitated. Training programmes in skill development and management etc. will be a priority area.

Women Cooperative Societies to be promoted and strengthened. Share capital to Women Cooperative Societies suggested to be increased to promote research in and development of implements/equipments particularly in agriculture sector to facilitate safe working of women agriculturist. Grain Banks could be set up through women SHGs. Assessment of poverty levels needs to be assessed regularly for appropriate management of supplies.

7

Women Entrepreneurship: Global Experiences

Historically, women all around the world concentrated in and performed low paid activities, jobs and occupations. They had limited ownership of land or other assets, limited access to credit and well paid jobs, and educational opportunities. Even though the data underestimated women's economic contributions, women's employment in developing countries over the post war period increased both absolutely and relatively. The available data shows that in 1950, 37 per cent of women participated in the total labour force of the developing countries. [1]

Since 1950, the proportion of adult women joining the labour force has risen in both developed and developing countries. The increased participation of women was primarily due to export led industrialisation, heavy use of low-wage female labour and labour market deregulation. [2] This has caused a relative increase in the employment of women in the manufacturing sector. Even in industrialised countries, before1970, women entrepreneurs were rare. Since then, however, their increase has been remarkable. The participation of women in entrepreneurship varies but the differences between men and women are remarkably stable across the countries.

There is no country where women are more active than men. [3] The proportion of women in the developed countries in the industrial labour force increased from 21 per cent in 1960 to 26.5 per cent in 1980. But the situation in developing countries was worst where women, in large numbers, participated in economic activities in informal and unorganised sector. Lack of education and training, the nature of jobs performed by women was inferior, repetitive, short cycled and stereo typed for which thorough technical knowledge was not necessary. Clothing and electronics are the two industries that universally employ large number of women. In developed countries, 57 per cent of all employed women worked in the service sector. They mainly engaged in community service (health, education and social service) commerce (retail service) and domestic service1. [4]

In the Western economies of the 1980s, there had been significant neglect of the contribution of women in the formation and growth of small scale businesses, which often provided services to their husbands' businesses during the crucial start up period. [5] By 1985, the participation of women in developing countries in the labour force s had risen to 42 per cent. In urban areas, women concentrated heavily in informal sector activities. Women mainly engaged in activities like petty trade, commerce, services and certain branches of manufacturing both as entrepreneurs and as dependent workers, whether in family enterprises or a wage workers in the informal sector, women concentrated in low-skilled repetitive work. In industry, they relegated to a narrow range of occupations-electronics, semi conductors, toys and sporting goods, textiles and apparels, footwear where in they performed the rote assembly line, manual and labour intensive operations.

In agriculture, landless women from the poorest households performed seasonal, casual and temporary work at low wages. Since World War II, there has been a growing influence of women into western labour market. Since the beginning of the Women's decade in 1975, a wide range of institutions has been involved in programmes to expand women's employment and income opportunities. [6] Surveys conducted demonstrate that women's primary entrepreneurial activity is focused on the small and medium enterprise (SME) sector. Approximately 60 per cent entrepreneurs are small-scale entrepreneurs, 15 per cent represent the large-scale manufacturers and the remainder comprise of cottage and micro entrepreneurs. They work in a wide range of sectors, from trade and services, to tailoring, beauty parlours, and printing. [7]

However, the involvement of women entrepreneurs in the production sector is minimal and the development of this sector is rather slow. Between 1997 and 2006, the number of majority women-owned businesses increased 42 per cent. [8] In 2006, majority women-owned businesses are expected to generate US$ 1.1 trillion in revenues. [9] According to World Bank Report, 2007 the business environment and business laws in the Middle East and North Africa Region are far less discriminatory than presumed. But, social attitudes and laws outside the business legislation heighten the barriers for women entrepreneurs and limit their opportunities. The report, titled 'The Environment for Women's Entrepreneurship in the Middle East and North Africa Region' finds that overall economic openness and reform of the business environment will reduce barriers and create opportunities for all investors, particularly women.

In recent years there has been a rising tide of female entrepreneurship around the world and female-owned firms have increased their work force faster in Egypt, Jordan, Saudi Arabia, and West Bank and Gaza than male-owned firms. The report finds that social attitudes that discourage women's employment can act as barriers, and that certain laws—such as those requiring a husband's permission to travel—can interfere with both a woman's opportunities and the implementation of business legislation. A large number of women have financial resources and educational skills, with an easier investment climate; they are more likely to start a business in the formal sector. This can help increase competition and diversify the region's economies." [10]

In the United States and Canada the number of women-owned businesses has been rising. In developed countries women are making progress in shipping, transport, tourism, financial brokerage and telecommunication. [11] However, their share of managerial job is only below 40 per cent. [12] A recent survey revealed that Asian women have highest confidence for tax planning anywhere in the world. South Asians were also the least likely to invest in alternative assets such as antiques and art. Some of the successful women entrepreneurs in Asia are Perween Warsi, the multimillionaire, Bhari British founder and CEO of S& A Foods, Kalpana Morparia. Joint MD of ICICI bank, Gerad Aqilina, head of Barclays Wealth's International Private Bank. [13] Female entrepreneurship is now considered one of the sources of growth, employment, and innovation. In Asia, women now out-number men in businesses. Across the world, women-owned firms typically comprise between one quarter and one-third of the business population. [14]

7.1 Estonia

Women entrepreneurs and their businesses is a growing segment of the business population in Europe. In the 1990s, there was a significant increase in the number of businesses owned by women. However, in the agricultural sector, approximately 41 per cent of women are self-employed. [15]

There is lack of information or statistical data on female entrepreneurs in Estonia. Several men and women organisations were established in Estonia during in the 1990s to provide women orientation, explore new employment opportunities and equip women to face new challenges of the dynamic world. Since 1991 organisations such as the Women's Training Centre were also established for providing women's business training and consultations, development of business women's networks, facilitating women to get international contact and participate in seminars. Business and Professional Women' Estonia organisation was established in 1992. Since 1995, Democracy training, integration into public life, gender equality etc. are ensured for women. International and local businesswomen's mentoring programmes were implemented since 1999 and Democracy training outside of Estonia Women's mobility programmes was initiated since 2001. [16]

7.2 Denmark

People in Denmark are well-educated because the educational systems of Denmark focuses on lifelong learning in the workplace as well as a high emphasise on research in both private companies and at universities. Interestingly, with the shifting of Danish society from an industrial nation to a society focused on knowledge, Danish government has implemented a new policy encouraging Danish people to become entrepreneurs in the fields of knowledge, knowledge-requiring industry and service-industry. As a result, the number of new established enterprises has increased, especially in the field of knowledge services but in areas such as technology and science, the numbers remain low compared to other European nations. The Business Development Education in Herning shows records that 25 per cent of their students start their own business upon graduation. How ever, in Denmark, the entrepreneurship is male prerogative, especially, in the Engineering Association of Denmark only 12 per cent of the employees are women while only one per cent of this sector consists of female entrepreneurs. In Denmark 30 per cent of entrepreneurs are women. At present, the enterprises in Denmark are characterised as small and medium size businesses with maximum 250 employees. [17]

7.3 Africa

In Africa, agricultural activities play a more prominent role within livelihood systems and women do most of the work. Although women keep a foothold in the household economy, increasingly they are dependent on self employment or wage work for survival. But they were not given equal participation in development .In the mid 1970s, women had been discovered by development planners who simultaneously discovered that aid programmes had failed to eradicate poverty. Since then much lip service has been paid to the equal participation of women in development. Numerous income-generating handicrafts and nutrition education projects have been implemented for women, some of which brought short term help to a few people. But in most cases, the double burden of work already carried out by women was ignored. The status of women was very low which limits women's access to land, credit, machinery, markets for their products and control over any income raised.

Colonialism established a capitalist economy, created urban migration of men from rural areas which caused excessive workload for women. The perceived inferiority of women to men- existed in most pre-colonial African societies was reinforced by the colonists and their religions. Even though national independence brought changes, no recognition was given for the central role played by women. Issues of women and development in most African countries are still dealt with by a Ministry of Culture and Social Development which is also responsible for youth sports, culture and destitutes. African women are still regarded as objects of recreation (as in sports), or art (as in culture) or social liabilities (as with destitute) rather than assets in development process. [18]

In Sub-Saharan Africa women predominantly producing food for subsistence and /or working as unpaid family labour on men's cash crop fields. In Sub-Saharan Africa, the informal sector offers opportunities for entrepreneurship, especially in trading or small scale agro industry where, women make up 80 per cent of the food producers in some countries. The proportion economically active women employed in manufacturing are only six per cent (UN 1991:88-9). Various national estimates indicate that in 1992, 10 per cent of the new enterprises in North Africa were started by women. African home-made products are known through out the Europe especially due to the enterprising spirit of African women who never miss a chance to bring along to international meetings and conferences things they can make themselves (clothes, decorative jewellery, coloured textiles). In West Africa, women control 60 to 80 per cent of marketing and trading. African women dominate in the traditional sector where as their representation in agriculture, manufacturing and commerce is very poor. But in Gabon, Liberia and Tanzania the percentage of women's participation in these areas are 50.6 per cent, 41.6 per cent and 51.1 per cent respectively. Dahomean monopolise in commerce (95 per cent). [19]

Women of Lesotho, in South Africa, have   established a special entrepreneurial incubator with the assistance of international institutions, where various products are being made and even exported in an organized manner. African home-made products are known throughout Europe especially due to the enterprising spirit of African women who never miss s chance to bring along to international meetings and conferences things they can make themselves(clothes, decorative jewellery, coloured textile). [20]

In South Africa, the constitutional and legislative framework is progressive and highlights the importance of gender equality. Broad-Based Black Economic Empowerment Act promotes "increasing the extent to which black women own and manage existing and new enterprises, and increasing their access to economic activities, infrastructure and skills training." Black women are the largest self-employed group of the population. But they have the least access to finance. In the year 2004-05 only 38 per cent of them had access to finance, compared to 96 per cent of white women. The study also shattered the myth that women were less likely to repay their debts, revealing in fact the opposite. [21]

7.4 United States of America

According to Kathy Peiss, in the women's history written in the 1960s and 1970s, the subject of women in business was virtually absent. Business was often characterised as a "capitalist patriarchy" that gained power by making women a commodity. However, as more women entered business and other professional schools, and as the women's movement matured and grew, there has been increasing interest among women's historians to study women's contribution and role in the development of American industry and businesses. [22]

According to Nancy Koehn, 'women played key roles in the early American economy through the development of cottage industries and in the organization and work of benevolent societies. The exhibit does a wonderful job in tracing women's ever-present role in the evolution of American businesses'. Women show interest in undertaking new ventures since they provide great opportunities to enter the national economy. In the mid-nineteenth century explosion within the textile industry and growing industrialisation; the development of the national railroad system and the telegraph from 1880-1920; and the more recent information revolution etc. the American economy and society were changing and women consistently took advantage of the opportunities. There has been significant increase in the number of women entrepreneurs during these periods. [23]

In ancient period much of Colonial America was agrarian, and most of the women assisted men in agricultural activities. In the early 19th century, with the spreading of factory system, only 24 per cent of manufacturing workers were women who produced clothes, shoes, cigars and other items. By 1890, nearly four million women in the U.S. worked for pay. The majority worked in domestic and teaching service, and in textiles factories. At the early 1900s, as a result of urbanisation and the availability of public education, more middle-class women joined the labour force primarily as teachers and nurses. [24] The proportion of married women in employment grew from less than 25 per cent in 1950 to 43 per cent by the late 1970s. [25]

Litrell, whose company publishes Working Woman and Working Mother magazines, said women in the 1970s were focused on finding a job; women in the 1980s were trying to fit into corporate America; women in the 1990s were finding the freedom to become "strong women and start businesses." [26] According to Howard Stevenson, Women are increasingly drawn to entrepreneurship, in 1972 women owned four per cent of all American businesses; by 1991, that figure had climbed to 38 per cent. [27].In U.S. women now hold about half of the managerial position up from 36per cent since 1976and while 11.2 per cent of all Fortune 500 companies had women officers—top executives—only 7 per cent of the corporate offices at Fortune 500 technology companies top executives are women.

Ms Carly Fiorina had been appointed as the first female chief executive officer of a blue chip American co. Hewlett-Packard. She will be running the second largest American Computer Co. which has 123000 workers and had sale of US$ 47 billion last year. Of America's Fortune 500 companies, 497 are still run by men. Other 6064 seats on the boards of the director of Fortune 500 companies, women hold just 671 .his sends a strong message to women that they can be business leaders, said Joweiss, Vice-president of advisory services at Catalyst Inc. a New York think-tank that studies women in the work place. [28] In the 1980s, there was significant increase in the number of women entrepreneurs as many women who had been in full-time or part –time paid employment acquired skills which were useful for business-start-up. A very large proportion of small firms in the service sector began on a very limited scale, often utilising domestic premises and the proprietors' own skills and the only finance required for such ventures was obtained from personal savings. [29]

Since 1987, the number of women-owned firms in the U.S. has doubled, employment has increased four-fold and their revenues have risen five-fold. The Organization for Economic Cooperation and Development estimates that women entrepreneurs in the U.S. increased from 29.7 per cent in 1980 to 35.2 per cent in 1990. [30] The women owned 32 per cent of the business in 1990. The areas chosen by women entrepreneurs are retail trade, restaurants, hotels, education and cultural, cleaning, insurance and manufacturing. Across the world, women-owned firms typically comprise between one quarter and one-third of the business population. [31] In 1998, women created 75 per cent of the new firms. [32] The U.S. Economic Census reports that women-owned business increased 16 per cent during the period 1992-97. [33] In the Unites States of America, 84.8 per cent of all businesses owned by women are sole proprietorships.

Sole proprietorships operated by women in the United States underwent dramatic increases from 1990 to 1998 in terms of numbers, gross receipts and net income. The OECD in 1998 estimated that 75 to 80 per cent of new enterprises in the United States are created by women. Women owned business is the fastest growing segment of the U.S. economy. The top growth industries for women-owned businesses between 1987 and 1999 were construction, wholesale trade, transportation, communications, agribusiness and manufacturing. Women-owned businesses are as financially sound and creditworthy as the typical firm in the U.S. economy, and are more likely to remain in business than the average U.S. firm. Since 1987, the number of women-owned firms in the U.S. has doubled, employment has increased four-fold and their revenues have risen five-fold. [34]

The fastest growing segment of the U.S. economy is women owned business. Women entrepreneurs are setting up establishments at twice the rate of that of men. The women owned 32 per cent of the business in 1990. In U.S. A. about 50 per cent of the manufacturing women operate units. The Organisation for Economic Cooperation and Development estimates that women entrepreneurs in the U.S. increased from 29.7 per cent in 1980 to 35.2 per cent in 1990. [35]. The U.S. Economic Census reports that women-owned business increased 16 per cent during the period 1992-97. [36]

The women owned 32 per cent of the business in 1990. The areas chosen by women entrepreneurs are retail trade, restaurants, hotels, education and cultural, cleaning, insurance and manufacturing. Across the world, women-owned firms typically comprise between one quarter and one-third of the business population. United States of America adopted several measures and mechanism for supporting women entrepreneurship, because the American government is aware of the fact that a Dollar invested into women entrepreneur start-up would be an investment much sounder as money for unemployed American women. The American small agency initiated the programme for active employment and self-employment for women in 1999.

American women also established 'women bank' to provide for the entrepreneurial projects initiated by women entrepreneurs. In America women entrepreneurial associations have a 25 years long tradition and it goes for west European countries. [37] Between 1997 and 2002, the number of women-owned businesses with more than 100 employees rose by 44 per cent. Women hold 13.6 per cent of board seats at Fortune 500 companies. The number of seats held by women of color has increased from 2.5 per cent in 1999 to 3 per cent in 2003. Of the Fortune 500, 54 companies have 25 per cent or more women directors in 2003. Women comprise 46.6 per cent of the U.S. labor force, 50 per cent of the managerial and professional specialty positions.

Women-owned firms continue to diversify across industries, with the fastest growth rates seen in non-traditional industries, including construction, agricultural services and transportation. As of 2004, nearly half (48 per cent) of all firms in the United States are 50 per cent or more woman-owned, for a total of 10.6 million firms 50per cent or more women-owned. Women-owned businesses are in all industries, with the fastest growth between 1997 and 2004 in construction (30 per cent growth), transportation, communications and public utilities (28 per cent growth), and agricultural serves (24 per cent growth).

Between 1997 and 2004, the number of women-owned

firms grew at twice the rate of all firms (17 per cent vs. 9 per cent). Women-owned firms are driving job creation, employment by women-owned firms expanded twice as fast as all privately held firms (24 per cent vs.12 per cent), the number of women-owned firms with employees grew 28per cent, three times the growth rate of all firms with employees. As of 2005, there are an estimated 10.1 million majority-owned, privately held, women-owned firms in the U.S. Women-owned businesses account for 28 per cent of all businesses in the United States and represent about 775,000 new startups per year and account for 55 per cent of new start ups. [38] The Small Business Administration (SBA) reports that small businesses in the U.S. represent more than 99.7 per cent of all employers, employ more than half of all private sector employees, pay 44.5 per cent of total U.S. private payroll, and generate 60 to 80 per cent of net new jobs annually, with Texas following such a pattern. [39]

7.5 Afghanistan

Women in Afghanistan have been reduced to pariah status by social, economic and cultural exclusion due to the epitome of religious extremism (U.N. Report).The conservative social structure in some parts of Afghanistan has traditionally been harsh on women, but the rights of women have been further degraded through the years of armed conflict, poverty and the immense under development of the war-torn territory. But the advent of the Taliban and their control over a vast part of the country and the restrictions imposed by them on women has made the latter the most seriously affected section of the population. Women are deprived of physical security, education, health, freedom of movement and freedom of association. [40]

7.6 China

Over the past few years, the Chinese Government has formulated and carried out supportive policies to encourage women to start businesses on their own initiative, and give them preferential treatment when granting employment training subsidies and small-sum guaranteed loans and conducting tax reduction and exemption. In the meantime, Governments at all levels have adopted many favourable policies toward women, such as creating public-welfare jobs, opening employment service centres, sponsoring special recruitment activities and vocational training courses, monitoring sex discrimination against women in employment and helping women, especially laid-off women, to find new jobs. In recent years, the tertiary industry has become the main channel for providing jobs to women, and an increasing number of women are entering the computer, communications, finance and insurance and other high- and new-tech industries, thus becoming an important force in these fields. In China, women founded 25 per cent of the businesses since 1978. [41]

At present, women owners of small and medium-sized enterprises account for about 20 per cent of the national total number of entrepreneurs, and 60 per cent of them have emerged in the past decade. By the end of 2004, women accounted for 43.6 per cent of the total number of professionals and technicians in State-owned enterprises and institutions nationwide, up 6.3 percentage points over the 37.3 per cent of 1995, among whom, the number of senior and intermediate-level women professionals and technicians rose from 20.1 per cent and 33.4 per cent to 30.5 per cent and 42 per cent respectively. [42]

7.7 Bangladesh

Bangladesh is one of the poorest countries of the world. Historically, it is an agricultural country where business is only a secondary occupation. It resulted in scarcity for entrepreneurs though there is abundant supply of manpower. People are ignorant in using their capability for income generation activities and lack risk taking ability. With the liberalisation of Bangladesh setting up of supporting institutions and gradual privatisation a new group of people emerged as entrepreneurs. Women constitute 48.65 per cent of the total population of Bangladesh. Approximately fifty per cent of the people live below the poverty line of which two-thirds are women. As far as a Bangladeshi woman is concerned, against the backdrop of overall socio-economic situation in the country, becoming an entrepreneur is a difficult task. The cultural environment of the country is also not congenial for women entrepreneurship development. However, this situation is gradually changing.

Today, more and more women are well educated, some others are working in various public and private sector organizations or self employed. Most of the women entrepreneurs are now engaged in rural activities especially in crafts and chose sectors on the basis of the availability of rural raw materials. Their activities include poultry, grocery, beauty parlour, stationery, boutique shop, handicrafts, food shop etc. In urban Bangladesh, the crafts women chose handicrafts such as readymade garments, boutique, loom, jute products, screen print, embroidery, leather goods, earthen ware and tapestry. These crafts small women entrepreneurs have to hinge on cheap and available raw materials around the location and their natural and traditional skills. However, the participation of women in non-traditional sector is not worth mentioning. Those women in cold storage, soaps, sanitary napkins, gold plated jewellery, furniture, emporium, press, travel agency, and advertising cannot run their businesses smoothly. [43]

7.8 France

In France, until 1965, a married woman could not open a credit account without her husband's consent (Veil 1994). [44] The first women entrepreneurial association was established in France in 1945 by a French woman Yvonne Foinant. From French Association, the World Association of Women Entrepreneurs (FCEM) evolved which helped many a woman to enter new markets world wide. Women represent 44 per cent of the entire population (the French working population amounts to 11 million): 26 per cent of all companies are run by women. In 1994 alone 30 per cent of all newly established companies were those formed by women, there are 150,000 young French women graduating and entering the vast number of first job seekers each year. [45] In 1998, France had 1400000 firms, of which 30 per cent (320,000) were owned and managed by women. Among these 320000 women-owned firms, 55 per cent had no employees, 38 per cent had from one to nine employees, and 7 per cent had 10 employees or more. Taken as a whole, female-owned firms are smaller than those owned by men. As in all other developed countries, these firms operate mostly in retail trade and services (INSEE 1998)

7.9 Slovenia

Economic need forced majority of Slovene women to join the work force. Women faced with a greater psychological threat of unemployment due to the economic crisis during transition period. Their representation in politics and management is also very low. As it was difficult for women managers to co-ordinate their business careers and family life, they concentrated in low profile activities with greater tax burdens resulted in common female-male wage differentials. Evidences show that women being sex discriminated in small firms. In Slovenia women who were employed in large self-managed companies got frustrated due to hidden discrimination. Lower levels of education contributed to over-representation of women in the unemployed labour force and under-representation in positions of management and politics. This pushes women towards entrepreneurial activities (Cromie, 1987; Hisrich & Brush, 1985). [46]

Slovenian women were also traditionally excluded from managerial ranks (male-female management wage differential was 16 per cent. [47] Most of the women entered in business because of unemployment. Therefore, the evidence implies that women are mostly motivated to entrepreneurial careers by push-factors instead of pull factors. However, they were involved in significant numbers in private small business activities and they increasingly opted for entrepreneurial career paths following the political and economic reforms at the end of 1980's in Slovenia. [48]

However officially, there was a prevailing thesis of gender equality during socialism, which was corroborated by statistical data. Even though several women's organisations were formed in Sloveneia, the significance of women's contribution to the national economy has come down due to the obscure and chagrin character of feminism. The Small Business Development Strategy for Slovenia (1996) identified women as a target group for support to develop their unrealised business potential. However, to date, there has been no significant implementation of this strategy. [49]

According to Glas & Petrin (1998) and Turk (1994) [50], the share of women-managed businesses within the Slovene small business sector approached the level for developed countries. The share of women in the work force was 20 per cent at the beginning of the century, 33.3 per cent in 1952 and 48.8 per cent in 1996, with the majority working full time. [51] Women tended to be educated in traditionally female spheres, and only gradually entered technical sectors; a typical feminisation of industries existed characterised as unskilled, relatively poorly paid occupations (textile 61.4 per cent, leather 76.6 per cent, service, teaching and culture 67.3 per cent, health 81.9 per cent);male-female wage differentials appeared, however lower than in western countries. [52]. Entrepreneurial research studies in Slovenia revealed that women showed less interest in acquiring marketing knowledge or technical skills which might imply that more women entrepreneurs are in service fields where technology does not play a direct role in productivity as it does in manufacturing. [53]

Slovenian women played an active role in the first entrepreneurial wave in Slovenia during the early 1990's. The transition from self-management to a market economy created new barriers to the progress of their political or managerial careers. In 1993, Slovene women represent almost 50 per cent of the Slovene working population, 30 per cent of them among top businesses professionals. European Commission Research observed that in Slovenia, 49 per cent of women- managed firms had female sole owners, 15 per cent had a women-held majority, and in 15 per cent women-owned at least half of the company. Literature states that women managed firms tend to be smaller as far as sales, employment and equity are concerned. Research highlighted the same case for Slovenia, especially for the self-employed group, although differences between groups were not significant. [54] Some other experiences of women entrepreneurs in Slovenia revealed that women entrepreneurs' establishment of micro-sized firms paralleled participation in Europe. [55]

Women-managed businesses tend to concentrate in certain sectors. Data was structured according to gender and sector for a study in 1997. [56] Only sectors with more than 10 women-managed firms were objects of further analysis. The share of women-managed companies was particularly low in the manufacturing basic metals, machinery and equipment, communications and wood processing sectors (7.9 per cent-12.5 per cent), but higher in the manufacturing (48.7 per cent) and sales (29.3 per cent) of textiles and textile products. Women-managed companies concentrated in wholesaling (23.5 per cent) and retailing (31.1 per cent). Some women businesses were in real estate (27.2 per cent), financial intermediation, data analysis and construction (13.3 per cent). [57] There is a large share of micro businesses in the Slovenian small business sector. [58]

The number of Slovenian women pursuing entrepreneurship is increasing and already represents a well-established stratum in the Slovenian entrepreneurial community, both in terms of numbers as well as in business accomplishments. Their business performance, when considering the timing of their entry, the average smaller firm size, as well as the clustering in highly competitive sectors, is similar and in some aspects even better than that of their male counterparts. Slovenian women tend to concentrate in so called feminised economic sectors. According to Marta Turk, vice-president, Association of Women Entrepreneurs [FCEM] in 2006, only 20per cent of the entrepreneurs in Slovenia are women. [59]

7.10 Latin America

In Latin America, in 1980, 16.7 per cent of economically active women were employed in manufacturing garments, electronics and in relatively unskilled occupations due to a shift of manufacturing industry from large to small enterprises and of increase in subcontracting, home working and other forms of unprotected employment. [60] In 1985, women's labour force participation rate was 25 per cent. The per cent of women in the informal sector was 25 per cent. The per cent of women informal sector was 25 to 40 per cent of informal businesses owners and operators and they had lower sales revenues, lower asset bases and smaller profit margins than men's. [61] In Latin America, according to the World Bank, fully half of all economic growth in the last decade through out the region is attributable to the creativity and hard work of female entrepreneurs. [62]

7.11 United Kingdom

Women enterprise has no definition other than that of a small enterprise in U.K. The history of growth of women enterprise in U.K. is the same as that of the growth of small enterprises. During 1960s no emphasis was laid on small firms. It is only after the Botton committee Report in 1971 that the need of small firm was recognized in U.K. The 1980s saw a remarkable growth in the number of businesses in U.K. from 1.8 million at the end of 1979, the number of businesses in U.K. went up to 3.8 million by the end of 1989. as per the study of the DTI in U.K. the number of businesses declined slightly to 3.5 million in early 1990s. However, the number of businesses closures has been falling since mid-1992 and the total number of businesses is now back to the level of late 1980s, i.e. around 3.8 million.

During the post war period, there had been significant increase in the proportion of women in paid employment. [63] In 1985, around 40 per cent of the labour force was women. [64] The growth in the number of businesses is largely the result of increasing micro businesses. This is linked to the considerable expansion in the number of self-employed people in 1980s. DTI estimates suggest that firms less than 100 employees account for 99.6 per cent of the U.K's total business population. They also contributed 54 per cent of total employment and 44.3 per cent of total turnover. [65] Knight could become the first British woman to head a high-tech company which makes components for computer networks because of the technology (Internet) 66.

7.12 Jamaica

In 1984, 38 per cent of economically active women in Jamaica were in the informal sector employment. A high percentage of the women working in the informal sector were hagglers i.e. petty vendors. The growth of informal sector employment was partly stimulated by Government's Seed Capital Programmes and partly by deregulation. During 1980-87, 24,000 women entered the distributive trades, many as 'commercial importers'. There was a 30 per cent increase in 1980-85 in women doing this work. Women working in the garment manufacturing industry were also increasingly doing so as home workers. [66]

7.13 Domain Republic

In Domain Republic, 70 per cent of the women in the informal sector are earning incomes below the poverty line. For women, informal sector work largely consists of low wage, unprotected domestic labour. The growth of the informal sector has been encouraged by the state and international policies supporting growth of micro enterprises and extending credit towards this sector which has not necessarily benefited poor women. [67]

7.14 Caribbean

Caribbean women's efforts to ensure and maintain an adequate livelihood for themselves and those in their care have been undermined during 1980s. In the Caribbean, in each territory; several regional institutions, viz. national government agencies with a focus on women and national umbrella women's NGO exist with varying degrees of interest and involvement in women's issues. All of these maintain links with the Caribbean women's association (CARIWA), a regional organisation, and with the women's desk of the regional CARICOM secretariat. 16-17 per cent of economically active women are employed in manufacturing, in sub-Saharan Africa the proportion is even lower   at around 6 percent (UN 1991:88-9) where women are employed in manufacturing they tend to be concentrated in specific industries (garments, electronics) and in relatively unskilled occupations, older women and especially female heads of households are more likely to be in the informal sector.

7.15 Saudi Arabia

Women in Saudi Arabia are making a significant impact on the economy. About 10 per cent of private businesses in Saudi Arabia are now run by women, compared with hardly any a generation ago. They are also making big use of the internet which helps them to do business online without having to meet male customers in person.   But in this highly conservative Gulf state, women still face many restrictions. Women entrepreneurs also conduct 'Women's Exhibition for Marketing and Investment' in Saudi Arabia. Although Saudi women are forbidden either to drive cars or to deal directly with men, an estimated 250000 of them have overcome these obstacles to form a growing part of the economy. Over 6,000 commercial licences have been issued to women; many of them run their own women-only businesses. [68]

7.16 Canada

Canada's economic conditions have changed dramatically over the years. One of the most exciting aspects of this trend is the entrance of women entrepreneurs with greater confidence into the new economy. In 1995, the number of women running small businesses in BC has grown from 97000 to over 137000. BC has almost 360 000 small businesses, in which the share of women entrepreneurs is about 35 per cent - the highest rate of small businesses ownership among women in Canada, which is higher than the national average of just under 34 per cent. The number is expected to double over the next decade. There are more than 821000 women entrepreneurs in Canada. Women in Canada make up a larger share of the self-employed than in any other country. In 1976, the average annual growth rate for self-employed women has been 5.3 per cent compared with 2.2 per cent for men.

One-third of self employed Canadians are women. Women entrepreneurs hold ownership in about 45 per cent of Canadian small and medium enterprises. Half of self-employed women work at home. Women tend to own firms in slower growth and higher risk sectors such as retail and service, in which access to financing is relatively more challenging. Between 1990 and 2003, the number of women entrepreneurs rose from 27 per cent to 33 per cent, which may indicate that women stay in business longer and their survival rates are higher. Small business trends show high levels of growth between 100 per cent—140 per cent in management services, educational services, and professional, sciences and technical services. The number of small businesses in Western Canada per thousand population is 40 per cent higher than in the rest of the country. One half of the numbers of self-employed men and women in

Western Canada possess either a university degree or a post-secondary diploma. [69]

According to Hughes, "There are now over 800,000 women owned businesses in Canada." while programs exist that encourage women to start businesses, women entrepreneurs still lack benefits, protections and social services typically granted to Canadian workers as their status as employees. [70] Ruth Bastedo, President of WEC stated that, "But while the increase of women entrepreneurship is rising dramatically, there has been very little statistical analysis of the contributions women-owned businesses are making on the Canadian economy." With women generating 40 per cent of new start-ups and one-third of self-employed proprietorships in Canada owned or led by women, women entrepreneurs have jumped by more than 200 per cent in the last 20 years. [71]

In 2004, 98 per cent of all businesses in BC were small businesses. Micro-businesses (those with fewer than 3 employees) comprised 83 per cent of small businesses. Statistics Canada's Labour Force Survey reports there were 866 000 self-employed women in Canada in 2005, accounting for about one third of all self-employed persons The number of employed women has been steadily climbing, and the number of self employed women has been rising even faster. Over the past 15 years, the number of female employees rose by 30 per cent, more than double the pace seen among male employees. But this impressive growth is dwarfed by the dazzling 50 per cent growth seen among women who were self-employed during the same period. 45 per cent of all SMEs have at least one female owner. For 34 per cent of all SMEs, women hold 50 per cent ownership or more.

This RBC report concludes that the generation of entrepreneurs that will emerge over the next 10 to 20 years will represent the biggest shift in the makeup of Canada's business community since the beginning of the 20th century. The new group is comprised of higher educated owners, more women and visible minorities, including new Canadians.

Canadian women's entrance into self-employment and small business ownership in recent years has been nothing short of dramatic. In a relatively short period of time, they have established themselves as a formidable presence, contributing an estimated US$ 18 billion to the Canadian economy and attracting much attention from policy makers and academic researchers alike. [72]

Women Entrepreneurs of Canada (WEC) is one of the pre-eminent non-profit making business associations for women entrepreneurs in Canada, a leading organization that champions and facilitates women's entrepreneurship. WEC members provide meaningful networking opportunities to connect with peers as well as the larger business community, Government and the international business world. WEC builds up entrepreneurship acumen and business leadership capacity. The Prime Minister's Task Force on Women Entrepreneurs was created to advance the contribution of women entrepreneurs to the Canadian economy. Women's Economic Club (WEC) was founded in Toronto in 1992 to undertake several on behalf of women entrepreneurs on the local, national and international level. WEC promotes and fosters the success of women entrepreneurs in Canada. It serves as a representative on the Prime Minister's Task Force to develop a national strategy to encourage women entrepreneurs in Canada. WEC is a resource, support and opportunity network for established Canadian women entrepreneurs.

WEC promotes the interests of women entrepreneurs in the larger business community; facilitates the transfer of relevant knowledge that is appropriate to WEC members; and partners with organizations both in Canada and abroad, such as NAWBO and FCEM, to bring the best-of-breed services, opportunities and resources to women in businesses. [73] The National Association of Women Business Owners (NAWBO) of Greater Detroit (NAWBO) and WEC connect women entrepreneurs and business owners in more than 40 countries. [74]

7.17 Italy

Female entrepreneurship in Italy is growing. According to the data from the Ministry of Equal Opportunities, every 3 out of 10 entrepreneurs are women and 35 per cent of new companies are driven by women. 69 per cent of the companies driven by women are in the tertiary sector. However, this is mainly confined to small companies, mainly due to the continuing problems of time management, work flexibility and finding initial funds to establish one's own company. [75]

The Law 215 'Positive action for female entrepreneurs', which was passed in 1992 aims to promote entrepreneurship and vocational training of women entrepreneurs, to support the creation and development of female entrepreneurship and t o promote the presence of female-run companies in diverse sectors of activity. The law aims to provide more funds and support to women who want to start up an entrepreneurial activity, women that have already founded their own companies and intend to develop innovative company projects and women that intend to acquire resources in order to improve their products, insert new technology, research new markets. Men are much more active in start-up enterprises than women. Most pressing issues are financial support issues, and labor market complications. Most of the start-ups are concerned with personal fulfillment. Therefore, there are not many start-ups in high technology sector, most concentrated in mature markets. Italians see entrepreneurship as more like self employment compared to seeing as a growth opportunity. [76]

7.18 Bulgaria

The transition from a centrally planned to a market economy in the former communist world has been characterized by the rapid formation of entrepreneurial new ventures. Private ,small- and medium-sized enterprises account for as much as 50-60 per cent of the gross domestic product (GDP) of countries such as Hungary, Lithuania, the Czech Republic, Poland, and Latvia, almost as much as in the industrialized West (World Bank, 2002). Entrepreneurship is seen as a major engine for job creation and social change in these economies (World Bank, 2002). The women-led entrepreneurial businesses in transitional economies have shown a lower propensity to grow and a higher propensity to exit under unfavorable industry and competitive conditions.

Resource scarcity, particularly lack of financial resources, plagues entrepreneurship in all transitional economies (World Bank, 2000). Another explanation for the lower growth propensity of women entrepreneurs' ventures in a transitional economy may be that, relative to men entrepreneurs, women have ex-ante lower growth expectancies for their ventures.

7.19 Russia

In the former USSR, the planned economy gave more emphasis on maximization of the labor force which resulted in women's increased participation in the economy and their participation was always one of the highest in the world. In poor families, women were forced to work outside the home or in a home-based business. Women had little opportunity to enter the business prior to the start of the market transition. Most of the private businesses that existed under the communist system in the former USSR operated in the underground economy. For decades, the terms "private property" and "private business" had been used in a negative context only. Private entrepreneurs were solely men as women were not willing to take up the risks of criminal prosecution inherent in entrepreneurial activities.

The legalisation of small private business in 1987 as part of Gorbachev's perestroika gave Russians an opportunity to develop their entrepreneurial skills for the first time in over 50 years. However, their massive influx into the ranks of private entrepreneurs began only after 1991, with the start of Russia's radical transition to the market. It was a transition that destroyed the "permanent full employment" guarantees inherent to the planned economy. Moreover, with the fall of the Communist State resulted in a decline in women's average wage levels from 70 per cent to 40 per cent of that received by men. Eight years of continued economic depression, followed by the financial crisis of August 1998, resulted in severe unemployment among women. Russian women massively turned to private entrepreneurship, both informal and officially registered due to sever unemployment and economic discrimination. At present, the estimated total number of women engaged in independent business of all kinds is over three million, which represents at least one-third of all self-employed in Russia. The explosion of unemployment and increase in economic discrimination against women in Russia since the start of market reforms has pushed many of them into the ranks of micro entrepreneurs. [77]

Karen Sherman, at a Kennan Institute lecture on 24 January 2000 stated that the overall transformation in the Russian and Ukraine societies in disproportionately affected women in different ways, viz. high unemployment, under employment, low mobility and opportunity etc. Women also suffer from a number of gender constraints such as the need to find daycare and support their family, a feeling of inadequacy in necessary technical skills, and gender discrimination. Women do not have suitable entrepreneurial environment to set up small businesses. Lack of access to financing, heavy taxation on businesses, non-supportive legislation, and inconsistent enforcement of laws relating to small businesses etc. are some of the constraints faced by them. For a majority of women in both Russia and Ukraine the macro-economic constraints were much more daunting than the gender constraints. Business training programme in Russia helped women in business planning and acquiring skills in various aspects of managing a business. Some women in Russia who had participated in business training and technical assistance programs had changed their way of doing business could increase the sales and employment in their business and obtained external finances.

In Ukraine, some of the women participants in training and technical assistance programmes were able to create small businesses, change the operation of their business, achieve growth in sales, income, and profit, create new jobs and enhance their self-confidence after the training. These training programs provide a forum and support mechanism for women to get the kinds of tools and resources needed to succeed in their businesses. [78]

Notes

1. Caren, A. Grown and Jennefer Sebstad, Introduction: Towards a Wider Perspective on Women's Employment, World Development, Vol.17, No. 7, 1989, p. 937.

2. Caren, A. Grown and Jennefer Sebstad, Introduction: Towards a Wider Perspective on Women's Employment, World Development, Vol. 17, No.7, 1989, p. 938.

3. enquiries@eupreface.org.

4. Anjali D' Souza', Empowering Women-A Key to a Developed Nation, Vikasini, vol.No.21, No.2, April-June, 2006, pp. 2-4.

5. Robert Goffee and Richard Scase, Women in Charge-The Experience of Female Entrepreneurs, George Allen and Unwin (Publishers) Ltd., London, U.K., 1985, p. 7.

6. Caren, A. Grown and Jennefer, Sebstad, Introduction: Toward a Wider Perspective on Women's Employment, World Development, Ox ford, U.K., Vol.17, No.7, pp. 937-952, 1989.

7. www. Justin.org.

8. Center for Women's Business Research, September 2006, Entrepreneur. COM, Inc.

9. Center for Women's Business Research, September 2006, Entrepreneur.com, Inc.

10. www.worldbank.org.

11. Anjali D' Souza', Empowering Women-A Key to a Developed Nation, Vikasini, Vol.No.21, No.2, April-June, 2006, pp. 2-4.

12. Reny Jacob, From Home Makers to Decision Makers-Women's Role Highlighted on Inter National Women's Day, Vikasini, Vol.No.21, No.2, April-June, 2006, pp. 7-8.

13. Rashmee Roshan Lall, Asian Rich Women Most Confident

in Tax Planning, Vikasini, Vol.No.22, No.2, April-June 2007, p. 30.

14. www.census.gov.

15. enquiries@eupreface.org]

16. enquiries@eupreface.org

17. enquiries@eupreface.org.

18. Wanjiru Kihoro, African women not helped by aid projects, Documentation on Women's Concerns, April-June 1992, p. 74.

19. www. asiasource. org.

20. Marta Turk, 'Women Entrepreneurship-Back to Traditional Values', PCMG Informator, 2000.

21. Ifcln001.worldbank.org

22. Kathy Peiss, Enterprising Women: 250 Years of American Business," the Radcliffe Institute for Advanced Study, 'two-day program entitled Women, Money and Power'. November 18, 2002.

23. Nancy Koehn, "Enterprising Women: 250 Years of American Business," the Radcliffe Institute for Advanced Study, 'two-day program entitled Women, Money and Power'. November 18, 2002.

24. infopedia-1995, Women, Employment of Funk and Wagnalls New encyclopedia.

25. Manpower Report, The changing economic role of women, in N. Glazer and H. Younelson Wachrer (eds), Women in Man-made World, 2nd edn. Chicago: Rand Mc Nally, 1977.

26. Jane Applegate, Tech economy helps women overcome cultural barriers in Greece, July 5, 2000.

27. Howard Stevenson, Enterprising Women: 250 Years of American Business" Radcliffe Institute for Advanced Study, 'two-day program entitled Women, Money and Power', Nov 18, 2002.

28. Chris Godwin, Have women finally shattered the glass ceiling? Documentation on Women's Concern, July-Sep 1999, p. 32.

29. Scase, R and Goffee, R. 1980a, The Real World of the Small Businesses Owner, London: Croom Helm, Women in Charge, p. 7.

30. www. Womensbusines sresearch.org

31. Center for Women's Business Research, Business Women's Network and the Dynamics of Women-Owned Sole Proprietorships by Dr. Ying Lowrey, 2004.

32. Jeanne Halladay Coughlin, Andrew R. Thomas, The Rise of Women Entrepreneurs, people, Processes and Global trends, Greenwood Publishing Group, New York, U.S.A., 2002, p. xii.

33. www. womensbusines sresearch.org.

34. Ying Lowrey, Center for Women's Business Research, Business Women's Network and the Dynamics of Women-Owned Sole Proprietorships.

35. www.cipe.org.

36. US Census Bureau 2004.

37. www.womensbusinessresearch.org.

38. www.census.gov.

39. www. sba.

40. Harsh Patriarhy Documentation on Documentation on Women's Concerns, Oct/Nov, 2000, p.26.

41. Estes, 1999; NFWBO, 1998; Women in Business-Lesotho, 1998; Jalbert, 1999c; Carter & Cannon, 1992.

42. www.chinadaily.com.

43. Shelina Akhter, Women Entrepreneurship in Urban Bangladesh: A Study, SEDME, Vol 32, No.2, June 2005, pp 77-99.

44. Women Business Owners in France: The Issue of Financing Discrimination. Orban, Muriel, Journal, 2001, All Business. COM, Inc.

45. Marta Turk, 'Women Entrepreneurship-Back to Traditional Values', PCMG Informator, 2000.

46 Cromie, S. (1987) "Similarities and Differences Between Women and Men Who Choose Businesses Proprietorship", International Small Business Journal, 5(3), pp. 43-60.

47. Kanjou Mrcela, A. (1996) Zenske v managementu (Eng.: Women in Management), Ljubljana: Enotnost.

48. Entrepreneurship: New Challenge for Slovene Women, Miroslav Glas, University of Ljubljana Tea Petrin, University of Ljubljana, University of Ljubljana, 1101 Ljubljana, Slovenia 1999.

49. Marta Turk, 'Women Entrepreneurship-Back to Traditional Values', PCMG Informator, 2000.

50 Glas, M. & Petrin, T. (1998) Entrepreneurship: new Challenges for Slovene Women, Ljubljana: Research Centre at the Faculty of Economics, Working Paper No. 74.

51. Ibid.

52. Petrin, T. & Humphries, J. (1980) "Women in self-managed Economy of Yugoslavia", Economic Analysis, 14(1), pp. 70-91, Glas, M. (1986) Delitev po delu v socialisticni druzbi (Eng.: Distribution According to Work in the Socialist Society), Ljubljana: Delavska Enotnost.

53. Entrepreneurship: New Challenge for Slovene Women,

Miroslav Glas, University of Ljubljana Tea Petrin, University of Ljubljana, University of Ljubljana, 1101 Ljubljana, Slovenia 1999.

54. Kovacic, P. (1997) *Zenske v samozaposlovanju* (Eng.: *Women in Self-Employment*), Ljubljana: Faculty of Economics.

55. Ambos, I (1989) Frauen als Unternehmerinnen und die Charakteristik ihrer Betriebe, Bielefeld: Kleine Verlag, Voigt, M. (1994) *Unternehmerinnen und Unternehmenserfolg– Geschlechtsspezifische esondeheiten bei Gruendung und Fuehrung von Unternehmen*, Weisbaden: Gabler, Brush, C. (1990) *Local Initiatives for Job Creation: Enterprising Women*, Paris: OECD.]

56. Glas, M. (1999) Slovenski podjetniki (Eng.: Slovene Entrepreneurs), Ljubljana: GEA College, Drnovsek, M. (1999) "Strategic Orientation of Slovene Small Businesses" Unpublished Data.

57. Miroslav Glas, Mateja Drnovsek, Various Financial Reports for 1997-98, Slovenian women as emerging entrepreneurs, Slovenke kot porajajoče se podjetnice, December 1999.

58. Miroslav Glas, Mateja Drnovsek, Various Financial Reports for 1997-98, Slovenian women as emerging entrepreneurs, Slovenke kot porajajoče se podjetnice, December 1999.

59. Slovene Press Agency, Public Relations and Media Office.

60. BRIDGE, Briefings on Development and Gender, Report No.15, December, 1993.p. 28.

61. BRIDGE, Briefings on Development and Gender, Report No.15, December, 1993.p. 24.

62. Jeanne Halladay Coughlin, Andrew R. Thomas, The Rise of Women Entrepreneurs, people, Processes and Global trends, Greenwood Publishing Group, New York, U.S.A., 2002, p. xi

63. Webb, M. 1982, The labour market, I. Reid and E. Wormald (EDS), in sex Difference in Britain, London: Grant McIntyre, 1982.

64. Women in Charge-The Experience of Female Entrepreneurs, George Allen and Unwin (Publishers) Ltd., London, U.K., 1985, p. 9.

65. P.K. Choudhury, Shashi Baijal and M. Asokan, Banks and women's enterprises development: a comparison of approaches in India and U.K., SEDME, Vol. XXIV, No.2, June 1997.

66. Jane Applegate, Tech economy helps women overcome cultural barriers in Greece, July 5, 2000

67. BRIDGE, Briefings on Development and Gender, Report No.15, December, 1993.p. 28.

68. BRIDGE, Briefings on Development and Gender, Report No.15, December, 1993.p. 28.

69. BBC Gulf Correspondent, Frank Gardner in Riyadh BBC News Online, September 21, 1998 Published at 10:50 GMT 11:50 UK

70. Prime Minister's Task Force on Women Entrepreneurs, Nov. 2003, BC Stats Small Business Profile, 2003, CIBC's Look at New Entrepreneurs in Canada, June 2004, HRDC Survey of Self Employment in Canada, A Portrait of Small Business Growth and Employment in Western Canada- Western Economic Diversification.

71. Karen Hughes, University of Alberta, 'Female enterprise in the New Economy' APRIL 26, 2006.

72. Mark Adler, Chairman of The Economic Club of Toronto. Introducing the New 'Women Entrepreneurs of Canada', http://www.wec.ca

73. Women Entrepreneurs: Statistics and Trends Reports, Studies, Women's Enterprise Centre, Canada.

74. Cathy-Anne O'Brien, WEC Public Relations, Blue Sky Communications, (416) 691-5206, cobrien@ yourbluesky.com or Julie O'Brien (416) 691-6657, jobrien@yourbluesky.com.

75. Ada LeeChairman and CEO, Glow Nutraceuticals Inc., Business Across Borders at the Detroit Conference Venter, Canada, October 3 & 4, 2004

76. www.pariopporunita.gov.it.

77. InternationalEntrepreneurship.com

78. Women entrepreneurs in Russia: Learning to survive the market, Izyumov, Alexei, Razumnova, Irina, Journal of Developmental Entrepreneurship, Apr 2000 , CNET Networks, Inc.

Appendices

Appendix 1

Women Entrepreneurship in Kerala and Tamil Nadu

Socio-Economic Status of the Women Entrepreneurs in Kerala and Tamil Nadu

Historically, Kerala has been quite different from the rest of the country, as far as the status of women is concerned. Kerala women enjoy a higher status due to progressive social movements and proper State action. In Kerala, education played a vital role in enhancing the status of women. The achievements of Kerala in the case of social development are ahead not only of all other States in India, but also most other developing countries. At the same time, in most parts of Tamil Nadu, women have little knowledge of their legal rights and depend largely on the male siblings or husbands. They also do not have much access to credit or income, as most of the family expenditure is controlled by men. Even when they have some measure of control, they spend most of their earnings on family needs. The position of women in the State has significantly improved with the starting of the S.H.Gs in 1989 in the rural areas.

Women Entrepreneurship in Kerala

Kerala presents a positive picture as far as women's development is concerned. The statistical data also show that the number of women SSI units is increasing every year. Even though women entrepreneurs in Kerala have essential education, they are not outstanding in their role as entrepreneurs, as the majority of them undertake less risky ventures. According to Soosy George Isaac, President of All Kerala Women's Industries Association, nowadays, women entrepreneurs are neither hard working nor willing to take risk which the women entrepreneurs of the previous generation took. Previously, most of the women entrepreneurs were engaged in some kind of manufacturing activities.

Today, most of the enterprises set up by women entrepreneurs are of simple consumer products, like ready made garments, food products, toys, handicrafts or are in the service sector, such as X-rays, clinic, tailoring, beauty parlours, data processing, advertising, departmental stores and photo-copying. Only a few have entered steel furniture, electronics, plastics and other industries that require higher technology and innovative production process. "Although the women of Kerala possess some personality traits necessary for successful entrepreneurship, they lack the critical factors necessary for entrepreneurship, like the ability to take risk, self-dependence, an experimental nature and innovativeness."

On the other side, in Kerala, entrepreneurs do not have a suitable entrepreneurial environment. Inadequate infrastructure facilities, existence of bureaucracy, etc. are some of the common problems faced by them. Rajula Chandran and R. Thiagarajan (2005) observed that the studies carried out in the field of agriculture indicated that in spite of the key role of women in crop husbandry, fisheries, animal husbandry and so on, those who formulated a package of technologies, services and public policies for rural areas had neglected the productive role of women.

Evolution of Women Entrepreneurship in Kerala

Kerala, being a 100 per cent literate State, has made significant progress in the area of social development but the performance in the industrial sector has not been keeping pace with the potential of the State. In Kerala, despite a high social capability (high literacy rates and good health status) women are economically dependent because of historical subordination. In the earlier period, the low caste women were the most massive work force in Travancore, Cochin and Malabar regions and were engaged mainly in the agricultural sector. British rule provided remunerative employment for women in rubber, tea, coffee and spices cultivation. It spread to coir, fishing industries, cashew, handloom and different sectors of construction activities, shop assistants, home nursing, hospital services, teaching, etc. Now the trend has changed. Their activities range from tailoring units to hi-tech IT centers.

Organisations Promoting Women Entrepreneurship in Kerala

Socio Economic Unit Foundation (SEU): SEU foundation was started in 1996 in Thiruvananthapuram. Issues and areas covered by SEU are water and sanitation, capacity building, women's empowerment, supporting women's skill development through training.

Centre for Collective Learning and Action (SAHAYI): SAHAYI has been working since 1990 towards capacity building of women collectives in Kerala. It also provides short-term entrepreneurship development training to women collectives.

Kerala State Women's Development Corporation (KSWDC): KSWDC is a public sector undertaking formed for the development of women and registered in 1988 under the Companies Act. It provides self-employment loans, employment based training, loans to mahila samajams and co-operative societies etc.

Self Employed Women's Association (SEWA): SEWA was established in 1986 and registered under the Charitable Societies Act. It is a membership-based organisation. The increasing marginalisation of women from their traditional occupation like fish vending and reed work was creating several problems, specially related to the sustenance of their families, which motivated the inception of SEWA in Thiruvananthapuram.

Dalit Women's Society (DWS): DWS is a voluntary organisation started in the year 1992 at Kurichi in Kottayam district. It is the first women's organisation which organised tuition programmes, self-employment programmes, workshop and computer training for dalit women.

Women's Endeavour: Women's Endeavour is a charitable society which was registered in Kochi on August 3, 2005 under the Charitable Societies Act for the social, educational and economic uplift of women through proper channel by conducting seminars, meetings, workshops and legal debates for the members.

Kerala State Women's Industries Association (KSWIA): KSWIA is an association of women entrepreneurs in Kerala, which was formed in 1980 for the promotion of women entrepreneurs. It safeguards the interests of its members and also provides a forum to discuss their common problems.

Schemes for Women Entrepreneurship in Kerala

Women's Industries Programme (WIP): WIP was introduced with a view to attract more women entrepreneurs to industrial sector. This scheme provides financial assistance to women industrial units engaged in small scale and cottage industries.

Special Schemes/Programmes of KSWDC: The Schemes/programmes of KSWDC include:

- **Organising Marketing Fairs** for marketing the products of small-scale women entrepreneurs.
- **Self-employment Scheme for Fisher Women:** Self-employment scheme for fisher women was implemented by KSWDC with the financial aid of the state Government and Fisheries Department in Kollam and Alleppey. State Institute of Training for women provides employment-based training to women in different trades. For this purpose a State Institute of Training has been started in Ernakulam. Training courses are provided in computer, food processing, electronic assembly, hardware maintenance etc. Cyber Café management training is

provided to women between the age group of 18to 35 to equip them to manage Cyber Café.

• **Operating Women Marketing Centres** in towns and cities of Thiruvananthapuram, Alleppey and Ernakulam for marketing the products of self-employed women.

Financial Institutions Assisting Women Entrepreneurship in Kerala

In Kerala, Kerala State Industrial Development Corporation (KSIDC), Kerala Financial Corporation (KFC), Small Industries Development Bank of India (SIDBI), Regional Rural Banks, Co-operative Banks, Public Sector Banks, Private Sector Banks, etc. provide financial assistance to women entrepreneurs. Commercial banks not only provide financial assistance but also offer consultancy services to women entrepreneurs. Some branches of commercial banks (e.g. Canara Bank's Mahila Banking Branch, Pattom, Thiruvanathapuram) act as a centre for the development of women, offering facilities such as a small library, credit-related counselling, guidance services and information about various schemes for women.

Kerala State Industrial Development Corporation (KSIDC): KSIDC, as facilitator and financier for medium and large scale industries offers wide assistance in building a dynamic economy. The key areas of focus include, identification of investment ideas, translating ideas into concrete proposals, feasibility study, technology sourcing, project evaluation, financial structuring, loan syndication, ensuring central and state Government clearances, tying up requirements in infrastructure, total project management support, development and administration of growth centres. KSIDC provides promotional supports by way of extending financial assistance share capital and loan to manufacturing project coming under different categories.

Kerala Financial Corporation (KFC): KFC was established in 1953 as a premier financial institution to provide medium and long term loans to industries in the small and medium scale sectors in the State.   KFC also conducts seminars and clientele meetings in different places.

Lending Schemes of Financial Institutions/Other Agencies in Kerala

Schemes of Kerala Financial Corporation: KFC offers Normal Term Loan Schemes and Special Schemes-Normal Term Loan Schemes   general scheme for SSI units, Single Window Scheme, National Equity Fund (NEF) Scheme, Scheme for financing activities relating to marketing of SSI products, Credit Linked Capital Subsidy Scheme for technology up gradation of small scale industries.

The special schemes of KFC include Technology Development and Modernisation Scheme for ISO Certification, Scheme for existing well run profit making enterprises, Equipment Leasing Scheme, Scheme for assistance for market research, advertisement, product launching, participation in trade fairs, exhibition etc., Hire Purchase Scheme, Bill Discounting Scheme, Working Capital Term Loan Scheme etc.

Margin Money Scheme of Khadi and Village Industries Board: This Scheme was launched by the KVIC during 1996-97. Under this programme, the beneficiaries are entitled to get Margin Money assistance as grant for the loans availed of from various financial institutions and banks, for establishing units in rural areas as approved by the KVIC. The beneficiaries have to submit project proposals recommended by the concerned project officer of the board to the banks for getting finance. On receipt of the orders of the bank sanctioning loan and release of first installment of loan, the board will release the Margin Money grant to the joint account of the beneficiary and the project officer concerned.

Margin Money is sanctioned at the following rates. For projects up to Rs. 10 lakh – Margin Money is 25 per cent of the Project cost. For projects above Rs. 10 lakh and up to Rs.

25 lakh – 25 per cent of the first 10 lakh and 10per cent of the balance amount. For beneficiaries belonging to SC/ST, women, minority community and their institutions, ex-service men, physically handicapped, Margin Money will be 30 per cent.

Schemes of KSIDC: The financial service of KSIDC ranges from equity and term loans to short term loans and bridge loans. Equity Participation is up to 11 per cent and debt- equity Ratio 1:1 Term Loans are granted up to Rs.1000 Lakh. No gap for term loan under direct financing. Bridge loans are granted against term loans sanctioned, against subsidy or against public issue. Short Term Loans are given for working capital and Emergencies Corporate Loans are given for existing profit making units up toRs.100 lakh.

For encouraging entrepreneurship in IT, Biotechnology and allied sectors, KSIDC in association with SIDBI and KFC has established Venture Capital Funding as an alternate financial source with a corpus of Rs.20 crore.

KSIDC is the operating agency for processing and disbursement of state investment subsidy for its assisted units.

The financial services of KSIDC range from equity and term loans to short term loans and bridge loans.

Schemes of Tamil Nadu Mercantile Bank: Loan for Women Entrepreneurs (Mahalir) Scheme: This scheme is exclusively tailored for women in business which is suitable for all the general business that need funding for the working capital and other business related funding necessities. Loan up to Rs.10 lakh is granted under this scheme with interest on diminishing balance. Loan is given to meet the working capital requirements/term loan to purchase fixed assets such as plant and machinery etc. Loan is also granted in the form of WCTL/WCDL/Term Loan/Demand Loan/Working Capital Limits such as OD, CC etc. Repayment of working capital limit is one year and for term loan/demand loan, the repayment period shall be fixed on the basis of income generation of the borrower up to the maximum of seven years. Primary security is hypothecation of stock/book debts/equipments/machinery and fitting and furniture etc. In addition to this collateral security and the guarantee from husband/father of (borrower) the proprietor/partner are also obtained.

Lending Schemes of Other Institutions in Kerala
Schemes of Kerala Women Development Corporation

- **Self-Employment Loan Scheme:** KSWDC has implemented three types of credit schemes to women viz. self-employment loan scheme to women below poverty line. Loans are granted for self-employment purposes subject to a maximum of Rs.50 000. Interest @ 8 per cent p.a. is charged on such loans. Loans are repayable in 60 monthly installments and loans to minority group. KSWDC is an agency of National Minority Development Corporation so as to implement the schemes of NMDFC in Kerala. Under this scheme women of the minority group can start any productive business. Under Temporary Loan Yojana scheme loans are granted by KSWDC for productive purposes after assessing the economic viability of the project. KSWDC is an agency of National Backward Community Financial Development Corporation for implementing the schemes of NBCFC in Kerala. Loans are granted to SC/ST categories at an interest rate of 7 per cent p.a., which are repayable in 60 monthly installments.

- **Loans to Women Co-operative Societies and Mahila Sangams:** These schemes are introduced mainly to provide employment to women who are below poverty line. Under this scheme, women commercial co-operative societies and Mahila Sangams can start any venture. Loans are granted after appraising the economic viability of the project.

Development Agencies in Kerala

District Industries Centre (DIC): District Industries Centre in Kerala plays a vital role in promoting industries at the District level. DICs provide necessary project assistance for the prospective entrepreneurs.

SISI Thrissur: The jurisdiction of the SISI covers all the districts of Kerala and the Union Territory of Lakshadweep. It has Extension Centres at Allapuzha, Shoranur, Kozhikode and Footwear Service Centre and Central Workshop in Thrissur. It provides technical, managerial consultancy services besides attending to revival of small-scale sick units. SISI, Thrissur undertakes promotional and developmental activities starting from creation of awareness, motivation, identification of products and entrepreneurs to setting up of industrial establishments and follow-up measures in the context of new era of liberalisation and globalisation. The Nucleus Cell of the Institute is also functioning at Cochin for the promotion and development of small-scale units in Lakshadweep Islands. Fruit and Vegetable Preservation Training Centre imparts training to the prospective entrepreneurs and also aims at upgrading the skill of the entrepreneurs in this line.

Kerala Bureau of Industrial Promotion (K-BIP): Kerala Bureau of Industrial Promotion (K-BIP) was constituted under the Industries Department during the year 1991 as an autonomous body of the State Government. It is an autonomous body under the aegis of Department of Industries, Government of Kerala and is the nodal agency for HACCP Certification. It is envisaged for promoting the potential business opportunities of the State to the foresighted entrepreneurs and to highlight the ideal business climate prevailing in Kerala. K-BIP works in close co-ordination with similar promotional agencies like KSIDC (Kerala State Industrial Development Corporation). K-BIP provides operational flexibility and acts as support mechanism for the Industries Department of the State Government. The Bureau also functions as an interface between the prospective entrepreneurs and other State agencies.

Small Industries Development Corporation (SIDCO) Kerala: SIDCO a promotional agency wholly owned by

Government of Kerala was set up in 1975. This corporation is rendering all kinds of assistance to SSIs in the State. At present the activities of SIDCO are confined to the distribution of raw materials to SSIs, marketing of the SSI products, maintenance of 17 industrial estates, 36 mini industrial estates and doing civil works for Industries Department and some other Governmental agencies. SIDCO is also running 11 production units which are undertaking various kinds of job works in metal and wood, bus body building, manufacturing bricks, furniture etc.

Kerala Industrial and Technical Consultancy Organisation (KITCO): KITCO is a public sector consultancy organisation established in 1972 by Industrial Development Bank of India (IDBI) in association with the Government of Kerala, other national and state level financial institutions and banks with a view to render consultancy services to industries and other entities. KITCO has gained considerable experience and expertise in various fields of consultancy including planning, design and implementation of projects, project management, plant engineering, electrification, asset valuation, energy audit, human resources development (HRD), etc.

Common Facility Service Center for Rubber at Manjeri: The CFSC at Manjeri, situated at the Functional Industrial Estate for Rubber provides services of costly rubber processing machines, services of tool room for designing, fabricating and repair of moulds, dyes, rubber processing machines etc up to date testing facility for rubber products training, technical advice, product development etc.

Kerala Industrial Infrastructure Development Corporation (KINFRA): The industrial parks developed by KINFRA have facilities like developed land, dedicated power, continuous water supply, communication facilities etc. in addition to supporting infrastructure facilities like administrative block bank, post office, round the clock security, etc. thus providing ready-made manufacturing environment for easy start up of industrial units with minimum time and cost.

Electronics Technology Parks-Kerala (Techno Park): Electronics Technology Parks Kerala at Thiruvananthapuram was established for development in the field of Electronics and Information Technology. TECHNOPARK covering an area of 184.72 acres of land was registered as an autonomous society on 28th July 1990 to create the infrastructure and provide necessary support for setting up hi tech electronics and software industries in Kerala.

Food Quality& Safety (HACCP) System in Kerala: To create awareness regarding Food Quality & Safety Hygiene, Food Processing Industry has been developed in Kerala. This is especially relevant with coming into effect of WTO agreement, standards, guidelines and recommendations of Codex Alimentarius Commission. Hazard Analysis Critical Control Point (HACCP) is internationally accepted as the most effective risk management technique in food safety and quality. All businesses involved in food supply chain from producers to retailers (fruits, vegetables, dairy products, meat and meat products, fish and fishery products, spices and condiments, nuts and nut products, cereals, bakery and confectionery, restaurants, hotels and fast food operations) can use HACCP for building and strengthening market relationships. K-BIP is the nodal agency for issuing HACCP certification.

Entrepreneurship Development Club: To provide a sustainable stimulus for industrial growth, Department of Industries & Commerce, Government of Kerala formulated a scheme to set up "Entrepreneurship Development Clubs" in schools and colleges of the State to inculcate "Entrepreneurial Culture" amongst youth and equip them with the skills, techniques and confidence to act as torch-bearers of "Enterprise" for the new generation.

Kerala Institute for Entrepreneurship Development (KIED): KIED is a premier institution promoted by

Government of Kerala and Government of India for promotion and development of entrepreneurial activities in the State. It was established in 1994. Its activities are managed by KITCO which include counselling, consultancy, training, identification of new entrepreneurs, and construction of industrial estates, feasibility studies, entrepreneurial guidance, surveys, sanctioning and disbursement of subsidies/incentives and escort services. It organizes seminars/workshops, cluster development programme and also buyer-seller meets.

Women Entrepreneurship in Tamil Nadu

Traditionally, Tamil Nadu is one of the well-developed States in terms of industrial development. In the post-liberalisation era, Tamil Nadu has emerged as one of the front-runners, by attracting a large number of investment proposals. It has been ranked as the third largest economy in India. But the Government's efforts come only from 1970 onwards for the promotion of self- employment among women.

In Tamil Nadu each city has its own set of products that are manufactured by women entrepreneurs using indigenous skills. Most of these products are made with locally available materials and the skills available in production are seldom found in other cities. Though traditional activities like production and sale of domestic items such as garments have been taken up by women since long, entrepreneurship on the modern lines has been found in industry and trade and service concerns only for the last one decade or so.

The modern Tamil Nadu woman is different from the housewife of the past, to whom selling or running a business carried a stigma which she found difficult to shake off. Women entrepreneurs in Tamil Nadu possess organisational abilities, marketing skills, entrepreneurial skills and efficiency and novel ideas. Many women have vaulted the barriers of conditioning and reaped the rewards of a globalising economy. According to Lakshmi V. Venkatesan, Founder Trustee of Bharatiya Yuva Shakthi Trust (BYST), "Women in Tamil

Nadu are the best entrepreneurs in the country; they have shown that they could make excellent entrepreneurs if they get support by way of finance and guidance."

However, the manager of Indian Overseas Bank, (SSI Branch), Guindy, Chennai is of the opinion that most of the women entrepreneurs prefer to start business in the service sector with minimum risk and efforts. They are not interested in any kind of manufacturing activities. According to Laxmi Narasimhan, Regional Manager, Indian Overseas Bank, Madurai, urban women have good ideas about business; the success rate is very high, whereas the success rate of individual woman in semi-urban areas is much less, i.e., 20 to 30 per cent. In rural areas, the relative percentage is only 10. In rural areas, individual woman is not successful, since she does not have any idea about the business. Women are successful when they undertake group activities like Self Help Group (SHG), since they get very good awareness from it about the Government agencies, financial institutions, their schemes and opportunity to utilise these facilities. Family support is the main criterion for running business. Otherwise, women can run business only at micro finance level.

Evolution of Women Entrepreneurship in Tamil Nadu

In most parts of Tamil Nadu, women occupied a very low status in medieval and early modern society in the Madras Presidency. Lack of educational facilities, child marriages, prohibition of widow remarriages, prevalence of Devadasi system, etc. were some of the social factors responsible for the low status and misery of women who were reduced to the position of glorified slaves. Social barriers, imposition of taboos and female ignorance reigned supreme. The heavy industrialisation and urbanisation in the State made significant development in the areas of women's empowerment and social development.

In Tamil Nadu, women were engaged more in agriculture than in manufacturing or services. In the manufacturing sector, women worked as beedi workers and as manual labour for cotton textiles, fish, and food processing and match industry. A few were involved in the manufacturing of electronic and electrical goods.

In a traditionally conservative society like Tamil Nadu, risk-aversion was common. Women were a further step behind the average man, having to contend with gender barriers in financial institutions, discouragement in families, lower levels of education and confidence. The position of rural women in the State has remarkably changed with the formation of SHGs, which started on an experimental basis in 1989 in the rural areas. It helped poor rural women to enter the entrepreneurial world and it also helped them to develop self-confidence, communication, independence, mobility, management and technical skills. Assisted by some NGOs and with a little Government support, this movement gained momentum and developed into strong local institutions. They provided legitimate avenues for social mobilisation with access to inputs, such as training, banking services, Government services, etc. Most of them in the informal sector are now running micro enterprises or home-based production units such as basket making, mat weaving, beedi making, lace making and the production of agarbathi, candles, garments, telephone mats, handicrafts, paper dice, ink, soaps, washing powder, snacks, fruit juices, pickles, jams, squash, vattal, etc.

Organisations Promoting Women Entrepreneurship in Tamil Nadu

The Integrated Women Development Institute: The institute was set up in 1989 to uplift women and girl children from the distressing situations they encounter, by setting up income generating programmes for deserving women to become self-employed.

The Tamil Nadu Corporation for Development of Women Ltd.: The corporation was set up on December 9, 1983 under the Companies Act, 1956 to focus on empowerment of women to encourage entrepreneurship among women, to identify trade and industries suitable for women, to undertake marketing activities for products manufactured by women and encourage women to form SHGs through giving training and extending credit facilities.

Women Entrepreneurship Promotional Association (WEPA): WEPA functioning in Chennai is an association of women entrepreneurs, providing training to women in various fields The association also conducts exhibitions for the members and assists in marketing of the products of members.

Marketing Organisation of Women Entrepreneurs (Regd.) (MOOWES): MOOWES provides comprehensive support to women entrepreneurs to achieve success in the business. Its main aim is to aid women in marketing their products through exhibitions and thus provide an opportunity to tour the country also.

Schemes for Women Entrepreneurship in Tamil Nadu

Indira Mahila Yojana (IMY): The IMY is a scheme aims at organizing women at grass root level to facilitate their participation in decision-making and their empowerment. The Scheme was launched in 1995 on pilot basis in 200 blocks over a strategy to coordinate and integrate components of sectoral programmes and facilitates their convergence to empower women.

Women Industrial Parks: Five Industrial Parks were set up in Tamil Nadu exclusively for women entrepreneurs in Chennai, Tiruchirappalli, Salem, Madurai and Coimbatore.

Vocational and Skill Development Programmes: The major focus of The Tamil Nadu Corporation for Development of Women Ltd. has been to provide support to economically disadvantaged women. The Corporation is funding entrepreneurial programmes, which is opened to all potential women entrepreneurs, preferably first generation. The EDP programme was commenced in 1998-99, which is conducted by the Industry and Commerce at Chennai and Madurai for

DeW. The major focus of the Corporation has been to provide support to economically disadvantaged women. The Corporation is funding entrepreneurial programmes, which is opened to all potential women entrepreneurs, preferably first generation.

Mahalir Thittam: Mahalir Thittam is a participatory, people centred and process oriented project, was started in 1997- 98 which is directed towards empowerment of women and capacity building of poor woman in rural areas through Self Help Groups. It covers the entire state of Tamil Nadu. Currently the coverage extends to rural areas of all the 30 districts of Tamil Nadu It is an unusual long term partnership between three agencies-the state government, non-governmental organizations and banks (including NABARD) and other financial institutions. It provides inexpensive and timely credit to SHGs. provides training for the development of communication skill, provides entrepreneurship development training, facilitates to participate in exhibitions, collective negotiation/bargaining, facilitate emergence of structures like marketing unions and dissemination of information about markets.

Support to Training and Employment Programme for Women (STEP): The programme of STEP launched in 1987 aims to upgrade the skills of poor and asset less women, mobilise, concentrise and provide employment to them on a sustainable basis in the traditional sectors of agriculture, small animal husbandry, Dairying, Fisheries, Handlooms, Handicrafts, Khadi and Village Industries and Sericulture, Social Forestry and Waste Land Development.

Women Entrepreneurs Development Programme: Women's development has been given top priority in 1997-98. The Government of Tamil Nadu has stressed the need to augment resource for such programmes. Women Entrepreneurs particularly, the first generation women entrepreneurs, face many constraints particularly paucity of margin money assistance to start their ventures by getting finance from the financial institutions. To overcome the difficulties experienced by these entrepreneurs, Government have sanctioned a sum of Rs.30.00 lakh to give the first generation women entrepreneurs a subsidy of 10 per cent Margin Money support to the project cost subject to a ceiling of Rs.50 000.

New Anna Marumalarchi Thittam: Government of Tamil Nadu has implemented New Anna Marumalarchi Thittam for the promotion of Agro based/food processing and other related industries in rural areas to generate rural employment and thereby improve the rural economy. The projects which have commenced production includes food products like mango pulp, fruit Pulp, edible oil refining, chips and Agro based projects like modern rice mill using polisher and colour sorter etc. The other projects include cold storages, manufacturing of eco-friendly products of coir such as coir pith block, Herbal products like aloe vera gel, herbal medicines, eucalyptus oil, Export oriented aqua-culture items like shrimp, fresh water prawns, flori-culture products like flower concentrates from jasmine, export oriented horticulture produces like cut flowers, etc. In order to enthuse the potential investors in the district to take up industrial venture in agro based and food processing sector in rural areas, the Government has ordered a Special Entrepreneurship Development Programme through reputed training institutions like Central Food Training and Research Institute, Mysore, Tamil Nadu Agriculture University, Coimbatore, National Institute of Small Industries Extension Training, Hyderabad.

The Tamil Nadu Women in Agriculture Project (TANWA): The Tamil Nadu women in Agriculture Project (TANWA) assisted by the Danish International Development Agency (DANIDA) introduced in Tamil Nadu in 1986 for involving the women in the agricultural activities through package of services rendered to them. The first phase of the project covered two districts viz., Tirunelveli and Sivagangai over a period of seven years ending 1993. The scheme was extended to all the districts except Chennai subsequently. The prime objectives of the project are to expose the farm women to a package of 10-12 skills of relevance to them in crop production and related activities and to enable them to choose and adopt relevant agricultural practices; to spread agricultural knowledge and skills from TANWA trainees to non-trained fellow farm women and to improve the access to existing agricultural extension services for women belonging to small and marginal holdings.

Financial Institutions Assisting Women Entrepreneurship in Tamil Nadu

In Tamil Nadu, Tamil Nadu Industrial Cooperative Bank Limited, Tamil Nadu Industrial Investment Corporation (TIIC), Tamil Nadu Adi Dravidar Housing Development Corporation (TAHDCO), Regional Rural Banks, Public Sector Banks, Private Sector Banks, etc. provide financial assistance to women entrepreneurs. In Tamil Nadu there are 36 specialised SSI commercial bank branches functioning in different places. Some banks (e.g. Indian Overseas Bank, Egmore, Chennai) have a Mahila Banking Branch which is meant mainly for women and managed by women.

Tamil Nadu Industrial Cooperative Bank Limited (TAICO Bank Ltd.): TAICO Bank Ltd was established in 1961 for providing credit facilities to the Industrial Cooperative Societies. The bank also extends loan assistance to SSI/Tiny Sector, small road transport operators and traders. The Reserve Bank of India has recognised the TAICO Bank to provide credit facilities to the Industrial Cooperative Societies under NABARD Refinance Scheme.

Tamil Nadu Industrial Investment Corporation (TIIC): TIIC was incorporated in 1949 as a banking company (exempted from Banking Regulations Act) under the Companies Act. It is a premier financial institution that fosters industrial development of Tamil Nadu. It provides financial assistance to tiny / small / medium / large scale industrial units, professionals and transport vehicle operators. Under the general scheme, term loan assistance is provided for small and medium scale industrial units to set up new industries and expansion / modernisation / diversification of the existing units. Women entrepreneurs could avail assistance to set up new projects if the project cost does not exceed Rs.10.00 lakh.

Development Agencies in Tamil Nadu

Tamil Nadu Industrial Development Corporation Limited (TIDCO): TIDCO, a wholly owned Government of Tamil Nadu Enterprise, was incorporated as a limited company in the year 1965 in order to identify and promote the establishment of large and medium scale industries within the State of Tamil Nadu in association with the private companies and individual entrepreneur. TIDCO is also registered with the Reserve Bank of India as non-banking financial company. TIDCO has been specified as public financial institution within the meaning of Section 4A of the Companies Act, 1956. TIDCO is the promotional arm of the Government of Tamil Nadu, which gives top priority to promotion of infrastructure development projects besides power generation, petrochemicals, pharmaceutical, telecom and agro-based industries in associated with private promoters. TIDCO has been a major player and facilitator in the state's industrial development. Over the years, TIDCO has moved away from public sector investments and currently focuses on equity partnership in joint ventures.

Tamil Nadu Corporation for Industrial Infrastructure Development Ltd. (TACID): TACID has been constituted to develop industrial infrastructure facilities. This is an exclusive agency, concentrating solely on development of appropriate infrastructure in industrial area. This corporation is involved in the establishment of new growth centres and development of ports, convention centres, finance and Business centres and water supply sector.

Tamil   Nadu   Small   Industries   Development

Corporation Limited, (SIDCO): SIDCO is a Government of Tamil Nadu undertaking, established in October 1970 with the specific objective of promoting and developing Small Scale Industries (SSIs) in the State. SIDCO has developed 41iIndustrial estates and manages 35 Government industrial estates on agency terms.

TANSTIA: TANSTIA is an apex body recognised by the state and central Government, which was established in 1956. It provides specific services to women through entrepreneurial development programmes.

Tamil Nadu Khadi and Village Industries Board: The Tamil Nadu Khadi and Village Industries Board was formed in April 1960 under the Tamil Nadu Khadi and Village Industries Board Act, 1959 to tap tremendous employment opportunities in rural industries and to provide employment opportunities. The object of the Board is to develop the Khadi and Village Industries in rural areas in collaboration with likeminded agencies engaged in rural development work. The Board is the authority to register co-operative societies formed by likeminded people under the Co-operative Societies Act to develop Khadi and Village Industries. The Board through these Co-operative Societies also promotes Khadi and Village Industries and thereby provides maximum possible level of employment opportunities to the rural artisans. The State and Central Governments provide financial support in the form of grants to the Board for supply of beehives to the rural folks and Tribals in Hill areas, for modernisation of looms to weavers and other equipments to village artisans.

Department of Industries and Commerce (DIC): The Department of Industries and Commerce is the Nodal Agency for development of Industries in general and small scale industries in particular in the State of Tamil Nadu. The role of this Department is to plan and implement various schemes for the promotion of Industries. Various activities undertaken by DIC are:

- To provide entrepreneurial guidance through Data Bank,

Information Centers and Technical Information Sections attached to various District Industries Centers.

- Registration and promotion of Small Scale Industries and Industrial Cooperative Societies.
- Assistance for import of capital goods, machinery and scarce raw materials.
- Offering various testing facilities for chemicals, metals, metallurgical, electrical, electronic gadgets and appliances.
- Implementation of Quality Control Act on household electrical appliances.
- Implementation of Centrally sponsored schemes like self-employment programme for the educated unemployed youth under Prime Minister's Rozgar Yojana Scheme.
- Creating awareness of the various policies and programmes of the Government through seminars and dissemination meets.
- Conducting of entrepreneur's development programmes.
- Sanction and disbursement of various subsidies and incentives such as State Capital Subsidy, Generator Subsidy, Power Tariff Subsidy, Interest Free Sales Tax Deferral/Waiver, Margin Money Assistance for sick units.
- Export promotion.
- Conducting of techno-economical surveys.
- Setting up of industrial estates with necessary Infrastructure facilities.
- Providing escort services to the entrepreneurs.
- Conducting sample and comprehensive surveys.
- Development and promotion of cottage and handicrafts industries.
- Training facilities in the field of light engineering tool and die designing etc.

District Industries Centres: The District Industries Centres are functioning in all the Districts of Tamil Nadu except Chennai District to render all help to small scale industry. In respect of Chennai District Regional Joint Director, Chennai provides the same assistance. The entrepreneurs are also assisted in getting clearance in Local Bodies, Town Planning, Pollution Control Board, Public Health Factories and other Departments and getting power connection under Single Window Scheme. Escort Cells have been set up in District Industries Centers for providing necessary assistance in arranging technical inputs to newly emerging SSI Units.

Central Electrical Testing Laboratory, Kakkalur: This unit provides a wide range of testing facilities for electrical and electronic products in the State. This Laboratory has been recognised by the Bureau of Indian Standards, Directorate General of Supplies and Disposals, Ministry of Railway, National Accreditation Board for Laboratories under I.S. Specifications.

Electro Medical Equipment Centres: There are 4 Electro Medical Equipment Centres under the control of this Directorate at Chennai, Thanjavur, Madurai and Coimbatore. These centres were established with a view to provide repairing and servicing of electro medical equipments in and around their location and neighboring districts.

Quality Control Order Enforcement Centre: This centre, which functions at Dr. Vikram Sarabai Instronic Estate, Chennai, enforces quality control order for household electrical appliances. The Deputy Director, Quality Control Enforcement Centre is the Enforcement Officer.

Data Bank and Information Centre: This Centre, functioning at Dr. Vikram Sarabai Instronic Estate, Chennai, provides guidance to needy entrepreneurs proposing to start new electronic units. The package of information and guidelines are selection of project, Government Policy, technical know-how, financial assistance, machinery, raw materials, subsidies, incentives, marketing etc.

Chemical Wing: The Chemical Industries Wing of the Department of Industries and Commerce caters to the needs of various types of industries in Tamil Nadu for speedy development by offering testing facilities, laboratory investigation on problems relating to chemical industries in chemical engineering wing, providing project profiles and answering technical enquiries on chemical and allied industries, assisting chemical industries in getting scarce raw materials both indigenous and imported, offering practical training in testing to technically qualified persons sponsored by industries as well as to unemployed graduates, offering of export opinion for import of chemicals, furnishing technical and industrial information on Chemical and Allied Industries, offering expert opinion on alcohol based industries as and when referred by Commissioner of Prohibition and Excise, coordinating the Commissioner of Prohibition and Excise in witnessing trial run to assess the performance and capacity of the unit and surprise inspection etc.

Industrial Co-Operative Societies: Industrial Co-Operatives have been set up to uplift the weaker sections including rural artisans, workers and labourers to enhance their inherited skills. They help the farmers in growing crops like green tea and tapioca, which form the raw materials for the ultimate industrial product and also help the small-scale industries to develop their industries. Tiny and small scale industries suffer due to the disadvantages of economies of scale owing to small size, less finance, employment of small machineries, high cost due to their inability to make bulk purchase and ineffective marketing. These deficiencies are overcome in a substantial way through the cooperative form of organisation.

Export Guidance Cell: In the world of globalisation, marketing of SSI products have always been a major problem for small-scale manufacturers due to severe competition in the market. The SSIs should have access to the export potential for expanding the marketing network. For this purpose, the Government has formed Export Guidance Cell in all the District Industries Centres. Export Guidance Cell provides information on existing export activities to the entrepreneurs and necessary assistance on procedural matters for export.

Entrepreneurship Development Institute: Entrepreneurship Development Institute provides skill development programme to the unemployed and under employed diploma holders to set up micro enterprises on servicing modern white goods, floated by the multi-national companies, especially split A/C, Washing machine, cell-phones, mixie, colour TV etc. Entrepreneurship Development Institute also organises entrepreneurship development programmes for tribals located at Nilgiris and Yercaud in cultivation of Anthurium, Ericulture etc.

Tamil Nadu Small Industries Corporation Limited (TANSI): The Tamil Nadu Small Industries Corporation Limited was formed in the year 1965 as a conglomerate of small industrial units spread all over the State, by taking over 64 such units originally started by Director of Industries and Commerce during the initial plan periods. TANSI has also established certain units for the assembly of watches, manufacture of spirit-based products, deep well Hand Pumps, Machine Tools etc. TANSI provides infrastructure facilities to the private entrepreneurs for the industrial development of the State.

Regional Industry Facilitation Council: The Government of Tamil Nadu has constituted 4 Regional Industry Facilitation Councils under the Chairmanship of the Industries Commissioner and Director of Industries and Commerce with headquarters at Chennai, Tiruchirapalli, Madurai and Coimbatore to ensure the prompt payment of money by buyers to small scale industries/ancillary industrial undertakings and payment of interest on the outstanding money in case of default.

Small Industries Service Institute (SISI): SISI Chennai is a wing of small industries which provides a comprehensive range of services to the small sale industrial sector in Tamil Nadu in terms of technical assistance, economic information services, workshop facilities, training and other general consultancy services industrial extension services to small industries through a network of Small Industries Service Institutes and its branches in the States and Union Territories. SISI, Chennai is the State Level office for Tamil Nadu and Union Territory of Pondicherry. In addition to the above, there is a Central Footwear Training Centre at Madras and one electric Motor Testing Laboratory at Coimbatore functioning under the jurisdiction of SISI Madras.

SSI Board: The SSI Board provides an effective platform for inter departmental coordination and inter-institutional linkages.

Electrical & Electronic Estates: Government   has established 8 functional industrial estates at Thiruvanmiyur and Perungudi in Chennai, Kakkalur in Tiruvallore, Coimbatore, Salem, Hosur, Tiruchirappalli and Madurai, based on the large-scale scope for establishment of electrical and electronics industries and to meet the growing demand for both common type of electrical goods such as lamps, transmission lines, accessories, motor starters, control equipment, overhead conductors, domestic appliances and heavy electrical equipment like transformers, circuit breakers, etc.

Centre   for   Entrepreneurship   Development: Entrepreneurship Development Centre was set up by the Government at Gundy to encourage educated unemployed men and women and others. It helps the entrepreneurs in identification of project, tie up for financial assistance and conducts continuous training programme on EDP.

Problems of Women Entrepreneurs in Kerala and Tamil Nadu

Adequate support of Government agencies and financial institutions is indispensable for enhancing the competitiveness of the State and also for fostering the pace of industrialisation. Several institutions have been set up in India in the public and private sectors to provide financial and technical assistance for entrepreneurship, particularly women entrepreneurship and are playing a pivotal role in giving financial and consultancy assistance to entrepreneurs for the setting up of new ventures and also for their modernisation, diversification and expansion. The Government of India has created a network of financial and development institutions to supply credit and other development and support services. Still, the small entrepreneurs, especially women, face the problem of credit and other services.

Several agencies have been set up by the Government of Kerala and Tamil Nadu for providing varied services to women entrepreneurs. The Government of Kerala implements the Centrally sponsored schemes and State schemes through different agencies such as DIC, Kerala SIDCO, KITCO, SISI, KINFRA, KSWDC, KVIC, CDS, DRDA, district, block and village Panchayats. In Tamil Nadu, DIC, TANSIDCO, ITCOT, TNCDW, SISI, TACID, CED, TANSI, KVIC, DRDA, etc. provide development/support services to entrepreneurs.

The activities of these agencies in Kerala and Tamil Nadu are more or less similar. The major activities include:
- Counselling and consultancy services.
- Clearance from various departments.
- Training programmes.
- Identification of entrepreneurs.
- Financial assistance.
- Dissemination of information.
- Entrepreneurial guidance.
- Escort services.
- Registration.
- Sanction and disbursement of subsidies.
- Creating awareness of various policies.
- Margin money scheme etc.

Besides the development and other support services, the Government agencies (in Kerala and Tamil Nadu) are carrying out continuous evaluation of performance (at the time when application for registration is received till the commencement of business) of the units for ensuring the utilisation of the development and support services provided. The methods adopted for evaluation include: i) survey, ii) enquiries through field staff, iii) direct visit by the officers themselves, iv) enquiries through letters/over phone, etc. Some Government agencies like KITCO and SISI do follow-up by organising meetings, seminars, etc. The Government agencies in Kerala evaluate the performance of the units through direct visit whereas in Tamil Nadu it is done through field staff.

Almost all the Government agencies in Kerala and Tamil Nadu mainly get funds from the State exchequer for carrying out these services. Only a few agencies like SISI, CED, etc. get funds from the Central exchequer.

Financial institutions play an important role in the development of women entrepreneurship, as credit is the prime input for sustained growth of business of the women entrepreneurs. Financial institutions provide both long term and short term credit. The availability of credit continues to be a matter of concern for poor women entrepreneurs as they do not possess any security.

With respect to the lending schemes of the financial institutions to women entrepreneurs, no significant difference is observed both in Kerala and Tamil Nadu, which include term loans, term loan and working capital under single window scheme, National Equity Fund Scheme, PMRY loan, soft loan, margin money loan, working capital loan, etc. The majority of the financial institutions in Kerala provide 'term loans and working capital assistance under single window scheme' to women entrepreneurs. Meanwhile, in Tamil Nadu most of them provide both term loans and 'term loan and working capital assistance under the single window scheme'.

Similarly, with regard to the development/support services of the financial institutions, no wide difference is observed in Kerala and Tamil Nadu. However, the major development support services of financial institutions in Kerala include counselling, entrepreneurial guidance and seminars. Meanwhile, in Tamil Nadu, they are trade enquiries and buyer-seller meets. All the financial institutions in Kerala and Tamil

Nadu utilise their own funds collected through deposits for their working.

The financial institutions both in Kerala and Tamil Nadu also visit the units before and after disbursing loans to ensure the requirement of the loan and its utilisation. In Kerala, a large number of financial institutions visit once in a month, some other institutions have limited their visit to once in every six months or a year. Meanwhile, in Tamil Nadu, most of them visit the units without any periodicity. Some others visit once in a month.

Like the Government agencies, the financial institutions also adopt different methods to evaluate the performance of the units. The majority of the financial institutions in Kerala and Tamil Nadu prefer direct visit and also give free counselling as a preliminary action to recover the loan amount from the women entrepreneurs, but in Tamil Nadu, financial institutions also give guidance along with free counselling.

Several barriers and constraints, viz. cultural, educational, technological, financial and legal lie in the way of women entrepreneurs throughout the world. In some parts of the globe, women are prevented by social customs from leaving their house and going to market. In other parts, women may be facing problems, such as lack of transport and storage facilities, market information, etc. and are also exploited by middlemen, due to poor bargaining power. It is often found that enterprises started by women and men alike mostly experience financial problems at the nascent stage of the enterprise. Thereafter, crucial problems are increasingly seen in connection with general management, marketing and delegation of the responsibilities. Further, for a female business owner, the process of starting and operating a new enterprise can be difficult, because they often lack the skills, education, and support systems that can expedite their business pursuits. They also face barriers in banking, legal aspects, political contacts, customs tariffs, bureaucracy and extortion.

In India, men who control operations and decision-making

in fact run many of the enterprises defined as being run by women in their names. Programmes for encouraging entrepreneurship among women are doomed to fail or at best to succeed partially when taken up in isolation. In addition to training, availability of finance and other facilities like land, industrial plots and sheds is often a constraint that many women-owned businesses face. Funding is not easily available for activities primarily pursued and this is mainly because the banks and money lenders are reluctant to advance cash due to the risk involved in these businesses and also due to the high operational costs. Another area in which women face hurdles is marketing. By and large, the problems faced by women entrepreneurs in Kerala and Tamil Nadu are not different from those faced by their counterparts in the rest of the country. Familial, social, and psychological factors often pose insurmountable obstacles for women even when credit, capital and skills are made available to them.

Recommendations

Women entrepreneurship has gained momentum in the last three decades with the increase in the number of women enterprises and their substantive contribution to economic growth. In the dynamic world, women entrepreneurs are likely to become an important part of the global quest for sustained economic development and social progress. There has been a rapid increase in the efforts to encourage women entrepreneurship in developing countries with the adoption of concrete industrial development goals and strategies. The role of women entrepreneurs is undergoing profound changes in the wake of technological innovations which have brought fresh opportunities to consolidate, enhance and derive the benefits reaped in promoting women entrepreneurship.

Women development is closely associated with national development. Since women constitute half of the total population and account for the second largest group of potential entrepreneurs in India, they also have to play a very important role in the advancement of the country. The Government of India has taken conscious efforts to substantially enhance the spirit of entrepreneurship among women from the Fifth Five Year Plan (1974-78) onwards. Since then, several developmental programmes have been implemented in this direction. Still, it is a major problem for the Government and promotional agencies to identify potential women entrepreneurs, their current status and problems and to decide, implement and derive optimum benefit of promotional measures to achieve sustained and speedy growth of women entrepreneurship.

Though the State of Kerala has made significant progress in the field of social development, its rank is relatively low with regard to the investment climate. Regarding women entrepreneurship, although Kerala has the maximum number of women-managed units and women enterprises in the SSI sector compared with those of the other Indian States (Third All India Census of SSI-2004), a generation of entrepreneurship has been lost for want of entrepreneurial skill. Further, in Kerala the atmosphere for women to start entrepreneurship, survive and flourish is not encouraging. But in Tamil Nadu, though the status of a woman is low when compared with that of a woman in Kerala, the entrepreneurial ambience of the State is favouring entrepreneurs to flourish and grow. A recent study by the National Council of Applied Economic Research (NCAER) reveals that Tamil Nadu offers the best incentive package for industries, among industrialised States in India and it ranks second at the all India level in terms of attractiveness of incentives. Evidently, as per the Third All India Census of SSI, 2004, Tamil Nadu ranks second in India with regard to the number of women- managed units and women enterprises in the SSI sector.

Based on the findings, the following proposals are advanced so as to promote women entrepreneurship in Kerala and Tamil Nadu.

Start Training Centres in Every District: The study

revealed that most of the women entrepreneurs in Kerala and Tamil Nadu faced different problems, viz. financial, marketing, production, labour, etc. in running the business. Even after entering business, they had poor access to information and communication technology. Further, the women entrepreneurs in Tamil Nadu did not possess leadership skill in managing the business. Training is found to be the best method to encourage women entrepreneurship, to develop the personality traits of women entrepreneurs, to face different problems daringly, to have more access to information and communication technology and to encourage women to undertake risky ventures. At present, training centres are functioning only in some districts of Kerala and Tamil Nadu. This causes inconvenience to the women entrepreneurs of other districts. The study also revealed that some women entrepreneurs in Kerala faced the problem of training because of this reason. Therefore, the Government of both the States may start training centres in every district which would help women entrepreneurs to remedy the various maladies that afflict them.

Set up District Women Entrepreneurship Promotion Cell: It is observed that there is a significant decrease in the investment, annual turnover, annual income, etc. of some of the women entrepreneurs (both in Kerala and Tamil Nadu), in the current period compared with that of the initial period, which is a symptom of sickness of their units. A review of the progress of the small scale units at least once in a year by the Government could help to revive the sick units. Setting up of District Women Entrepreneurship Promotion Cell would facilitate to monitor and review the functioning of the women SSI units and this may also help to avoid or reduce the incidence of sickness. This Cell could also operate 'single window clearance system' which would facilitate women entrepreneurs to avoid delay in the setting up of their businesses.

Conduct Periodical Meeting of the Women Entrepreneurs: The study observed that most of the women entrepreneurs in Kerala and Tamil Nadu had no awareness about financial institutions and their schemes and had not attended training or utilised other development/support services of the Government agencies. Further, the Government agencies and financial institutions in Kerala and Tamil Nadu feel that the performance of the women entrepreneurs in running and expanding businesses is only satisfactory. It is also observed that training programmes offered by the Government agencies in both the States are excellent, and those who had availed themselves of the services of both the Government agencies and financial institutions were satisfied with the services. But these facilities were unutilised by most of the women entrepreneurs. Some of the women entrepreneurs did not approach financial institutions or could not take loan from them because of the problem of unwanted delay in the sanctioning of loan, indifferent attitude of the staff and neglect. Hence, it is suggested that periodical meetings organized at the block and district level by the Government agencies would enable the women entrepreneurs to get clear ideas about the various Government agencies, financial institutions and their current schemes. Also it provides a forum for expressing their needs and grievances.

Improve the Quality of Service of the Government Agencies and Financial Institutions: It is observed that some women entrepreneurs in Kerala and Tamil Nadu, who had utilised the services of the Government agencies and financial institutions, were not satisfied with the services, due to unwanted delay and apathetic attitude of the staff. Some women entrepreneurs in Kerala faced the problems, viz. delay in getting documents like statement of account, income tax certificate, etc. after taking loan from banks. Some others, who utilised PMRY loan, were denied subsidy without any genuine grounds. Hence, it is suggested that the quality of services of Government agencies/financial institutions could be improved by retaining customer-friendly Government/bank staff, especially in rural areas, for assisting genuine the women entrepreneurs.

Formulate Liberalised Loan Schemes to Women Entrepreneurs: The study revealed that the major problem faced by the women entrepreneurs in Kerala was financial and they ranked 'poor security', as the first nature of the financial problem. Further, some women entrepreneurs in the service sector (driving school) were denied bank loan. Also, some banks in Kerala insisted on collateral, from women entrepreneurs who were unaware of the Government policies and schemes, for granting PMRY loan. Government may take steps to ensure that conditions are applied uniformly to all women entrepreneurs, irrespective of their financial position. Again, owing to poor or non-availability of credit from financial institutions, women entrepreneurs were compelled to borrow from money lenders , which increased their financial burden. So it is proposed to formulate liberalised loan schemes for women entrepreneurs. Further, they should be provided with adequate credit not only at the initial stage but also subsequently for expansion, diversification and modernisation. Introduction of credit guarantee schemes for the women entrepreneurs by the Government would also enable the genuine women entrepreneurs to utilise required credit from banks without any collateral.

Open Women SSI Bank Branch in Every District: An SSI bank branch specifically for women and operated by women would be helpful to women entrepreneurs, which is not functioning at present in all the districts of Kerala and Tamil Nadu. Therefore, it is proposed that a women SSI bank branch may be opened in every district of Kerala and Tamil Nadu to carry out their banking activities freely.

Constitute Separate Section for Women Entrepreneurs in DICs: No separate data relating to women entrepreneurs are maintained by the DICs in Kerala and Tamil Nadu. A reliable data base, especially for women entrepreneurs, is imperative to assess their performance and contribution to the national economy. Therefore, maintenance of a separate section for women entrepreneurs in DICs to deal with all matters relating women, viz. promotion of women entrepreneurship, maintenance of separate data for women SSI units, organisation of women entrepreneurship development programmes, guidance, redress of grievances etc. would make it easier for the Government and other agencies to effectively implement their policies and programmes for the promotion of women entrepreneurship.

Provide Concession and Preference in Trade Fairs/Exhibitions: Women entrepreneurs consider trade fairs/exhibitions as one of the best ways for marketing their products. But owing to financial constraints, they could not participate in trade fairs and exhibitions organised by the Government agencies during festival or other seasons. For encouraging the marketing of the products of women's enterprises, the women entrepreneurs must be given opportunities to participate in trade fairs/exhibitions by giving preference and also giving concession in stall rent (In Tamil Nadu, concession in stall rent is in vogue). Further, some women entrepreneurs (in both the States) who participated in the trade fairs/exhibitions organised in other States, faced language problem, which seriously affected their marketing. This problem could be solved if the Government makes necessary arrangements to hire local people to present the products to the buyers in regional language.

Create Good Employer-Employee Relationship: It is observed that in Tamil Nadu, the employer-employee relationship is not good. For the success and expansion of the business, good employer-employee relationship is a must. Therefore, the women entrepreneurs must cultivate a new labour-management culture in the organisation by adopting innovative schemes of industrial relations.

Change the Attitude towards Women Entrepreneurs: It is observed that women entrepreneurs are facing several problems from their family members, local people, Government officials and other organisations, which seriously affected the setting up and functioning of their businesses. Their attitude badly needs a marked change. They can be more sympathetic, positive and encouraging. This may help them in the successful functioning of their businesses in a big way. Encouragement on the part of the society is also essential to prompt more and more women to enter this field.

Conduct Periodic Inspection: It is observed that seven per cent of the Government agencies in Kerala and 33 per cent in Tamil Nadu felt that the utilisation of loan amount by women entrepreneurs was poor. Also, 50 per cent of the financial institutions in Kerala 6 per cent in Tamil Nadu had only a satisfactory opinion in this regard. In the case of loans like margin money loan, bridge loan, working capital loan, etc. there is the possibility of utilisaton of loan amount for consumption purpose by some women entrepreneurs. Periodic inspection of the units by the officials of Government agencies/financial institutions, after granting of the above mentioned loans may prevent this tendency.

Circulation of Brochures in Local Languages: It is observed that a large number of women entrepreneurs are not able to understand the contents of the brochures and other materials supplied to them at the time of attending the training, since they are in English. Therefore, the Government agencies and financial institutions, while conducting training, seminars, workshops and meetings, may make sure that all the women entrepreneurs get the printed materials in a language intelligible to them.

Ensure Marketing of Women Products through Government Outlets: The study also revealed that most of the women entrepreneurs in Kerala and Tamil Nadu are exploited by the wholesalers and retailers by way of huge commission, free samples, low price, and return of dead stock after the expiry period, etc. So the Governments of Kerala and Tamil Nadu may ensure the marketing of the products of women's enterprises through Government outlets.

Develop Competitive Mind: Though the women entrepreneurs in Kerala and Tamil Nadu are facing a number of problems, viz. financial, marketing, etc. they should not always look for help from the Government or any financial institutions. They should work with confidence and courage and also develop a competitive mind. This will help them to succeed in businesses.

Introduce Pension Scheme: It is inferred from the study that a significant number of women entrepreneurs in Kerala and Tamil Nadu (21 per cent), are either single/divorced or widowed whose source of livelihood is exclusively their business. As they could not continue their businesses in their old age, a support from the Government by way of pension would give them protection in life. Therefore, it is proposed that the Government may introduce a pension scheme for women entrepreneurs and this may attract more women to the entrepreneurial field.

Appendix 2

Alphabetically Arranged List of 376 NGOs (with brief description of their activities) Engaged in Women Welfare and Development in India

Literature about self-employed women often discusses the supportive role of NGOs. Associations in market-based economies have played a significant role, not only in shaping investment and performance decisions for free enterprises, but also in determining public policy decisions affecting private business interests.

Women organise NGOs because of several reasons, viz. as a solution to isolation, education, training, achieve goals, market products and services, support, promote common interest, expand business, financial assistance and economic independence. Rural entrepreneurship has emerged for the empowerment of women during the last decade through the formation of self-help groups (SHGs) especially among women; and, clusters among similar or mutually related enterprises. S.H.G. is a mechanism through which women are empowered by developing various skills. The formation of SHGs among women has fetched noticeable results in many developing countries. The economic conditions of the women has significantly improved through the SHG approach. It not only facilitated income generation but also created awareness about health and hygiene, sanitation and cleanliness, environmental protection, importance of education and better response for development schemes. In handicrafts, handlooms, forest based enterprises etc. cluster approach has been used and was very effective for promotion of rural enterprises.

Women's business organisations offer a venue and

resources for them to set up a business of their own. While NGOs are important as they provide a collective voice to advocate for public policies which benefit members. Voluntary organisations facilitate empowerment of women through economic independence and in building up of self-confidence. Women's grassroots organisations (SHGs) have played a vital role all over the world in improving the socio-economic status of their members and eliminating gender gap. NGOs act as catalysts, educators, monitors, mediators and activists. The development organizations have the additional responsibility to ensure that their members become more empowered with their participation in the developmental activities. The benefits received by the members are to a great extent influenced by the participatory processes adopted by the NGOs.

Associations cover a wide spectrum of activities encompassing credit, business skills training, business training, credit, technical and technology training, employment creation, marketing services, legal assistance, psychological counselling, and some social welfare programmes. They are specialised agencies of micro credit. They encourage solidarity and collective action between the groups and help to organise the members to enhance their bargaining power and self confidence.

With the introduction of financial sector reforms in 1991, the banks are providing finance to SHGs. The NGO engaged in the activities related to community mobilisation for their socio economic development have initiated savings and credit programmes for their target groups. Most of the NGOs like SHARAN in Delhi, Federation of Thrift and Credit Association (FTCA) in Hyderabad, or SPARC in Bombay have adopted the Group Based Financial Intermediary Model where they initiate the groups and provide necessary management support. Others like SEWA in Ahmedabad, or Baroda Citizen's Council in Baroda pertain to the NGO Linked Financial Intermediary Model.

Some of the NGOs which promote women

entrepreneurship in India are the following:

1. **Aastha**, Udaipur, helps in formulating groups for economic and social upliftment, education and training, movement against social discrimination, networking etc. for women's empowerment.

2. **Aawaz-e-Niswan**, Mumbai, undertakes activities for the empowerment of women with the aim to make them self reliant and independent.

3. **Abalashrama** in Bangalore provides rehabilitation services to women through education, vocational training and job placements and also for initiating ITI level vocational training.

4. **Abhayashrama Association for Social Health in India** , Bangalore, imparts training with the aim of providing better employment opportunities.

5. **Action Research Institute**, Kolkata, undertakes a self employment scheme for the aged people and unemployed women.It provides training on how to prepare Indian and western dishes. It provides training for the preparation of jelly/jam, pickle etc.

6. **Adarsh Sarswati Mahila Kalyan Prashikshan Samiti** , Bundi, conducts skill development programmes for women, the handicapped and other weaker sections of society and help them to be self dependent. It undertakes training programmes of activities related to knitting, embroidery, weaving carpets and making leather bags.

7. **Adarsh Sewa Sansthan, Lucknow** provides formal and non formal education, vocational training to the youth and vulenerable groups and undertakes women employment and gender issues, income generation programmes.

8. **Affus Woman Welfare Association**, Anantapur, works for the socio-economic upliftment of women.It imparts training with the aim of providing better employment opportunities and education to poor and destitute. And also provides training facilities for the needy.

9. **Aid The Weaker Trust (ATWT),** Bangalore constituted

by a group of activists imparts training to women in printing. It is the only one in Asia. Its benefits are available to women all over Karnataka. The emphasis is not merely on providing economic assistance but also on equipping the girls with the expertise in various aspects of printing and building up self- confidence.

10. **Akhand Jyot Foundation** at Ahmedabad in Gujarat helps to bring women into the mainstream of development. It focuses on income generation and training programmes.

11. **Akhil Bhartiya Mahila Parishad,** Sagar, is set up to uplift the socio-economic status of women in the society. It provides education and training to women to make them self-dependent.

12. **Akshaynagar Pallisri Sangha**, 24 Parganas (S), imparts education and training, works for empowerment of women through the formation of self-help groups.

13. **Alaukik Seva Samiti**, Bhopal, imparts vocational training to women and empowers women through self-employment.

14. **Alert Rural and Tribal Development Society**, West Godavari, involves in income-generation activities through savings and credit and assists to form mahila mandals.

15. **All Bengal Women's Union**, Kolkata, promotes and undertakes activities that raise the socio-economic, cultural and moral status of women. It provides vocational and educational training to handicapped people and conduct awareness generation programmes against exploitation of young girls.

16. **All India Women's Conference** at Kolkata in West Bengal works for the welfare of women and children. It undertakes vocational training activities like handicraft, weaving, tailoring and knitting.

17. **All India Women's Conference,** Rewari, organises social welfare programmes and provide vocational training for income generation activities.

18. **All Kerala Youth Centre**, Kollam, promotes programmes

in micro-credit for women and is running a vocational training centre.

19. **All Tribal Women's Welfare and Self Employment Society,** Low Sabansiri, works for the overall development of the tribals. It makes the women aware of their rights and works for the overall empowerment of the women with the aim to make them self reliant and independent.

20. **Allepey Diocesan Chairtable and Social Welfare Society,** Alappuzha, promotes socio-economic and cultural development for the welfare of women and organises various training programmes for women and promotes educational activities.

21. **All-Women Management School,** Punjab has been has set up by Aryans Business School for offering programmes exclusively for women with aim of making them efficient managers in corporate world.

22. **Area Networking and Development Initiatives,** Bhavnagar, provides training, planning and field support to organisations that work with rural women. It works towards building local tribal women's organisation to improve their position and conditions of living.

23. **Area Networking and Development Initiatives,** Chhabutra Sheri , empowers communities, especially rural poor women and provides support to their endeavours to become equal partners in socio-eco-political development. It undertakes training programmes and coordinates with other NGOs regarding information dissemination.

24. **Arthik Samata Mandal,** undertakes income generation activities for the disadvantaged communities enabling them to have a sustainable source of livelihood. It develops women as decision makers and managers in the community by equipping them with different skills. It promotes women groups, youth associations, grama sabhas in the target villages for gender equity, empowerment and environmental sustainability.

25. **Arundhathi Mahila Mandali,** Guntur, works for the

development of women through different social and educational programmes and promotes cultural and recreative activities for women.It provides training to women in handicrafts to enhance the economic development of the country.

26. **Arya Samity**, Kolkata, undertakes various skill-development training programmes for women.

27. **Asha Community Health and Development Society** of New Delhi has been set up to improve the quality of life of slum dwellers in Delhi. It provides training through mahila mandals for the empowerment of women.

28. **Asha Nivas Social Service Centre**, Chennai, co-operates and co-ordinates with Governmental and Non-Governmental agencies to enable the community to carry out development programmes. It organises women into Madhar Sangams.

29. **Ashoka** in New Delhi identifies helps and launches individuals with innovative ideas for solving social problems around the world and to build an international network of social entrepreneurs who have the ability to initiate and develop far-reaching programs for systemic change - change that can be replicated on a national and international scale. It promotes and strengthens the profession of social entrepreneurship so that practitioners can field their knowledge and experience in collaborative ways.

30. **Ashoka** of Kolkata, has been set up with the objective to identify and help launch individuals with innovative ideas for solving social problems around the world, to build an international network of social entrepreneurs who have the ability to initiate and to develop far-reaching programs for systemic change - change that can be replicated on a national and international scale. It promotes and strengthens the profession of social entrepreneurship so that practitioners can field their knowledge and experience in collaborative ways.

31. **Ashoka,** an organisation functioning in Hyderabad identifies and supports women who possess vision, creativity and determination of the business entrepreneur with ' truly new ideas for solving a public need ' through fellowships and support services.

32. **Ashurali Vivekananda Smriti Sangha**, 24 Parganas (S), works to increase awareness about income-generation activities and provides non-formal education and vocational training to the girl children.

33. **Asian Network of Women in Communication**, New Delhi, works for the socio-economic upliftment of women. It undertakes activities for the empowerment of women with the aim to make them self reliant and independent. It works for improvement of the economic, social and legal status of women through counselling, legal aid, education and vocational training.

34. **Association for Bottom Strata**, Pudukottai has been set up to improve the standard of living of tribal and dalit communities through training and awareness programmes. It works for women development by forming women self-help groups and conducts income-generation programmes.

35. **Association for Community Training**, Viluppuram, facilitates empowerment of the marginalised communities by supporting and strengthening the people's organisations and movements. It gives special attention to the dalits, women and the poor.

36. **Association for Rural Education and Development Services**, Krishnapuram, conducts leadership training workshops for women.It promotes development through education and common cooperated action through income generation programmes.

37. **Association for Rural People's Education and Development**, Tiruvannamalai, promotes self help groups among women.It motivates Dalits for their liberation.

38. **Association for Social Health in India,** Chandigarh, provides training in crafts to poor destitute women and

their children.

39. **Association for Social Health in India,** Mumbai , imparts vocational training to the same.

40. **Association for Social Hygienic Interest and National Awareness**, Kullu, works for the social and economic development of women and to create awareness generation activities and income generation programme.

41. **Association for the under Developed Beneficiaries of India**, Nayasesh, initiates development of women and children through education. It provides vocational training to the women.

42. **Association for Welfare and Comprehensive Rural Development**, Bhimavaram. It works for the upliftment of poor labour dalit families with income earning programmes and raising awareness among them. It empowers women with education and self-help training.

43. **Association for Women and Rural Development**, Angul, works for the development of women and provides vocational training to the women. It organises and conducts various rural development programmes.

44. **Association for Women Education and Rural Development**, Arani, imparts vocational training programmes to dalits young and aims at empowerment and economic independence of women through income generational programmes.

45. **Association for Women's Awareness, Knowledge and Education**, Thoothkudi, undertakes activities for the empowerment of women with the aim to make them self reliant and independent. It provides educational and training facilities and micro credit to the needy with the aim to make them self reliant and independent.

46. **Association of Non-Governmental Orgainsations** set up in New Delhi improves networking with other NGOs, works for the overall welfare of women and children and provides guidance to people about good health and nutrition.

47. **Association of Rural Women Welfare Society**, Tiruvannamalai, promotes developmental activities for the upliftment of the rural grass-roots people.

48. **Association of Voluntary Agencies for Rural Development**, in New Delhi, has been set up promote co-operation and understanding among voluntary organisations working for the rural community in India .It act as a cleaning house for information and knowledge for voluntary action. It works for the overall welfare of women and children and promotes development, democracy and equality in society through voluntary action and active citizenship as a complement to public action by the State to achieve these objectives.

49. **Association of Women Entrepreneurs of Karnataka (AWAKE)** is one of India's premier institution of women entrepreneurs which was formed in Dec. 1983 by a team of women entrepreneurs .It is totally devoted to the development of women entrepreneurship among women. It helps women in different ways –to prepare project report, to secure finance, to choose and use a product, to deal with bureaucratic hassles, to tackle labour problems, and so on. This organisation is based in Bangalore. Through an exclusive arrangement with consultancy service, technical knowledge is also shared. Membership is open only to those women entrepreneurs who have proved their business credibility in the market. AWAKE has built up a strong support net work with Government and non-government development agencies working with them to provide the expertise in entrepreneurship development.

50. **Association of Women Entrepreneurs of Small scale Industries (AWESSI)** was founded in Ambattur in Chennai in 1984 to promote, protect and encourage women entrepreneurs and their interest in South India. The primary aim of the organisation is to seek work and co-operate with the central and state Government services and other Government agencies and promotes measures for the

furtherance and protection of small-scale industries.

51. **Avilash**, 24 Parganas (S), is involved in women's development through related activities for the less-educated, less-advantageous, poor women of villages and semi-urban areas. It gives special emphasis on training for skill or capacity building, works on education, general awareness and health education.

52. **Avinashalingam Institute for Home Science and Higher Education for Women**, Coimbatore, undertakes women and child development programmes and imparts education to the target groups.

53. **Ayodhya Lal Kalyan Niketan**, Gopalganj, works for all-round development of women in the villages through formation of self-help groups. It works in the fields of income generation, education, environment awareness, health and nutrition.

54. **Azad Welfare Society**, Howrah, empowers weaker sections, particularly women through various programmes like jari work, health clinic, income generation and self-employment.

55. **Bharat Children Shiksha Samithi**, in Jaipur undertakes programmes for the welfare of women. It provides better educational and training facilities for women with the aim of making them self reliant and independent.

56. **Bhartiya Kisan Sangh**, Ranchi, promotes self help group and works for the empowerment of women in tribal areas.

57. **Bhartiya Yuva Shakti Trust (BYST)** assists young people in the age group of 18-35, who are either unemployed or under employed with sound imaginative business ideas, along with the will and determination to succeed. BYST supports ventures both in the manufacturing and servicing sector, turning job seekers into job creators by supporting a wide variety of enterprises; from Doll Making to Desktop Publishing, and Herbal Cosmetics to Hi-Tech Electronics, thereby enabling wealth generation. The Indian business community

supports the trust. Presently BYST is operational in six regions of India - Delhi, Chennai, Rural Haryana, Pune, Hyderabad and Rural Maharashtra. Out of these six regions four regions run the urban programme, while two regions run the rural programme.

58. **Brahmo Samaj Mahila Bhavan**, Kolkata, helps shelterless destitute women and undertakes teaching and self-employment orientation programmes. It imparts training on handicrafts and preparation of confectionary items to women to develop vocational skills for self-reliance.

59. **Bullock-Cart Workers Development Association**, Villupuram, encourages the formation of women self help groups. It provides better educational, training for the needy.

60. **Bunyad**, Patna provides professional training with the aim to promote income generation activities. It provides better training for the needy. It provides financial assistance to women with the aim to make them self reliant and independent. It co-ordinates and provides linkage with funding agencies for financial assistance to minority groups.

61. **C.S. Parekh and R.S. Parekh Public Charitable Trust** , Ahmedabad, establishes cottage industries for economic upliftment of poor women in rural and urban areas. It provides vocational training centres for women.

62. **Catholic Church Lok Sewa Kendra**, Vadodara, undertakes community development programmes and to work for the empowerment of the rural community. It encourages the formation of credit co-operatives and mahila mandals.

63. **Catholic Relief Services,** Calcutta, works for the empowerment of the slum communities through community-based, women's projects and income-generation programmes.

64. **Centre for Action in Rural Development,** Kanchipuram ,

promotes the establishment of self-help groups and to work for the empowerment of women It undertakes skill development activities with the aim of making the people self reliant and independent.

65. **Centre for Community Development**, Gajapati, works for the overall development of the society, undertake poverty alleviation projects through natural resource management. It promotes the formation of self-help groups and undertakes income generation activities. It facilitates the empowerment of women and inculcates advocacy of leadership amongst tribal women to cope with the decentralised Pachayati Raj administration.

66. **Centre for Community Economic and Development Counsultants Society**, Jaipur, promotes community-based economic development by encouraging decision-making at the village level through village development committees and women's organisations.

67. **Centre for Development Action and Appropriate Technology**, Guwahati, is formed to eradicate poverty through awareness generation and income generation activities. It works for the rights of the marginalised community. It provides micro credit to the needy with the aim to make them self reliant and independent. It provides opportunities for underprivileged women for entrepreneurship and community businesses and implements Information and communication Technology tools that are tailor made for the social sector. It encourages capacity building of local NGOs by imparting training.

68. **Centre for Development Action**, Kottayam, conducts seminars on environmental issues and promotes vocational training and education for women.

69. **Centre for Human Action and Resource Management,** Bhubaneswar, mobilizes local resources skill and management by the people to bring them towards economic empowerment. It empowers the women through

the formation of micro-credit/Self Help Groups.

70. **Centre for Rural Education and Development** , Madurai, works for the overall development of the rural communities with main focus on women empowerment. It organises several women upliftment programmes in the fields of education, vocational training, awareness programmes, self employment, thrift and credit, formation of self help groups and other important issues including health, child labour, etc.

71. **Centre for Social Development** at 24 Parganas in Barrackpore works for the overall development of women and children and provides financial support to small voluntary organisations.

72. **Centre for Social Development,** Kolkata , encourages women to adopt income generating programmes like poultry, paper bag-making with the aim of making them self reliant and independent.

73. **Centre for Social Reconstruction**, Kannyakumari, provides educational and training facilities for the needy. It undertakes activities for the empowerment of women with the aim to make them self reliant and independent and encourages the youth to participate in various development activities.

74. **Centre for Women's Development Studies**, New Delhi, organises and provides training programmes for scholars, communicators and members of women organisations. It collaborates with grassroots organisations and provides consultancy services to other institutions and organisations. It promotes action programmes especially for the under privileged women so as to enable them to be to self-dependent.

75. **Chaithanya Samskarika Kala Samithi**, Kannur, conducts programmes for the development of women, SC/STs and other backward communities of the society. It generates employment opportunities for the unemployed youth, especially from the weaker sections of the society

and works for the promotion of art and culture.

76. **Chamarajangar Parikh Society**, Mysore, empowers women through education and training and to look after the development of rural areas by providing good health, water and sanitation.

77. **Chanchalba Amin Charitable Trust**, Vadodara, promotes welfare activities for women and provides training for employment generation.

78. **Chandrakala Mahila Grah Udhyog Sahkari Mandali Limited**, Ahmedabad, promotes income generation programmes and to impart vocational training to rural women.It provides professional services to the craftsmen and rural artisans to improve their productivity, market access and income generation capability. It undertakes employment generation activities for women with the aim to improve their family's economic conditions.

79. **Chassad Avenue Tribal Women Development Organisation**, Imphal, works for the betterment of tribal, marginalised women. It trains the rural poor on livestock management.

80. **Chetana Foundation for Social Awareness, Research and Development**, Kolkata creates opportunities for employment and self-employment for women and undertakes activities related to funding of social welfare projects and training for small organisations.

81. **Chetana Vikas**, Madurai, works for the development of women by conducting income generation programmes.

82. **Chetna Bharti**, Chatra, works for the overall development of the women and provides better educational and training facilities for the needy and undertakes income generation programmes with the aim of making the people self reliant and independent.

83. **Chetna**, Sonebhadra, works for the empowerment of women by promoting income generation programmes.

84. **Child and Social Welfare Society**, Midnapore, works for the empowerment of women by providing better training

facilities. It enhances the standerd of living of the people through promotion of alternative sustainable agriculture and income generation activities.

85. **Children's Garden School**, Chennai, assists destitute women by providing training to rural and urban women in activities designed to make them economically self-reliant.

86. **Chirasabuj**, Silchar, imparts training and jobs to poor women in the valley.

87. **City Health & Small Welfare Association**, Kolkata, works for the development of the community through promotion of skill development programs especially for women.

88. **Commmunity Development Information and Action Centre,** Chennai, assists the economically backward and weaker sections of the society. It works for the empowerment of the women by providing better educational and training facilities, easier access to micro-credit and income

89. **Community Action For Rural Development,** Puddukkottai, promotes income generating activities for women and the aged. It promotes the formation of self help groups and to extend credit to the needy.

90. **Community Aid and Sponsorship Programme** in Mumbai, promotes income generation activities for women and initiates vocational training courses with the aim of making the people self reliant.

91. **Community Development Centre,** Vishakapatnam, works for the empowerment of women and encourages them to undertake income generation activities with the aim to make them self reliant and independent.

92. **Community Project Centre,** Thiruvananthapuram, promotes socio-economic development activities for the women. It organises several educational, income generating for helping the target people improve their economic conditions.

93. **Council for Advancement of Rural Education,**

Bhubaneshwar, undertakes schemes for women and organises income generation programmes.

94. **Creative Handicrafts**, Mumbai, provides opportunities for underprivileged women for entrepreneurship and community businesses. It encourages self-employment among poor and needy women and provide training to the needy of the marginalised community to build and operate own businesses.

95. **CSI Embroidery Industry**, Neyyoor, provides employment to the poor women folk of rural areas and improves their self-respect and social status.

96. **CSI Women's Industrial School**, Chittoor, provides vocational training in cross-stitch, embroidery, sewing, tailoring for school dropout girls and to market their products to make them economically self-reliant and independent. It imparts training with the aim of providing better employment opportunities.

97. **Cuddapah District Grama Seva Samithi**, Cuddapah, undertakes income generation, community development, micro entrepreneurs and other such activities related to women.

98. **Dakshin Kalikata Sevasram**, Kolkata, imparts various types of vocational training to women for skill-development.

99. **Dalit Vikas Vandu**, Jamui, works for all round development of weaker section of society particularly the tribals and harijan women of remote villages residing in the jungles of the border of Kharia, Tisri of Jamvi, Geredih & Nawada districts of Bihar.

100. **Dalit Women's society** is a voluntary organisation started in the year 1992 at Kurichi of Kottayam district. It is the first women's organisation, which organised tuition programmes, self-employment programmes, workshop, and computer training for dalit women.

101. **Damodar Mahila Mandal**, Kodarma, promotes income generation programmes. It works on all women issues.

102. **Damodar**, Hazaribagh, improves status of women through awareness generation activities.
103. **Danida-Women Youth Training Extension Project**, Bangalore, encourages women participation in agriculture. It imparts training and form self help groups.
104. **Darabar Sahitya Sansad**, Khurda, undertakes activities related to formation of self help groups, developing entrepreneurial skills, employment generation etc.
105. **Darshana Mahila Samajam**, Pathanamthitta, works for the socio-economic upliftment of women and provides employment training in various trades.
106. **Deccan India Foundation**, Bangalore, undertakes activities for the empowerment of women with the aim to make them self reliant and independent and imparts vocational training and coaching for competitive examination to the educated youth. It provides free consultancy to small NGOs.
107. **Deen Dayal Vanavasi Seva Samiti**, Bilaspur, imparts training to women for self employment. It undertakes agricultural development programmes. It helps the poor to set up small cottage industries.
108. **Desa Sevini Mahila Samajam**, Malapuram, conducts development activities for the welfare of women. It undertakes income generation programmes and generates awareness among women.
109. **Development and Educational Society**, 24 Parganas (S), encourages agricultural development through training on self help, savings and credit promotions among the rural poor. It imparts non formal education among the women and children.
110. **Development Dialogue**, Kolkata, promotes income generation among the rural poor women.
111. **Development Education and Environment Protection Society**, Dharampuri, provides micro credit to the needy with the aim to make them self reliant and independent.
112. **Development Education Exchange Service**, Varikkal,

undertakes integrated rural development. It works for the empowerment and financial development of women and increases awareness in income generation activities.

113. **Development Education Society**, Bangalore, empowers women through community organisations and income enhancement. It provides micro credit to the needy with the aim to make them self reliant.

114. **Development of Underprivileged through Integrated Economic Societies,** Nellore has been set up to eradicate evil social practices like the practice of Devadasis (Matangis) and promotes rural entrepreneurship and environmental awareness.

115. **Development Promotors**, Solan, works for sustainable development of weaker section of rural communities with special focus on all round development of women, through awareness creation and empowerment.

116. **Development Services Society**, Chennai, undertakes activities for the empowerment of women with the aim to make them self reliant and independent by providing micro credit. It also undertakes youth development programs.

117. **Dharani Roy Memorial Self-Employment Training School**, Birbhum, provides vocational training services for ladies.

118. **Dharaninagar Milan Bithi Seba Sansad**, Birbhum, provides training for women in weaving, tailoring, net-making.

119. **Dharti Vikas Mandal**, Ahmedabad, improves the status of women by promoting income generating programmes.

120. **Dhoraninagar Rural Development Society**, Mollarpur, works for the upliftment of economically backward people who are living below poverty line by providing income generation activities to the rural women.

121. **Dhubri District Mahila Samity**, Dhubri, develops economic, social and educational programmes for women members of the low income group of the society. It

conducts adult educational and vocational training courses for destitute women and help them to earn their livelihood with their hand made products; distribute food, medicine and clothes to the victims of calamity and natural disaster.

122. **Dhulapur Vivekananda Club**, Howrah, promotes education programmes for rural women and promotes rural development and self employment programmes by providing vocational education for rural youth and women.

123. **Dinasevanasabha**, Kannur, works for upliftment of the economic conditions of the poor and downtrodden. It provides vocational training to the rural women.

124. **Diocese of Baroda**, Vadodara, initiates development programmes for women. It promotes income generation programmes for the welfare of women.

125. **Disaster Mitigation Institute** at Ahmedabad in Gujarat undertakes activities related to training, planning, advocacy, action research and employment generation programmes for women.

126. **Diverse Women for Diversity**, New Delhi, works for improvement of the economic, social and legal status of women through counselling, legal aid, education and vocational training.

127. **Divya Chaya Trust**, Kolkata provides financial and technical assistance to small organisations working in the field of social development. It provides better educational and training facilities for the needy. It promotes employment and income generation activities and works for the empowerment of the women and children.

128. **Dr Annie Besant Mahalirmandram**, Chennai, helps poor women for their betterment and provides vocational training for poor girls.

129. **Dr. Ambedkar Welfare Trust**, Nowshera, initiates welfare operations for the disadvantaged. It empowers women and make them self reliant by providing better educational and training facilities with the aim of promoting income and employment generation

programmes.

130. **Dr. Radhajrishnan Publi Silai Kadai Prashikshan Kendra**, Jhansi, imparts training to unemployed youth and women with the aim of providing better employment opportunities.

131. **Dr. Rajendra Prashad Anand Vidyapith**, Unnao, undertakes educational, social and economic development of rural women and children.

132. **Drishti Media Group** of Ahmedabad aims to use media to strengthen women's movement. It facilitates the expression of women's experiences and concerns and document women's struggles as part of feminist histonography. It works with mainstream media to project constructive role models for women and place women's perspectives on public agenda and also undertakes training sessions and networking with social organisations.

133. **Drusti**, Puri, works for the development of the weaker sections of the society especially women of the backward regions of the region by building up self help groups.

134. **Dum Dum Park Mahila Samity**, Kolkata, imparts training for development of skills among women for their economic development.

135. **Durga Women's Organisation** at Kumbakonam in Thanjavur assists women of lower income groups in the rural villages to strengthen their economic base by providing them

136. **Ecumenical Church Loan Fund of India**, Nagpur, facilitates socio-economic growth of marginalised groups by providing fair credit for socio-economic activities. It promotes self-employment, self-reliance and poverty alleviation using micro-credit judiciously to economically disadvantaged groups, especially women.

137. **Edamon Vanitha Society**, Kollam, conducts socio-economic activities for the upliftment of women in backward community.

138. **Educational Society Vidya Niketan**, Sirmour, provides

vocational training for women.

139. **Ekatma Samaj Kendra**, Sangli, brings about improvement in the living conditions of backward classes (Mahars and others) through cooperative milk production and cooperative farming. It has established mahila ashrams and Balwadis. It promotes self employment schemes for women and youth.

140. **Eklavya Sanstha**, Hoshangabad, promotes education among illiterate women and conducts vocational training and adult education programmes.

141. **Eklavya,** Bhopal, works for the upliftment of backward communities. It improves the status of women through awareness generation activities.

142. **Ernakulam Women's Association**, Ernakulam, provides training for women and youth and promotes income generation programmes.

143. **Family Welfare Foundation of India**, New Delhi, provides better health care, educational and training facilities for the needy. It promotes income generation programmes and to impart vocational training to rural youth and women.

144. **Foundation for Entrepreneurship Development of Orissa**, Khurda, develops self-reliance among the women. It promotes entrepreneurship among the youth.

145. **Foundation for Fisheries Welfare and Management India**, Kottaipattinam, works for a good future of the fisher workers of Palk Bay in South Tamil Nadu. It organises traditional fisher women into self help groups and conducts education educational programmes.

146. **Friends Association for Ladies and Orphan Welfare**, Srinagar, rehabilitates destitute women, orphans and handicapped children. It stands against exploitation, oppression and social injustice against women.It raises educational, social and economic status and literacy level of women by imparting formal and informal education and training for self employment and income generating

schemes. It makes the target group aware of the schemes and privileges introduced by private and public sectors.

147. **Friends' Association for Rural Reconstruction,** Rourkela, provides equal opportunity to the poor people, women in particular to strengthen their stand in the people centered developmental process which will be ecologically, socially and economically sustainable.

148. **Friends of Women's World Banking, India,** Ahmedabad assists to build a society based on equality and social justice where women are the leaders in social change. It extends as well as expands informal credit support and network within India and link them to a global movement. It provides training, revolving loan funds and support to women's groups through NGOs.

149. **Gandhi KasthuriBai Village Development Society,** Puliyampatti, works for the socio-economic development of the rural people. It implements various developmental programmes on self employment, income generation activities, non formal education and formation of self help groups of women.

150. **Gandhi National Memorial Society,** Pune, provides training programmes for women in social service, khadi and skill development programmes, including entrepreneurship.

151. **Gandhipet Women's Collective,** Ulundai, works for the development of the socio-economic condition of the women. It undertakes activities for the empowerment of women with the aim to make them self reliant and independent.

152. **Gansoville Association** , Sivaganga, assists to form self help groups among women.

153. **Garib Nawaz Mahila Evam Bal Kalyan Samiti,** Ajmer, organises vocational training and self-employment programmes for women and unemployed youth.

154. **Gautam Buddha Sevabhavi Sanstha,** Parbhani, undertakes activities for the empowerment of women with

the aim to make them self reliant and independent.

155. **Gayatri Shiksha Sadan Sansthan**, Udaipur, propagates income generation programmes among rural and tribal women.

156. **Gharib Nawaz Mahila Avam Bal Kalyan Samiti**, Ajmer, works in the field of women and undertakes self employment programmes for unemployed youth and poor women for self reliance.

157. **Good Shepherd Health Education Centre and Dispensary**, Coimbatore, undertakes poverty alleviation programmes by promoting income generation activities. It provides micro credit to the needy with the aim to make them self reliant and independent. It promotes overall development of the dalits, tribals and other backward classes. It undertakes activities for the empowerment of women with the aim to make them self reliant and independent and encourages the youth to participate in various development activities.

158. **Gram Vikas Trust,** Bharuch, provides better educational and training facilities for the needy. It works among the rural communities and groups particularly the under privileged and women, in the areas of education, health and community development.

159. **Grama Vikas**, Kolar, improves the conditions of rural women belonging to the marginalised sections. It engages in developmental activities and assists women to form organisations thereby helps them to become self sufficient.

160. **Grama Vikasa Vidya Samsthe**, Bijapur, encourages rural development programmes like dry land agriculture, shepherd groups and watershed development. It integrates women's self-help groups with income generating activities and health programmes.

161. **Gramanchala Unnayan Parishad**, Boudh, implements welfare programmes for women and children in rural areas. It undertakes urban and rural community development programmes.

162. **Gramayan,** Aurangabad works for the socio-economic upliftment of women. It promotes principles of equality and social justice so that women and men can develop capacities and participates equally in all aspects of social, political and economic life. It promotes overall rural development.

163. **Grameen Development Services,** Mumbai , works for the overall rural development. It undertakes programmes for the welfare of women, artisans and other grass root level organisations. It mobilises the rural community by encouraging them to form self-help groups around savings and credit, and encourages self-management and decision making capacity through a process of community organisation building. It promotes income and employment generation activities. It provides professional assistance, technical know-how and institutional credit to the needy. It works for the economic upliftment of the poor.

164. **Grameen Koota**, Bangalore, helps poor women in rural areas and urban slums with micro credit. It constantly delivers need based financial services in a cost effective manner. It guides women in the financial matters. It builds a micro-finance institution which will eventually be owned, managed and used by poor women.

165. **Grameen Vikas Sansthan**, Mau, undertakes activities related to educational, social and economical development of women, children and people living in the rural areas. It has established women's organisations for the development of women.

166. **Gramin Seva**, Madhubani, promotes employment generation activities for the underprivileged families and provides technical and financial assistance to those who wish to start their own business.

167. **Gramin Vikas Mandal,** Beed, enhances women's empowerment through development of self-help groups.

168. **Gramin Vikas Mandal,** Bhiwani , provides education and

vocational training to the needy and promote income generation activities in the villages.

169. **Gramin Vikas Mandal, Himachal**, Mandi provides technical education and vocational training to the tribal women.

170. **Gramin Vikas Sansthan,** Rai Bareilly, helps dalits and poor women through income generation from agarbathi. It conducts women awareness programmes and assists in forming self help groups.

171. **Gramin Vikas Seva Sanstha,** Delhi, implements programmes designed to lead to self sustaining village republic gramswaraj. It implements income generation programmes for rural women like cottage industries, livestock improvement etc. It encourages women for entrepreneurial development so as to make them self-sufficient and to have respectable earnings.

172. **Gramin Vikas Sewa Sanstha**, Barasat, implements income generation programmes for rural women like cottage industries, livestock improvement etc.

173. **Gramin Vikas Shikshan Sanstha,** Amravati , undertakes rural and urban development programmes particularly, socio-economic development. It works towards the implementation of development programmes related to rural poor, women and youth. It conducts training programmes for women and youth.

174. **Gramin Vikas Shikshan Sanstha,** Latur , works for the overall development and welfare of rural population. It provides better educational and training facilities to make women independent and self-reliant. It administers socio-economic development programmes for women.

175. **Gramium**, Tiruchirapalli works for integrated rural development through organisation of women and promotion of self-help groups. It promotes income generation programmes for the person in general. It provides educational and training facilities for the needy.

176. **Gramiya Social Welfare Society**, Nagapattanam,

promotes welfare of women, widows, old and socially handicapped people in rural areas. It promotes and develops agriculture oriented rural programmes.

177. **Gramoday Chetna Kendra,** Chatra works for women's empowerment and promotes income generation programmes for the self reliance of people.

178. **Gramodaya,** Gaziabad, generates self employment for rural youth and women. It caters to the educational and health care needs of the rural poor.

179. **Gramothan Bal Mahila Kalyan Sansthan**, Mau, promotes integrated rural development through development of self help groups. It works upon watershed management and micro-credit systems.

180. **Gramshakti Shramjivini Sanghathan**, Ahmedabad, works towards poverty eradication with emphasis on rural women. It brings rural women in the mainstream of development.

181. **Gramya Mahila Vikash Samiti**, Cuttack, facilitates all round sustainable development of rural women by helping them to become self reliant and independent.

182. **Gramya Research Centre for Women**, Secunderabad, works for the overall development of women and encourages them to participate in rural development activities.

183. **Groupious Social Welfare Society**, New Delhi, promotes literacy movement, environmental, agricultural, forestry and fisheries programmes. It has set up vocational training centres for generating employment and income opportunities for women.

184. **Gudibanda Gramodyoga Sangha**, Kolar, provides better health care, educational and training facilities for the needy. It works for improvement of the economic, social and legal status of women through counselling, legal aid, education and vocational training.

185. **Guild of Service,** Chennai, works for the overall development of rural women through self awareness and

income generating activities.

186. **Guild of Women Achievers**, Bangalore, maximises women's potential by organising interactive workshops, seminars, contests and creating an environment for women in different walks of life to reach out to each other.

187. **Gujarat Rajya Bal Kalyan Sangh**, Ahmedabad, provides vocational training to women.

188. **Gujarat Stree Pragati Mandal**, Ahmedabad, provides training to women in some kind of skill which would ultimately help them to augment their income.

189. **Gujarati Mahila Vikas Parishad**, Ahmedabad, provides education to the backward women to make them independent in the society.

190. **Guru Angad Dev Sewa Society** at Ludhiana in Punjab, provides vocational training to girls. It conducts income generation programme for the upliftment of women in rural areas.

191. **Gyan Bharti Mahila and Bal Vikas Parishad/Trust**, Jalaun, works for education, health and economic development of women and children. It undertakes development of agriculture, livestock and rural enterprise. It has established women's organisations, micro credit and farmer clubs.

192. **Habitat Technology Group** in Kollam, Kottayam, Malappuram, Mavelikkara, Palakkad, Thiruvalla, Thiruvananthapuram, Changanasser, Ernakulam, Idukki, Kayamkulam, Chennai, Coimbatore and Bhubaneswar undertake projects for the empowerment of women in the shelter sector by educating and training women in the field of architecture.

193. **Haria Girish Sangha**, Midnapore, provides vocational training to women.

194. **Harijan Christian Seva Samajam**, Cuddapah, provides financial assistance poor women and creates opportunities for self-employment.

195. **Harijan Mahila Anadha Saranalayam**, Cuddapah,

provides skills training to women.

196. **Haryana Rural Development Farmers Association**, Rohtak, has launched community based programmes with special emphasis on the development of women and children in the state of Haryana. It provides vocational training to the children.

197. **Health and Integrated Rural Development Agency**, Koraput, involves in community-based development programmes using methodologies like participatory rural appraisal and strategic planning with women.

198. **Health Education Agriculture Development Society**, Ananthapur, provides training on economical developmental activities and financial assistance to women.

199. **Health Education Leadership Promoting Society**, Cuddapah, promotes sustainable development and income-generating activities in rural areas through programmes like thrift and credit for women, agriculture, joint forest management and rehabilitation of child labourers.

200. **High Range Social Service Society**, Idukki, promotes welfare activities for rural people especially women. It provides income generation programmes for the village people.

201. **Himalay Rachnatmak Jan Kalyan Samiti**, Chamoli, imparts education and conduct income-generation programme. It **works** specially for women.

202. **Himalayan Society for Alternative Development**, Chamoli, works for women's empowerment. It provides income generation, skills development training and imparts education.

203. **Himalayan Study Circle**, Pithoragarh, undertakes activities for the empowerment of women with the aim to make them self reliant and independent.

204. **Himalayan Women Welfare Association** promotes research and action in the area of women's education and development by opening centres for comparative studies

with focus on girls, women and disadvantaged sections of society.

205. **Himaliyan Gram Vikas Samiti**, Pithoragarh, conducts women development programmes.

206. **Hindu Kusht Nibaran Sangha**, Kolkata, helps marginalised women to regain their self esteem through skill development and vocational training.

207. **Hit Kalyan Mahila Mandal**, Wardha, provides better educational and training facilities. It makes the women aware of their rights with the aim of making them independent and self-reliant. It works for the welfare of the tribal community, artisans and the village community.

208. **Holy Cross Social Service Centre, Hazaribagh**, works for the empowerment of women and women groups and promote self help programmes for them.

209. **Janpad Vikas Evam Samaj Kalyan Samiti**, Mauo, provides both formal and non formal education to the underprivileged women. It works for the empowerment of women.

210. **Janta Kalyan Samiti**, Rewari, provides vocational education and training. It also looks after all aspects of women development.

211. **Jayashri Mahila Sangham**, Khammam, imparts education to the poor and the marginalised sections of the society. It undertakes activities for the empowerment of women with the aim to make them self reliant and independent.

212. **Jeeva Poorna Women Masons Society** supported by SEU foundation, Royal Netherlands Embassy, BILANCE, district, panchayat, and grama panchayat is established in 1995 in Kerala for skill development and empowerment of women. Major activities are giving training in skills, running of production centre, social managerial training.

213. **Jeevadhara Society**, Udupi, organises self-help groups for women thereby enabling empowerment and sustainability.

214. **Jeevan Nirman Sansthan**, Bharatpur, provides training to

unemployed youth and women.

215. **Jeevan Rekha Parishad,** Bhubaneshwar, promotes overall development of women by promoting micro enterprise programmes.

216. **Jeevika Development Society,** 24 Parganas (S) organises self-help credit groups for women.It provides vocational training in tailoring and assists other voluntary organisations to set up broiler farming, piggery and self-help groups for women.

217. **Jila Vikas and Gramodyog Kalyan Samiti**, Gazipur, provides vocational training with the aim of making people self reliant and independent.

218. **Joint Action Council for Women**, Chennai, conducts projects and programmes focusing on women empowerment and privileges of women.

219. **Joint Women's Programme,** Chennai, facilitates campaigning and action programmes for women. It organises women and the community in rural and urban areas at the grassroots level.

220. **Joint Women's Programme,** New Delhi, organises women and the community in rural and urban areas at the grassroots level.

221. **Joseph Memorial Mahila Samajam**, Thiruvananthapuram, works for the upliftment of women and provides training to various traders to generate employment opportunities.

222. **Jyoti Sangh,** at Ahmedabad in Gujarat, creates awareness amongst women to become self reliant. It creates awareness at grassroots levels .It has established training centres for making women self reliant. It conducts vocational and skills development programmes. It undertakes activities related to counselling, consumer protection, income generating.

223. **Kachuberia Development Action Group**, 24 Parganas (S), promotes rural poor women by providing education, training, and income-generation activities.

224. **Kailash Gramya Vikas Sansthan**, Rudra Prayag, promotes non-formal and regular education, training in carpet and shawl weaving among the rural poor. It conducts awareness programmes for women.

225. **Kairali Mahila Samajam**, Thiruvananthapuram, provides training for self employment.

226. **Kallar Development Society**, Idukki, organises women's welfare activities and promotes income generation programmes formation of self help groups.

227. **Kalpavruksha Rural Development Society**, Tumkur is engaged in developmental activities with special attention to women .It assists women in employment.

228. **Kalyankari Mahila Mandal**, Parbhani, undertakes activities for the empowerment of women with the aim to make them self reliant and independent.

229. **Kamalpur Adivasi Mahila Unnayan Samity**, Bankura, provides vocational training to women and promotes income generation programmes for them. It encourages small savings through self help groups in the society.

230. **Kamdar Swasthya Suraksha Mandal,** Ahmedabad, creates awareness and provides training to industrial and sewerage workers (dalits) including women.

231. **Karma Kutir,** Kolkata, promotes community organisation with special focus on women.It creates income generation activities among women through tailoring, weaving and knitting. It encourages women to learn various skills for their economic development.

232. **Karnataka Integrated Development Services**, Dharwad, works for the upliftment of women. It provides training and assistance to women to form self help groups.

233. **Karnataka Rural Education Development Society**, Bijapur, provides opportunity for rural self employment through income generation programmes and thereby improves the standard of living for rural women.

234. **Karnataka Rural Service Society**, Belgaum, works for the promotion of economic status of women through

formation of self-help groups. It works for the promotion of job oriented training and entrepreneurship development training and there by aiding women to take up income generation activities, for sustainable development.

235. **Karunaya Trust**, Dindigul, works for marginal groups, tribal people and women and helps to develop self-help group.

236. **Karwar Diocesan Development Council**, Uttar Kannada, works for ultimate social change through organising marginalised people including women and provides training for personal development and development of community.

237. **Kasturba Vanwasi Kanya Ashram** , Khargone, works for the overall development of women through education and integrated rural development.

238. **Kaushalya Artisan Welfare Council of Karnataka**, Bangalore, designs and assists marketing of handicrafts produced by craftsperson and women entrepreneur organisations.

239. **Keirao Women Welfare Association**, Imphal, undertakes activities for the empowerment of women with the aim to make them self reliant and independent.

240. **Keliapathar Sabut Sangha and Library**, Bankura, undertakes various development programmes for the rural poor women .It organises training programmes for the rural people. It undertakes income generating programmes for women.

241. **Kerala Association for Social and Women's Welfare**, Kollam develops a scientific outlook in society on issues relating to women, and other socially and economically backward sections of society. It works for the promotion of gender equity and women empowerment. It associates and co-operates with Government in the implementation of developmental programmes.

242. **Kerala Catholics Services Centre**, Kolkata, imparts skill development techniques to women for their sustainable

development.

243. **Kerala State Unemployed Service Society**, Thiruvananthapuram, works for the elimination of poverty. It organises self help groups for community development and women and child development.

244. **Khadi Gramodyog Niketan, Nainital**, works with rural scheduled caste and scheduled tribe women and promotes production and sale of handloom textiles.

245. **Khadisilk Gramodyoga Samiti**, Cuddapah, works for the overall development of women, children and youth, and encourage them to participate in rural development activities.

246. **Khela Ghar1**, Kolkata, imparts training to marginalised women so that they can attain self sufficiency.

247. **Kirti Abudhya Sansthan**, Gwalior, promotes women education and provides training on fabric painting.

248. **Kishan Adarsh Siksha Samiti**, Padrona, works for the welfare of women and provides better educational facilities to the backward classes. It promotes integrated rural development programmes.

249. **Kizhakkumkara Mahila Samajam,** Thiruvananthapuram was established in1966 and registered under the Travancore Cochin Literary Scientific Charitable Societies Act in 1974 with a view to promote the living conditions of women of Attipara Panchayat in Thiruvananthapuram. Since its very inception, it has been striving towards the socio-economic, political and cultural well being of the women, so as to make them self-reliant and self-sufficient. This Mahila Samajam has launched several training–cum–production units and employment generation activities. They provide training in tailoring, composing, printing & binding, fruit preservation, vocational training in DTP & offset printing, screen-printing, soup soap power making, mushroom & prawn cultivation, bio-mass processing.

250. **Kodumon Grama Vikasana Samithy**, Pathanamthitta, provides welfare activities for disabled people and helps in

the formation of self help groups.

251. **Kolathur   Educational   Social   and   Cultural Organisation**, Malappuram, provides income generation programmes for women and unemployed youth.

252. **Koottay   Ali   Akbar   Smaraka   Mahila   Samajan**, Malapuram, provides vocational training and education for the empowerment of women in rural areas.

253. **Kottapuram Integrated Development Society**, Trichur, develops programmes for women's welfare and provides training for income and employment generation.

254. **Kshetriya Gramin Vikas Sansthan**, Kanpur, conducts self employment training programmes especially for women and rural artisans.

255. **Kutch Mahila Vikas Sanghatan**, Bhuj, empowers women through education and vocational programmes and eradicates gender disparities. It has set up literacy centres and skills development centres. It provides legal aid, vocational training and health education to people in rural and urban areas. It undertakes activities related to savings and credit schemes, water harvesting and watershed management schemes and documentation of traditional crafts of women.

256. **Kyamgei   Khoiram   Leikai   Women   Welfare Organisation**, Imphal, undertakes developmental activities for women and promotes weaving, knitting and embroidery.

257. **La Martiniere SEOMP Society**, Kolkata, promotes self help and self reliance activities among the young men and women. It provides opportunities for livelihood through training and other support services to the underprivileged.

258. **LAKSHYA for Sustainable Development**, Allahabad, works for the empowerment of rural women with micro-finance and micro-enterprise development.

259. **Late Vijay Gundewar Gramin Vikas Pratishthan**, Parbhani, promotes comprehensive rural development programmes and provides better educational and training

facilities for the needy. It works for the welfare of women.

260. **Laxmi Chand Shiksha Prasar Samiti**, Shivpuri, provides better employment opportunities for women.

261. **Laxmi Mahila Evam Bal Kalyan Sanstha**, Lucknow, works for the welfare of the economically weaker sections of the society, mainly women, both in urban and rural areas. It works for the empowerment of women by promoting income generation activities and the formation of self-help groups.

262. **Legal Aid Centre for Women**, New Delhi, provides supportive services to the women in distress.

263. **Liberation Movement for Women**, Villupuram, works for the development of the dalit women through education organisation, training, agitation and demonstration. It liberates women from all sorts of exploitation and provides various training programmes to enrich their skills and knowledge.

264. **Life Academy of Vocational Studies**, Bhubaneswar, works for the overall development of women with the aim of making them self reliant and independent.

265. **Lohardaga Gram Swarajya Sansthan**, Lohardaga, organises rural people and women for leadership development and development of people's pressure and vigilance committee. It collaborates with the Government and voluntary agencies in promoting developmental activities.

266. **Lok Chetna Manch**, Nainital, works for women's empowerment and assists them to form self-help groups.

267. **Lok Chintan Samitee**, Jhabua, undertakes educational programmes for women.

268. **Lok Seva Mandal**, Ahmedabad, works for the development of women and undertakes free non-formal, vocational and educational training programmes.

269. **Lok Unnaty Chinta Kendra**, Sundargarh, organises youth groups and mahila mandals for the empowerment of people.

270. **Loka Seva Parishad**, Midnapore, provides vocational training to women on carpentry and carries out plantation programmes.

271. **Lokhit Pashu Palak Sansthan**, Pali, empowers the marginalised communities through training in animal husbandry. It preserves traditional knowledge, conducts appropriate animal health programmes, and helps to develop additional income of women from livestock and transfer skills to women.

272. **Lord Gautam Shikshan Prasarak Mandal**, Amravati, provides assistance to tribal communities through training for self employment.

273. **Lotus India Foundation for Excellence**, Bangalore works for the overall welfare of women. It provides educational and training facilities ,and micro credit to the needy with the aim to make them self reliant and independent.

274. **Louis-Braille Drishtiheen Vikas Sansthan** of Jaipur provides service to the visually impaired and disabled with emphasis on women, socially backward and weaker sections of society. It imparts education and vocational training. It undertakes survey, social research and networking with other voluntary organisations.

275. **Lupin Human Welfare and Research Foundation,** Bharatpur, accelerates infrastructure development in key rural sectors through government institutions, NGOs, professional experts and people representatives; empowerment of women and deprived sections by providing credit facility, entrepreneurship skills and creating an environment for value-added produce from micro enterprises and informal sectors at village level.

276. **M. Rakho Multipurpose Society**, Phek, undertakes developmental programmes for women and provides employment opportunities to the educated youth.

277. **M.P. Mahila Samakhya Society,** Raisen, works for the empowerment of rural women and to make them aware of

their basic human rights and provides better educational facilities.

278. **Ma Sarada Sishu Tirtha**, Nodia, imparts vocational training to women.

279. **Madhar Nala Thondu Niruvanam**, Cuddalore, organises several developmental programmes in the areas of education, income generating activities and vocational training for women.

280. **Madhavimandiram   Loka   Seva   Trust**, Thiruvananthapuram works for the development of rural women and inculcates self-confidence in women and imparts education to women. It works towards establishment of communal harmony.

281. **Madhuri Mahila Mandali**, Karimnagar, undertakes activities for the empowerment of women with the aim to make them self reliant and independent.

282. **Mahabhagya Mahila Mandali**, Kurnool, undertakes activities for the empowerment of women with the aim to make them self reliant and independent.

283. **Mahadevi Tai Mahila Vidya Vardhaka Sangha**, Gulbarga, works for the betterment of women.

284. **Mahalakshmi   Welfare   Society**, Vizianagaram, implements socio-economic programmes, promotes the welfare of women and imparts training in crafts, arts, sports and cottage industries.

285. **Mahalaxmi Mahila Mandali**, Nalgonda, undertakes activities for the empowerment of women with the aim to make them self reliant and independent.

286. **Maharana Pratap Jan Kalyan Sanstha**, Simla, works for the overall development of the weaker sections of the society especially women and backward classes.

287. **Maharashtra State Women's Council**, Mumbai, sponsors programmes and homes for socially handicapped women and children.

288. **Maharshi Sambamurty Institute of Social and Development Studies**, Kakinada, promotes overall urban

and rural development, undertakes poverty alleviation programmes by promoting income generation activities and works for the welfare of women.

289. **Mahatama Gandhi Mahila Avam Bal Kalyan Sansthan**, Bastar, works for upliftment of the downtrodden and brings them to the main stream of society and promotes development of the women.

290. **Mahatma Gandhi Institute of Socio Economic Changes**, West Champaran District, provides with legal aid, self-employment training and shelter to deserted women.

291. **Mahatma Gandhi Krida Va Samaj Kalyan Mandal**, Akola, promotes education among children and women and provides vocational guidance to the youth.

292. **Mahesh Drashtihin Kalyan Sangh**, Indore, provide better educational and training facilities for the visually impaired with the aim to work for their rehabilitation. It imparts education and vocational training to the visually-impaired girls/women.

293. **Mahila Abhivrudhi Society** at Hyderabad in Andhra Pradesh works for the empowerment of women by making them self reliant and independent.

294. **Mahila Ashram**, Bhilwara, promotes education of girl child and to provide training to women to make them self-sufficient.

295. **Mahila Bunkar Sahakari Samiti**, Noida, provides training to women to weave products like durries, bed-covers, sheets and table-mats that were in demand and offered good profit margins.

296. **Mahila Chetna Manch** at Sirohi in Rajasthan works for the upliftment of rural women and help to make them self-sufficient.

297. **Mahila Chetna Manch**, Bhopal, provides better educational facilities and works for the welfare and development of women with the aim of making them self reliant and independent.

298. **Mahila Dakshata Samiti,** Mumbai works for the upliftment of women in distress and to elevate the status of women in society

299. **Mahila Dastkari Vidyalaya**, Ranchi, provides training and non-formal education to women.It promotes self employment activities.

300. **Mahila Gramydogya Vikas Aur Prashikshan Sansthan**, Pauri, works for the promotion of small scale industries by providing the necessary training and encouraging women participation.

301. **Mahila Haat**, New Delhi, has been set up for the promotion of women's empowerment and advancement. It develops the collective strength of the self-employed women producers and promotes their self-confidence and upgrades their skills in the traditional trades and crafts.

302. **Mahila Hakka Saurakshan Samiti**, Nasik, improves the economic conditions of the women by providing various employment generation activities.

303. **Mahila Harijan Pichhra Warg Utthan Samitee**, Muzaffarpur, imparts education and training to rural women.

304. **Mahila Hitkari Grih Udyog Sahkari Samiti**, Kota, provides economic support and employment to women and works for the development of cottage industry.

305. **Mahila Jan Kalyan Samiti**, Jabalpur, generates interest in women regarding education, disseminates development related information and imparts vocational training to women.

306. **Mahila Kalyan Evam Janam Niyantran Samiti**, Azamgarh, works for the overall development of women .It aims at making women self reliant and independent and provides better educational and vocational training facilities.

307. **Mahila Kalyan Samiti,** East Singhbhum, promotes income generation activities to improve the living conditions of women.

308. **Mahila Kamla Ben Sah Silai Kadai Kendra**, Khandwa, develops the condition of the women by providing them education and vocational training. It increases self reliance among the backward section of the society.

309. **Mahila Krishi Sanshodhan Sanstha**, Mumbai, works for the overall welfare of women. It undertakes activities for the development of agriculture and agricultural intensification programmes. It spreads awareness and unity among the agricultural labourers, promotes research and provides training in the field of agriculture, encourages the use of modern technology in the field of agriculture and provides better health care, educational and training facilities for the needy.

310. **Mahila Mandal Baiswas**, Ambikapur, works for development of the rural women.

311. **Mahila Mandal Chak Khurd**, Kapurthala, provides employment to poor women of the village and enables them to have a better standard of living.

312. **Mahila Mandal Silai Center**, Balaghat, helps for the empowerment of women through self-help schemes. It looks after the welfare of the people and implements balbarhi programs.

313. **Mahila Mukti Wahini**, Patna, helps the weaker sections of the society especially women and children. It focuses on issues related to education, health, capacity building of the women, elimination of child labour and their rehabilitation.

314. **Mahila Navjagran Samiti**, Garhwal, facilitates the formation of self-help groups.

315. **Mahila Panchayat**, Hingoli, undertakes activities for the empowerment of women with the aim to make them self reliant and independent.

316. **Mahila Pragati Praristhan**, Pauri, promotes overall rural development. It provides training and educational facilities to rural women and promotes income generation programmes by encouraging local handicraft industry and

other alternative sources of income.

317. **Mahila Samaj Kalyan Samiti**, Ropar, works for the upliftment of the rural people, especially women through awareness and literacy. It provides training in cottage industries and assists in the formation of self help groups.

318. **Mahila Samakhya,** Mysore, empowers women through education and promotes employment generation activities for them.

319. **Mahila Samannwaya Committee**, Kolkata, works for the overall welfare of women with the aim of making them self reliant and independent.

320. **Mahila Samiti**, Kandhamal, works for women development and works for tribal development.

321. **Mamta Samajik Sanstha** in Dehradun provides both formal and non-formal education to women, children and other disadvantaged groups. It helps women, children and other disadvantaged groups to identify their problem and seek solutions through their own group effort activities and co-operation.

322. **Mauli Mahila Mandal (Mauli Women's Organisation) (MMM),** a non-profit making charitable organisation was registered and established in the year 1986 by a group of women with the inspiration to help needy and destitute women and children. MMM works in the Sindhudurg district of Maharashtra state in India which has been actively involved in extending training and inputs to the women of the area in income generation as well as marketing of the products made by women, many of these products possess local demand and hence developing a chain or network of consumers within the district works successfully. MMM has initiated a number of programmes for women entrepreneurs to ensure information sharing on different Government schemes and facilities. Through the 'Prerna Mahila Audhogik Sahakari Sanatha' MMM is preparing food items such as papad, masala, kokam aagal, kokum sol, roasted cashew etc. The products are marketed

in the district and surrounding areas. This project has given a stable income generation source to the women in surrounding area.

323. **MOOWES (Marketing Organisation of Women Entrepreneurs (Regd.)** Madras, provides a comprehensive support to women entrepreneurs to achieve success in the business. Its main aim is to aid women in marketing their products through exhibitions and thus provide an opportunity to tour the country also. One of its major annual programmes is Shakti, a women entrepreneurs' exposition comprising workshops, seminars and sale of their products. MOOWES consists of 50 members, mostly housewives, who wish to spend their time profitably. Now MOOWES is focusing on personality development and imparting communication skills to novice women entrepreneurs.

324. **MRD Sports Club**, 24 Parganas (S), promotes the lifestyle of rural people through various development activities and generates savings and credit and set up self-help groups for women.

325. **Nari Mukti Sanstha (Women's Liberation Forum)** is a state level Communist Party of India (Marxist-Leninist) led women's organisation which concentrates its activities in rural and tribal areas of Assam. It helps women to transform their backwardness through consciousness-raising about class, caste and gender based social relations.

326. **Network of Entrepreneurship and Economic Development (NEED)** in Lucknow works for the development of natural resources in rural areas. It encourages women to undertake trade based on entrepreneurship, income generation and employment generation. It helps women to form self help groups and organizes other capacity building programmes for them.

327. **New Life,** Tiruchirapalli, provides micro credit to poor women and facilitates their empowerment by encouraging compulsory savings, credit management, skills

enhancement and income generation.

328. **New Mahila Agarbati Udyog Centre**, Ahmedabad, undertakes developmental activities for women. It promotes income generation activities for the village youth and works on various agricultural development schemes.

329. **Purnea Pramandal (Zila) Smagra Vikas Parishad**, Purnia, promotes overall development of the weaker section of society specially the women and youth. It provides formal and non-formal education with the aim of making the people self reliant.

330. **Purvanchal Vikas Sansthan**, Gazipur, provides better education and training facilities to women and better employment opportunities to the unemployed.

331. **Pushpanjali Chhatra Samitee**, Jabalpur, promotes social service and brings up women to the mainstream of society. It imparts vocational education to women from poor families. It generates employment for the poor and disseminates information about welfare schemes of the Government.

332. **Radha Bal Mandir Vidhyalay Academy**, Jodhpur, works for the upliftment of the disadvantaged sections of the society, mainly widows, poor and the weaker sections. It conducts several activities in the field of education, health, employment, training etc.

333. **Radhika Seva Sansthan**, Motihari, promotes awareness on social activities among women and provides training to the rural population so that they can establish and run small industries.

334. **Rajachana Krida Shikshan Prasarak Mandal**, Solapur, provides training to rural women for self employment. It undertakes watershed development and management programmes.

335. **Rajasthan Adivasi Sangh Zila Sakha**, Dungarpur, works among tribal people with emphasis on economic development and women's empowerment.

336. **Rajiv Gandhi Foundation**, New Delhi, acts as a catalyst

in promoting effective, practical and sustainable programmes in areas of national development and empowers the underprivileged women.

337. **Ramakrishna Vivekananda Mission**, 24 Parganas (S), imparts general education and vocational training to visually and speech impaired women.

338. **Rani Luxmibai Mahila Mandal**, Chandrapur, promotes the development of women and youth in the rural communities. It   has introduced skills development programmes, libraries, vocational training, panchayati raj training for generating income and encourages saving and credit schemes.

339. **Rashtriya Gramin Vikas Nidhi** at Guwahati in Assam, promotes, supports and develops voluntary organisations engaged in economic uplift of rural and urban poor, physically and socio-economically handicapped people. It assists women for their economic self-sustenance. It provides financial and human resource support to non-governmental organisations (NGOs) working in the realm of poverty alleviation.

340. **SAHAYI, (Centre for Collective Learning and Action)** has been working since the 1990s towards capacity building of small and medium sized development oriented NGOs, VDOs, and citizens groups such as women collectives in Kerala. It has two resource centers in Kasargod and Kollam districts of Kerala. These two districts resource centers work for the cause of the marginalized people, strengthen their capacity, work for the best practices in governance, strengthen the governance institutions, build the capacity of the people to ensure the effective participation in Gramsabha/Wardsabha, influence the policy making bodies for pro-poor policies by conducting studies, and work for keeping social cohesion and peace in the community. It also provides short-term entrepreneurship development training to women collectives in market analysis, marketing skills,

marketing strategies, salesmanship, production, and inventory and financial management. The training programmes aim towards making the enterprises of women collectives a sustainable profit-making unit. SAHAYI's interventions have largely focused on capacity building of SHGs and consequently have had little role to play in building coalitions in terms of federation.

341. **Sakhi** is a resource centre for women which was set up in 1996 in Thiruvananthapuram to bridge the gap between the women SHGs and NGOs and other civil society organisations' and the international and national organisations and net works by empowering women through information sharing, education communication and advocacy.

342. **Self-employed Women's Association (SEWA)** is a trade union registered in1972. It is an organisation of poor self-employed women workers. SEWA's main goals are to organise women workers to obtain full employment and self- reliance. SEWA conducts exhibitions also.

343. **Shramik Naari Sangh** , Mumbai, is engaged in various activities for economic and moral upliftment of women in general and especially creating employment opportunity and education for Tribal (Adivasi) women of Parli villages.

344. **Socio Economic Unit Foundation (SEU)** was started in 1988 and SEU foundation in 1996. Its registered office is situated in Thiruvananthapuram and regional offices in districts. They get financial support from Royal Netherlands Embassy, UNICEF, World Bank, District Panchayat, Municipalities and blocks. Issues and areas covered by SEU especially for women are water and sanitation, capacity building, women's participation, supporting women's skill development especially in masonry, vermin composition, stand post maintenance, skill training to women in plumbing, carpentry etc. SEU established a training centre for women's empowerment

and doing gender workshops like skill education in schools for gender development for setting up of small scale industries in the state.

345. **Swargiya Annasaheb Tatha Sudhir Baburao Pethkar Shikshan Sanstha**, Malegaon, Dist. Nashik, is engaged in training computer education, and vocational courses like fashion designing and beauty parlor courses for women.

346. **Tagore Society for Rural Development (TSRD)**, Kolkata, provides opportunities to women, in the formulation and implementation of the project activities to shape their future destiny. It gives more emphasis on women empowerment.

347. **Tambaram Community Development Society**, Chennai, works for self dignity, self reliance, and self governance of women through empowerment by undertaking women development project and through the formation of self help groups

348. **The Consortium of Women Entrepreneurs of India (CWEI)** is a registered civil society, a voluntary organisation that works for the economic empowerment of women in the country and world over. It gives manpower training, undertake product development activities and also act as an intermediary between Indian entrepreneurs and overseas agencies for marketing and exports. The most effective function of all these associations is their lobbying for the cause of the SSIs. It acts as a springboard for entrepreneurship, provides all escort services leading to higher productivity, competitive prices and stringent quality control for export, facilitates technology transfer, improves access to natural resources, product and design development, explore marketing linkages within and outside the country through various Haats, Buyer Seller Meets, Exhibitions and Fairs in India and abroad, disseminates timely information on policies and programs, implements and monitors govt. schemes and programs for sustainable growth of enterprises. This consortium

consisting of NGO's, voluntary organisations and self-help groups, both from rural and urban areas, helps the women entrepreneurs in finding innovative techniques of production, marketing and finance.

349. **The FLO (FICCI Ladies Organisation)** is an arm of the Federation of Indian Chamber of Commerce and Industry (FICCI). FLO regularly holds workshops for women entrepreneurs in various enterprises.

350. **The Integrated Women Development Institute** was set up by Celinal Paul Daniel in 1989, a woman inspired by the ideology of Gandhian thoughts and Christianity, who wanted to implement programmes and rural development works that would benefit the people living in Gummidipoondi and Ponneri taluks of the Thiruvallur District, Tamil Nadu. IWDI fulfills its mission to uplift women and girl children from the devastating situations they encounter by setting up income generating programs for deserving women to become self-employed. The IWDI targets homeless women, low income bonded labourers, the destitute, the deserted aged, and nutrition lacking girl children and provides them with better water facilities, proper sanitation, hygiene education, and savings micro credit programs. Under the rehabilitation of manual scavengers programs, IWDI has formed four sanitary Mart Groups in the Ambattur and Kattivakkan municipalities (slum areas). IWDI also would like to educate and motivate women through Leadership Training Camps with a view to utilise their potential for creation of a new society which is free from exploitation.

351. **The National Association of Disabled's Enterprises** , Mumbai, provides training, guidance and support to the unemployed disabled. It works for the rehabilitation of the aged and women in distress by introducing to income generating activities.

352. **The Rayalaseema Rural Development Society**, Cuddapah, organises self-help groups for women for

social, political and economic empowerment of rural poor.

353. **The Refuge**, Kolkata, provides shelter and training to marginalised women for regaining self-sufficiency.

354. **The Saraswathy Shanmugam Public Charitable Trust**, Kalasapakkam, undertakes activities for the empowerment of women with the aim to make them self reliant and independent.

355. **The Social Centre**, Ahmednagar, creates sustainable livelihood opportunities for the marginal rural people, especially women. It provides women with guidance on the benefits of small savings.

356. **The Swallows of India,** Chennai works in the field of poverty eradication through formation of self-help groups and helping the people to take advantage of the plans and resources from the government to the grass-roots level. It conducts programmes in the field of health care, education and day care centres for children of working women and income generation programmes for the poor women.

357. **Udyogini** is a Delhi based organisation which works for the empowerment of poor women, viz. capacity building, providing marketing net work through its retail out lets, viz. Jeevika. This organisation sells pickles, spices, cotton, woolen textiles, jute and bamboo, handicrafts, leather products and body care products like oils, creams and lotions.

358. **Women Entrepreneurship of Maharashtra (WIMA)** was set up in 1985 with its head office in Pune. The main objective is to provide a forum for members and to help them sell their products. WIMA also provides training to its members. It has established industrial estates in New Bombay and Hadapsar.

359. **Women Entrepreneurship Promotional Association (WEPA)** is an association of women entrepreneurs, which is functioning in Chennai, provides training to women in various fields (simple chemicals, paper products, jute bags, food processing, organic products, bio tech and bio–

products etc.). The association also conducts exhibitions for the members and assists in marketing of the products of members. Consultancy service is also provided to the needy by charging a fee of Rs.250.

360. **Women's Endeavour** is a charitable society which was registered on August 3, 2005 under the Charitable societies Act for the social, educational and economic upliftment of women through proper channel by conducting seminars, meetings, work shops, legal debates for the members. Its registered office is situated at Palarivattom in Kochi. It was founded by Rabiya A.P. Membership is open to all women who are above the age of 25.The society markets the products produced by its members and also conducts fairs and exhibitions for its members.

361. **Women's India Trust (WIT)** is charitable organisation established by Kamila Tyabji in the year 1968, which has helped many women to develop skills to earn a regular income, which has changed their lives and the lives of their families. With a two shops in Mumbai and a training and production centre known as the Kamila Tyabji WIT Centre at Panvel, Mumbai. The Kamila Trust, UK, was set up in the early 1990's with the aim of selling in England items produced by the WIT family of women in India. Hundreds of women have benefited from WIT not only financially but also to become more self-assured, self-confident and self-reliant. WIT has provided training and employment opportunities to needy and unskilled women of all communities in and around Bombay. Beginning with stitching sari petticoats, WIT has helped many such women to develop sewing skills and enables them to earn a regular income, which has changed their lives and that of their families. With the establishment of the training and production centre being set up at Panvel, WIT was able to launch an education programme in nursing and kindergarten training, block printing, screen-printing, toy making and catering. The products these women make are

marketed through our own shops in Bombay as well as outlets throughout India and abroad.

362. **Women's Action for Rural Development**, Madurai, has set up vocational training centres for the rural and urban youth.

363. **Working Women's Forum (WWF)** also known as National Union of Working women, was founded in 1978 in Chennai for the development of self employed women, especially poor in rural and urban areas. All of them run their own small enterprises. The WWF has rescued petty traders from the clutches of middlemen and has made them confident entrepreneurs in their own right. It unites more than half the number of women labour in the unorganised sector in Chennai working micro-enterprises. The beneficiaries of WWF are fisher women, lace makers, bidi making women, landless women, labourers and agarbatti workers.

364. **Young Utkal Project,** Balasore generates awareness on environment and provides employment opportunities to women.

365. **Young Women's Christian Association** in Chandgarh, Hyderabad and Secunderabad work   for the socio-economic upliftment of women irrespective of caste or creed. These organisations provide vocational training to women rural areas with the aim to make them self reliant and independent.

366. **Youth Service Centres** in Angul and Bolangir undertake agricultural intensification programmes; promote women banking systems and works for micro enterprises development.

367. **Youth Technical Training Society**, Chandigarh works for the rehabilitation of poor rural/urban women through vocational training and basic education to make them economically independent. It works for the overall welfare of women.

368. **Youth Welfare and Cultural Society**, Howrah, organises

vocational training for women and undertakes awareness generation programmes for women.

369. **Yuva Evam Bal Vikas Samiti**, Deoria, promotes integrated community development by organising educational and income generation programmes and works for the overall welfare of women belonging to backward communities.

370. **Yuva Janiv**, Amravati, provides education for women in rural areas and it conducts vocational training programmes.

371. **Yuva Mahamandal Dhartidhar**, Sirmour, works in the field of the upliftment of women and works specially on income generation and technology transfer to villagers.

372. **Yuva Rasmi Mahila Samajam**, Thiruvananthapuram, undertakes welfare and rural development activities for women and encourages the weaker sections to obtain education.

373. **Yuvak Sangh**, Patna, imparts training for skill development as well as for the empowerment of women and the weaker sections.

374. **Zanana Dastkari Production Limited**, Srinagar, imparts training and provides jobs to poor women in the valley.

375. **Zonta Resource Centre** at Mylapore in Chennai works for improvement of the economic, social and legal status of women through counselling, legal aid, education and vocational training.

376. **Zonta Resource Centre**, Alwarpet, Chennai, works for improvement of the economic, social and legal status of women through counselling, legal aid, education and vocational training.

Bibliography

Bibliography

A. Books

Acharya, Women *and Society in India,* Ajantha Publications, Jawahar Nagar, New Delhi, 1979.

Adisheshiah Malcom, S., Entrepreneurship *for Tamil Nadu,* Tamil Nadu State Council for Science and Technology, Madras, 1985.

Aldrich and Sakano, *Entrepreneurship in a Global Context,* Edited by Sue Birley and Macmillan, New Fetter Lane, New York ,1997.

Allen, H., Anderson et al, *Effective Entrepreneurship,* Blockwell Publishers Inc., USA, 1999.

Anuradha Prasad, Kuldeep Mathur, *Entrepreneurship Development Under TRYSEM,* Concept Publishing Co., New Delhi, 1988.

Baud, I.S.A, Forms *of Production and Women's Labour: Gender Aspects of Industrialisation in India and Mexico,* Krips Repro. Meppel, 1989.

Brigitte Berger, The *Culture of Entrepreneurship,* Tata McGraw-Hill Publishing Company Limited, New Delhi, 1991.

Brydon, L. and Chant, S., *Women in the Third World, Gender Issues in Rural and Urban Areas,* Aldershot, Edward Elgar Press, 1989.

Caplan, P., *Women United, Women Divided: Cross-Cultural Prospectives on Female Solidarity,* London, Fontana, 1978.

Caroline Sweetman, *Women Employment and Exclusion,* Oxfam (U.K. and Ireland), Oxford OX2 7DZ, U.K., 1996.

Chakravarti, *Women Employees and Human Resource Management,* Nalini Sastry, Subrata Pandey, University Press (India) Ltd., Hyderabad, 1995.

Creevey L., *Changing Women's Lives and Work,* IT Publications, 1996.

Dhanalakshmi, Bhatia, B.S. and Batra, S., *Entrepreneurship and Small Business Management*, Deep and Deep Publications Pvt. Ltd., New Delhi, 2000.

Dharmaja, S.K., Bhatia, B.S. and Saini, J.S., *Women Entrepreneurs: Perceptions, Attitudes and Opinions-Entrepreneurship and Education*, Rawat Publications, New Delhi, 2001.

Dwijendra Tripathi, *The Dynamics of a Tradition Kasturbhai Lalbhai and His Entrepreneurship*, Ramesh Jain, Manohar Publications, New Delhi,1981.

Ganesan, S., *Status of Women Entrepreneurs in India*, Kanishka Publishers, Distributors, New Delhi, 2003.

Geecrtz, C., Peddlers and Princes, University of Chicago Press, Chicago, 1963.

Gianotten, V. Riofrio G., Bueningen C. Van and C. Van Kooten, *Las mugeres del grupo destinatario:La mujer en programas de promicion urbana en el peru.lima, Informe de evaluacion* DGIS-CEBEMO,1990.

Gupta, C.B. and Srinivasan, N.P., *Entrepreneurship Development,* Sultan Chand and Sons, New Delhi. 1992.

Hisrich, R.D. and Brush, *The Women Entrepreneur: Starting, Financing and Managing a Successful New Enterprise,* Washington D.C. Health and Co., 1986.

Jain, S.C., *Women and Technology*, Rawat Publications, Jaipur, 1985.

James, J. Berna, *Industrial Entrepreneurship in Madras State*, Asia Publishing House, Bombay, 1960.

Janaki, D., *Women's Issues (Perspectives from Social History)*, Dhana Publications, Anna Nagar, Chennai, 2001.

Jayan, Nair K.G.C. and Biji, *A Systematic Approach to Entrepreneurship Development and Management,* Chand Publications, Thiruvananthapuram, 2000.

Jose Paul, Ajith Kumar, N. and Paul T. Mampilly, *Entrepreneurship Development*, Himalaya Publishing House, Mumbai, 1996.

Khanna, S.S., *Entrepreneurship in Small Scale Industries*,

Himalaya Publishing House, Bombay,   1990.

Krishna Lal Sharma and Harnet Singh, *Entrepreneurship Growth and Development Programmes in Northern India, A Sociological Analysis,* Abhinav Publications, New Delhi, 1980.

Lalitha Iyer, *Women Entrepreneurs, Challenges and Strategies*, Friedrich Ebert Stiftung, New Delhi, 1991.

Lallan Prasad, *Industrialisation- Concepts and Issues,* S. Chand and Co. New Delhi, 1983

Mac Coby, E.E. and Jacklin, C.N., *The Psychology of Sex Differences,* Standford, Calif, Styaford University Press, 1974.

Manohar , U. Desh Pande, *Enterpreneurship of Small Scale Industries. Concept. Growth. Management,* Deep and Deep Publications, New Delhi, 1982.

Mira Seth, *Women and Development, The Indian Experience*, Sage Publications India Pvt. Ltd., New Delhi, 2001.

Martin Robertson, *What Unemployment Means*, Oxford University Press, New York, 1981.

Moore Perrin Dorothy and Butner, E., *Holly Women Entrepreneurs – Moving Beyond Glass Ceiling*, Sage Publications, New Delhi and International Educational and Professional Publishers, Thousand Oaks London, 1997.

Morrison, A.M., White, R.P., Van Velsor, E. and Centre for Creative Leadership, Breaking *the Glass Ceiling: Can Women Reach Top of America's Largest Corporations?* Reading M.A. Addison Wesley Publishers Inc.1987.

Mumtaz Ali Khan Noor, *Status of Rural Women in India-A Study of Karnataka*, Uppal Publishing House, New Delhi, 1982.

Narendra, S. Bisht and Pamila K. Sharma, *Entrepreneurship Expectations and Experience,* Himalaya Publishing House, Bombay, 1991.

Papalo, T.S. and Alkah N. Sharma, *Gender and Employment in India,* Vikas Publishing House, New Delhi, 1999.

Paramjeet Kaur Dhillon, *Women Entrepreneurs Problems and*

Prospects, Blaze Publishers and Distributors Pvt. Ltd., New Delhi, 1993.

Palmer, I, *The Impact of Agrarian Reform on Women. Women's Role and Gender Differences in Development,* Monograph, No.6, West Hartford, Kumarian Press, 1985.

Patel, V.G., *Women Entrepreneurship Development, Developing New Entrepreneurs,* Entrepreneurship Development Institute of India, Ahmedabad, 1987.

Peter Berger and Richard J. Neuhas, *To Empower People,* The American Enterprise Institute, 1978.

Poonam Smith-Sreen, *Accountability in Development Organisations, Experiences of Women's Organisations in India,* Sage Publications India Pvt. Ltd., New Delhi,1995.

Richard Swedberg, *Entrepreneurship-The Social Science View,* Oxford University Press, 2000.

Robert Goffee and Richard Scase, *Women in Charge-The Experience of Female Entrepreneurs,* George Allen and Unwin (Publishers) Ltd., London, U.K., 1985.

Robert, F. Hebert, Albert N. Link, *The Entrepreneur,* Prager Publishers, New York, U.S.A., 1982.

Schumpeter Joseph, A., *The Theory of Economic Development,* Oxford University Press, New York, 1961.

Sen Gupta Padmini, *Women in India : Information Services of India,*
New Delhi, 1964.

Sextan and Kent, The *Art and Science of Entrepreneurship,* Cambridge, Mass, Ballinger, 1981.

Sexton, D.I. and Simlor, R.W., *The Arts and Science of Entrepreneurship,* Cambridge, Mass, Ballinger, 1986.

Shah, Hina, *Fostering Women Entrepreneurs in India,* Mittal Publications, New Delhi,1987.

Shally Joseph, *A Study on the Socio-Psychological Background of the Entrepreneurs - Managers of Small Scale Industrial Units in Ernakulam District, Kerala,* Northern Book Centre, New Delhi, 2003.

Shanta Kohli Chandra, *Development of Women*

Entrepreneurship in India, Mittal Publications, New Delhi 1991.

Sharma, R.A., *Entrepreneurial Performance in Indian Industry*, Inter-India Publications, New Delhi, 1985.

Sharma, R.A., *Entrepreneurial Change in Indian Industry*, Sterling Publishers Pvt. Ltd., New Delhi, 1980.

Sharma, D.D., Dhameja, S.K. Gurjar, B.R, *Entrepreneurship, Strategic Management and Globalisation,* Rawat Publications, Jaipur and New Delhi,1999.

Shilendra Vyakarnam, *Developing Rural Entrepreneurship*, Oxford and I BH Publishing Co. Pvt. Ltd.,1990.

Shirley Nuss and Ettore Denti, David Viry, *Women in the World of Work: Statistical Analysis and Projections to the Year 2000.* International Labour Office, *Geneva,* Switzerland, 1989.

Sumi Guha, *Entrepreneurship and Empowerment of Women Entrepreneurship and Education*, Rawat Publication, New Delhi, 2001.

Taylor R.R, *Exceptional Entrepreneurial Women: Strategies for Success*, Praeger Publishers, New York, 1988.

Thea Hilhorst Harry Oppenoorth , *Financing Women's Enterprises-Beyond Barriers and Bias*, Royal Tropical Institute, The Netherlands Intermediate Technology Publication, U.K. UNIFEM- USA, 1992.

Tinker, I., *Women in Micro- and Small-Scale Development,* West View Press, 1995.

Unger, R.K., *Female and Male: Psychological Perspective'*, New York, Harper and Row, 1979.

Van Dijik, M.P. and Secher Marcussen H (eds.), *Industrialisation in the World: The Need for Alternative Strategies',* Frank Cass London, 1990.

Vasant Desai, *Entrepreneurial Development,* Volume-1, Himalaya Publishing House, Bombay, 1991.

Vasant Desai, *Dynamics of Entrepreneurial Development and Management,* Himalaya Publishing House, Mumbai, 1996.

Vinayshil Gautam, *Enterprise and Society (A study of some*

aspects of Entrepreneurship and Management in India), Concept Publishing Company, New Delhi, 1978.

Vinze Medha Dhubhashi, *Women Entrepreneurs in India - A Socio-Economic Study of Delhi,* 1975-85, Mittal Publications, New Delhi, 1987.

Yasodha Shanmuga Sundaram, *Women Employment in India with Special Reference to Tamil Nadu,* Institute for Advanced Studies and Research, Madras, 1993.

B. Journal Articles

Ahmed , I. (ed.), *Technology and Rural Women: Conceptual and Empirical Issues,* London, George Allen and Unwin for the ILO World Employment Programme, 1985.

Alsos and Ljunggren in Schultz Grafisk A/S Danish Agency for Trade and Industry November, 2000.

Anil Kumar, 'Enterprise Location: Choice of Women Entrepreneurs', *SEDME,* Vol. No.31 (3), September, 2004.

Anjaneya Swamy, G. and Deepak Rajan, 'Women Entrepreneurship-Need for a Fresh Look', *Indian Economic Panorama,* Vol.13, No.3, October, 2003.

Anju Gupta and Inderjeet Khanna, 'Constraints Analyses of Women Entrepreneurs', *SEDME,* December, 1997.

Archana Mahanta, 'Impact of Development on Women', *Documentation on Women's Concerns,* October-December, 1991.

Aravinda, Ch. and Renuka, S., 'Women Entrepreneurs: An Exploratory Study', *SEDME,* Vol.28, No.3, September, 2001.

Aruna Prasad, Shashi Raja Gopal, Tara Appachoo and Narayan Prasad, 'A Review of the Schemes for the Development of Women in the Past Decade with Special Reference to Karnataka State', *Second National Conference on Women's Studies,* Institute of Social Studies Trust, Thiruvananthapuram, April 9-12 , 1984.

Aurora Business Women's Network in partnership with DTI Small Business Service, 2004.

Baker et al. in Schultz Grafisk A/S, Danish Agency for Trade and Industry, November, 2000.

Barefoot Bankers are Women's Best friends-*Documentation on Women's Concerns*, July-December, 1997.

Batra and Narinder Kaur, 'Promotion of Women Entrepreneurship in India, An Empirical Study of Punjab', *National Seminar on Current Research in Indian Entrepreneurship*, 29-31 March, 1994.

Beena, C. and Sushma, B., 'Women Entrepreneurs Managing Petty Business-A Study from Motivational Perspectives', *Southern Economist*, Vol.42, No.2, May 1, 2003.

Belcourt, M., Burke, R.J. and Lee H. Gosselin, 'The Glass Box: Women Business Owners in Canada', Ottawa, Canadian Advisory Council on the Status of women, Back Ground Paper, 1991.

Berik, G., 'Women Carpet Weavers in Rural Turkey: Pattern of Employment, Earnings and Status', *Women, Work and Development*, International Labour Office, Geneva, No.15, 1987.

Bequele, A. and Boyden, *Combating Child Labour*, Geneva, ILO, 1988.

Birely, S., 'Female Entrepreneurs: Are They Really Different?' *Journal of Small Business Management*, XXVII-1, 1989.

BT/Aurora Women Entrepreneurs and ICT Research Source-Albert Buildings, London , 2004.

Bowen, D.D and Hisrich, R .D., 'The Female Entrepreneurs: A Career Development Perspective', *Academy of Management Review*, 11(2) ,1986.

Brady Anderson, J., 'Women: The Emerging Economic force', *CIPE Conference*, U.S. Agency for International development (USAID), June 15-16, 2005.

Bruce, J. 'Home divided'. *World Development,* 1989, Vol.17, No.7.

Brush, Cromie and Hayes in Schultz Grafisk A/S- Danish Agency for Trade and Industry, November 2000.

Buvinic, M. and Berger, M., 'Sex Differences in Access to a

Small Enterprise Development Fund in Peru', *World Development*, Vol.18, No.5, 1990.

Chittawadagi, M.B., Women Entrepreneurship in Co-operative Banking Sector, *Southern Economist*, Vol.42, No.19 Feb.1, 2004.

Choudhury, P.K., Shashi Baijal and Asokan, M., 'Banks and Women's Development: A Comparison of Approaches in India and U.K.', *SEDME*, Vol. XXIV, No.2, June, 1997.

Creevey, L., *'Changing Women's Lives and Work'*, IT Publications, 1996.

Downing, J., 'Gender and The Growth of Micro Enterprises'. *Small Enterprise Development*, Vol.2, No.1, 1991.

Erard, B., Josette and Donna Brown, *Services to Women Entrepreneurs n~ The Western Canadian Case*, Western Economic Diversification Canada n~Mantioba Office, August 19, 1994.

ESCAP Study, 'Fewer Changes for Asian Women', *Documentation on Women's Concerns*, October-March, 1991.

Expert Meeting on Mainstreaming Gender in Order to Promote Opportunities, *United Nations Conference on Trade and Development*, DISTR GENERAL TD/B/OM. 3/EM.14/2 28 August, 2001.

Filomina Steady, 'Women's Projects and Programmes-Resources Power and Women', *Proceedings of the African and Asian Inter –Regional Workshop on Strategies for Improving the Employment Conditions of Rural Women*, Arusha, ILO, Geneva ,Switzerland, 1987.

Francke, BRIDGE,-Briefings on Development and Gender, *Report No.15*, December, 1993.

'Gender and Poverty in India', *World Bank Report*, Prepared by World Bank in Collaboration with Government of India, 1991.

Gita Sen, *Paddy Cultivation, Processing and Women Workers in India: The South Vs North-East,* Centre for Development Studies, Thiruvananthapuram, 1983.

Goffee, R. and Scase, R., 'Business Ownership and Women's Subordination: A Preliminary Study of Female Proprietors', *Sociological Review*, Vol.31, 1983.

Goffee, R. and Scase, R., 'Female Entrepreneurs; Some Preliminary Research Findings', *Service Industries Review*, Vol.2, 1983.

Gopala Krishnan, B.K, 'Self-Help Groups and Social Defense', *Social Welfare*, 44 (10), 1998.

Gurumoorthy, T.T., 'Self-Help Groups Empower Rural Women', *Kurukshetra,* Vol.48 (5), 2000.

Haan, H.C., 'Community-Based Training for Employment and Income Generation', Geneva, ILO, 1994.

Hariram and Chitra Narayanan, 'Train a Woman and She is Better Than a Man', *Documentation on Women's Concerns*, July-September, 1992.

Helen Pickering, Ellen Kajura, George Katongole and James White Worth, 'Women's Groups and Individual Entrepreneurs: A Uganda Case Study', Women Employment and Exclusion, *Focus On Gender* Vol.4, No.3, October,1996.

Hirata and Humphrey, BRIDGE, *Report No.15*, December,1993.

Hisrich, R. and Brush, C.G., 'The Women Entrepreneur: Management Skill and Business Problems', *Journal of Small Business Management,* XX11-1, 22 January, 1994.

Fisher, E., Rouber, R. and Dyke, L., 'A Theoretical Overview and Extension of Research on Sex Gender and Entrepreneurship', *Journal of Business Venturing,* VIII, 1993.

Hisrich, R.D. and Brush, C.G, 'The Women Entrepreneur; Management Skills and Business Problems'. *Journal of Small Business Management*, January 22, 1984.

Hisrich, R.D. and O'Brien, 'The Women Entrepreneurs from a Business and Sociological Perspective', Frontiers of

Entrepreneurship Research, *Proceedings of the 1981 Conference on Entrepreneurship,* Wellesley, Mass, Bobson College, 1981.

Hisrich, R.D. and O'Brien, 'The Women Entrepreneur as a Reflection of Type of Businesses' Frontiers of Entrepreneurship Research, *Proceedings of the 1981 Conference on Entrepreneurship,* Welleslay, Mass, Bobson College, 1982.

Holt, S.L. and Ribe, H., *'Developing Financial Institutions for the Poor: Reducing Gender Barriers'.* World Bank Policy, Research and External Affairs Division, Washington,1990.

Huntley , R.L, 'Women Entrepreneurs and Career Choice', *Dissertation Abstracts International (Part A),* 46, 1755-A., 1985.

ILO Report, 'Women in the Informal Sector-Overview – Gender, Poverty and Employment Turning Capability into Entitlements-ILO, Governing Body 261st Session ,GB/ESP/2/2, Geneva, ILO, 1994.

INFOPEDIA, 'Women, Employment of Funk and Wagnalls' New Encyclopedia, Soft Key International, Funk and Wagnalls, Corporation, 1995.

Izyumov, Alexei, Razumnova, Irina, 'Women Entrepreneurs in Russia Learning to Survive the Market', *Journal of Developmental Entrepreneurship,* April, 2000.

Jaya Arunachalam, 'Credit and Marketing, Women's Projects and Programmes, Resources Power and Women', *Proceedings of the African and Asian Inter–Regional Workshop on Strategies for Improving the Employment Conditions of Rural Women, Arusha, United Republic of Tanzania, 20-25 August 1984,* ILO, Geneva, Switzerland, 1985.

Jayasree, S., 'Entrepreneur's Access to Household Resources', *VIII National Conference of Women's Studies (Bombay) - Abstracts,* Survival and Sovereignty Challenges to Women's Studies, May, 1998.

Jockes, BRIDGE, Briefings on Development and Gender, *Report No.15*, December, 1993.

Komarovsky, M., 'Cultural Contradictions and Sex Roles: the Masculine Case', *American Journal of Sociology*, 1973.

Krishnaveni Motha, 'Women Entrepreneurship in Rural Areas of India', *SEDME*, Vol. No.31, No.3, September, 2004.

Lalitha Shivakumar, N., 'Self-Help Groups', *Social Welfare*, 42 (4), 1995.

Levitsky, J., 'Micro Enterprises in Developing Countries', *Papers and Proceedings of an International Conference*, London, Intermediate Technology Publications, 1989.

Ljunggren, Schultz Grafisk A/S, Danish Agency for Trade and Industry, November, 2000.

Loyola Joseph, 'Inter-City Marketing Net work for Women Micro-Entrepreneurs Using Cell Phone: Social Capital Brings Economic Development', *An Initial Survey of The Foundation of Occupational Development (FOOD)*, Based in Chennai, India, February 5, 2005.

Lycklama, A. Nijeholt, 'The Fallacy of Integration: The UN Strategy of Integrating Women in to Development Revisited', *.Netherlands Review of Development Studies*, Vol.1, 1987.

Mac Coby, E.E. and Jacklin, C.N., 'The Psychology of Sex Differences', Stand Ford, Calif, Styaford University Press, 1974.

Mc Clung and Parker J., 'A Study of Female Business owners in Oklahoma and the Association Between Specified Entrepreneurial Characteristics and Financial Performance Based on the Strategies Profit Model', *Dissertation Abstracts International (Part –A)*, 46(12) 3811-A, 1986.

Mac Donald, J.L., 'The Traits and Characteristics of Women Entrepreneurs: Criteria for Predicting Success in Business Management', *Dissertation Abstracts International (Part-A)*, 46(8) 2169-A., 1986.

Malathi V. Gopal, Manimala Mathew , J., Srinivas Prabhakhya and Joseph Shields, 'Role Conflicts of Women

Entrepreneurs', *GEM India 2001 Report*, Global Entrepreneurship Monitor; Entrepreneurship learning, Indian Institute of Management, NISIET, Government of India, Hyderabad, 2005.

Mallika Das, 'Women Entrepreneurs from Southern India: An Explorative Study', *The Journal of Entrepreneurship,* Sage Publications, Vol.8,(2), July- December, 1999.

Marlow in Schultz Grafisk A/S Danish Agency for Trade and Industry November 2000.

Marta Turk, 'W*omen Entrepreneurship-Back to Traditional Values',* PCMG Informator, 2000.

Mayoux, Linda, 'Women's Empowerment and Micro-Finance Programmes: Approaches, Evidence and Ways Forward', *Discussion Paper,* Open University, Milton Keynes, U.K., 1998.

McKee, K., 'Micro Level Strategies for Supporting Livelihoods Employment and Income Generation of Poor Women in the Third World: the Challenge of Significance'. *World Development,* Vol.17, No.7, 1989.

Mohiuddin, Asghari, 'Entrepreneurship Development Among Women, Retrospects and Prospects', *SEDME*, Vol. 10(1), 1983.

Moser, BRIDGE, Briefings on Development and Gender, *Report No.15*, December,1993.

Nadkarni, Sulochana, 'Women Entrepreneurs, A Socio-Economic Study of Pune City', *The Economic Times,* September14, 1983.

Nagendra. P. Singh and Rita Sen Gupta, 'Potential Women Entrepreneurs, Their Profile , Vision and Motivation- An Exploratory Study', *Research Report Serial II ,*New Delhi, NIESBUD, 1985.

Nandini Azad, 'Women in the Informal Sector', *Documentation on Women's Concerns,* October-March , 1991.

Narasaiah, P.V., Ramakrishnaiah, K., 'DWCRA Programme in Cuddapah District: An Evaluation', *SEDME,* Vol. 31,

No.3 , September,2004.

Neider, L., 'Á Preliminary Investigation of Female Entrepreneurs in Florida', *Journal of Small Business Management*, XXV-3, 1987.

Noeleen Heyzer and Gitazen, *Gender, Economic Growth and Poverty*, Asia and Pacific Development Centre, New Delhi, 1994.

Paramjeet Kaur Dhillon, *Women Entrepreneurs Problems and Prospects*, Blaze Publishers and Distributors Pvt. Ltd., New Delhi, 1993.

Prasanna, S. and Pal, M.S., 'Women Innovation - Their Contribution and Experience in Organised Industry', *Papers Presented at the UNESCO sponsored International workshop*, National Institute for Training in Industrial Engineering, 29 October through 2 November, 1984.

Punithavathy Pandian and Eswaran, R., 'Empowerment of Women Through Micro-Credit', *Yojana*, Vol. 46 (11), November, 2002.

Radhika Sachdev, 'Where is the Queen Bee'-*Documentation on Women's Concerns*, July- September, 1999.

Rejula Devi, A.K., 'Women Entrepreneurs', *Yojana*, New Delhi, Vol. XXII, No.13, July16, 1978.

Randeep Wadehra, 'Write View, Of Enterprise and Empowerment of Women', *Review of Papers Presented During the UGC Sponsored Seminar*, University of Kerala's Department of Commerce, 2002.

Richard Kibombo and Samuel K. Kayabwe, 'A Baseline Study on Economic Empowerment of Women Through the Use of ICTs in Uganda', *Final report,* Compiled for the Council for Economic Empowerment of Women of Africa (CEWA), Uganda Chapter-IDRC, October,2000.

Rhokit Khilani, 'Law Needed for Work Place Hazards Faced by Women', *Documentation on Women's Concern*, January-March, 2001.

Rupande Padaki and Anne Mara Sillevis Smitt, 'Women Entrepreneurs: Significance of Personality Theory',

National Seminar on Current Research in Indian Entrepreneurship, Entrepreneurship Development Institute of India, Ahmedabad, 29-31 March, 1994.

Sara Carter, 'Securing a Business Loan: How Women Entrepreneurs View Banks and How Banks View Them', Lancaster University Management School, Lancaster, 2004.

Saraswathy Amma, K.P. and Sudarsanan Pillai, P., 'A Study on Women Entrepreneurs in Garment Making Industries in Kerala – A profile', *Management Researcher*, VI -VII, October 2000- March 2001.

Schwartz, E.B., 'Entrepreneurship: A Female Frontier'. *Journal of Contemporary Business winter*, 1979.

Shane S., Kolvereid, L. and Westhead, P., 'An Exploratory Examination of the Reasons Leading to New Firms Formation Across Country and Gender', *Journal of Business Management*, XXXV-1,1991.

Shirley Nuss, Ettore Denti and David Viry, *Women in the World of Work: Statistical Analysis and Projections to the Year 2000*, International Labour Office, 1989.

Seminar on Women's Empowerment Through Training, Development and Entrepreneurship Organised by the Ishan Institute of Management-Noida, March 29, *Documentation on Women's Concerns*, April-June, 1999.

Sharon Hadary, Center for Women's Business Research, Center for Women's Business Research, Washington, 2004.

Shaver, Gartner and Gatewood in Schultz Grafisk A/S, *Danish* Agency for Trade and Industry, November, 2000.

Shoma A. Chatterji, 'Under the Thumb', SIETI, *Documentation on Women's Concern*, April-June, 1999.

Shoma Chatterji, 'Small Entrepreneurs Among Women', *Documentation on Women's Concerns*, October- March, 1991.

Shramshakti, National Commission on Self Employed Women and Women in the Informal Sector, New Delhi, June,

1988.

Simel Esim, 'Why earn less?', Gender Based Factors Affecting the Earnings of Self-Employed Women in Turkey, JAI Press, July, 1999.

Singh, N.P. and Senguptha, R., 'Potential Women Entrepreneurs; Their Profile, Vision and Motivation - An Exploratory Study', *Research Report Serial-1*,New Delhi, NIESUBUD, 1985.

Singh, N.P., Sehgal, P., Tinani, M. and Senguptha, R., 'Successful Women Entrepreneurs-Their Identity, Expectation and Problems, An Exploratory Research Study', *Research Report Serial II*, New Delhi, MDI Collaboration, 1986.

Sosamma, D.P., 'Margin Money Assistance for Women may be Enlarged', Chennai, *Documentation on Women's Concerns*, April-June, 1999.

Stolen, K.A., 'The Social and Cultural Context: Women and Development Assistance'. *Paper Presented at the Symposium Sharing Poverty or Creating Wealth, Access to Credit for Women's Enterprises,* Amsterdam, The Netherlands, 7th-9th January, 1991.

'Study on Women's Industrial Programme in Kerala', Department of Economics and Statistics, Government of Kerala, 1984.

Sulochana, A. Nadkarni, 'Women, Entrepreneurship and Economic Development', *Paper of First National Conference on Women's Studies-*Bombay, April,1981.

Sundin and Holmquist ,Carter and Allen ,Electronic Edition by Schultz Grafisk A/S. in Danish Agency for Trade and Industry November, 2000.

Sumangala Naik, 'The Need for Developing Women Entrepreneurs', *Yojana*, Vol.47 (7), July, 2003.

Surti, Kirtidas and Dalpat Sarupria, 'Psychological Factors Affecting Women Entrepreneurs - Some Findings', *Indian Journal of Social Work*, 44(3) , October , 1985.

Swatko, 'Breaking in Experience in Male Dominated

Professions', *Women and Theory* 2(3), 1981.

Tara S. Nair , 'Entrepreneurship Training for Women in the Indian Rural Sector: A Review of Approach and Strategies', *The Journal of Entrepreneurship*, Volume 5(1), 1996.

The World Micro Credit Summit, 'Government to Give Facilities to Women Entrepreneurs, *Documentation on Women's Concerns*, July'- December, 1997.

Tovo, M., 'Micro Enterprise Among Village Women in Tanzania'. *Small Enterprise Development*, Vol.2 (1), 1991.

Tripp, BRIDGE, Briefings on Development and Gender, *Report No.15*, December, 1993.

UN 1991, *Economic Survey of Europe in 1991-92*, United Nations Economic Commission for Europe, United Nations, New York, 1992.

United Nations, 'Women in a Changing Global Economy, *1994'*, *'World Survey on the Role of Women in Development*, 1995', In Women Entrepreneurs in Small and Medium Enterprises, National Foundation of Women Business Owners (NFWBO) OECD, 1998.

Williamson, L.C., Joyce Eddy, *A Successful Female Entrepreneurs'*. *Dissertation Abstracts International (Part A)*, 46(9), 2739-A., 1986.

Wees C. Van der and Romijn, *Entrepreneurship and Small Enterprise Development for Women in Developing Countries, An Agenda of Unanswered Questions*, Geneva ILO, Management Development Branch, 1987.

White, B., Studying Women and Rural Non-Farm Sector Development in West Java, *Project Working Paper Series, No.B-12* , Institute of Social studies and Banding Research Project Office, 1991.

C. Government Publications

Department of Economics and Statistics, *Statistical Hand Book of Tamil Nadu, 2002*, Special Commissioner and Director, Chennai, 2003.

Industries Department, Government of Tamil Nadu, *Guide to Entrepreneurs*, Tamil Nadu, 1984.

Magalir Nala Membattu Niruvanam, *Unnal Mudium Thozhi*, Tamil Nadu, 2001.

Ministry of Small Scale Industries, Government of India, *Final Results: Third All India Census of SSI units 2001-2002*, Development Commissioner (SSI), New Delhi, 2004.

Ministry of Labour, Government of India, *Indian Labour Year Book*, Labour Bureau, New Delhi, 1982-83.

Ministry of Small Scale Industries, Government of India, *Final Results: Third All India Census of SSI units 2001-2002*, Development Commissioner (SSI), New Delhi, 2004.

Ministry of Small Scale Industries, Government of India, *State Level Report on Third All India Census of SSI- (2001-2002)*, Development Commissioner (SSI), New Delhi, 2004.

Ministry of Statistics and Programme Implementation, Government of India, *Statistical Abstract India*, Central Statistical Organisation, New Delhi, 2000.

Planning Commission, Government of India, X Plan - *Five Year Plans, Sectoral Policies and Programmes,* New Delhi, Vol.11, 2002-2007.

State Planning Board, Government of Kerala, *Economic Review*, Thiruvananthapuram.

State Planning Board, Government of Kerala, Census of India 2001, Chapter 18, Gender and Development, Economic Review, 2001.

D. Articles in News papers

Bindu Shridhar, 'Women as Entrepreneurs', *The Hindu*, Kochi, December 14, 2005.

'Minister Regrets Fall in Number of Women Entrepreneurs', *The Hindu*, January 22, 2005.

Savitri Ramamurthy, 'Women Entrepreneurs in Delhi', Tinani, Madan, "Women Entrepreneurs', *The Economic*

Times, Sunday, April 10, 1988.

'TN Women Hailed as First-Rate Entrepreneurs', *The New Indian Express,* Thursday, March 4, 2004.

E. Research Studies

Arulappan, A., 'A Study of Entrepreneurship in Small Scale Industries in North Arcot Ambedkar District - Tamil Nadu', *Ph.D. Thesis,* University of Madras, Madras, June, 1996.

Anna, V., 'Women Entrepreneurship in Industrial Manufacturing Sector of Kerala', *Ph.D. Thesis,* Cochin University of Science and Technology, Kochi, June,1989.

Francis, C., 'Women .Informal Sector Workers in Chennai city: A Study', *Ph.D. Thesis,* University of Madras, Madras, 2000.

Kerala Women's Commission, *'Status of Women In Kerala',* Kerala Women's Commission, Thiruvananthapuram, May 30, 2002.

Khondkar, Mubina, 'Women's Access to Credit and Gender Relations in Bangladesh', *Ph.D. Thesis,* University of Manchester, U.K., 1998.

Lokeswara Choudary, Y., ' Women Entrepreneurs-A Case Study of Vikram Sarabhai Industrial Estate in Chennai City', *M.Phil. Dissertation,* Madras University, October,1999.

Marline Morais, 'Development of Women Entrepreneurship in Tamil Nadu', *Ph.D. Thesis,* Madras University, 1996.

Mathialagan, R, 'Women Entrepreneurs in Tamil Nadu – A Socio-Economic Study of Selected Women Entrepreneurs at Chennai City', *Ph.D. Thesis,* Madras University, Madras, March, 2002.

Nirmala Karuna D'Cruz, *'Constraints on Women Entrepreneurship Development in Kerala: An Analysis of Familial, Social, and Psychological Dimensions',* Centre for Development Studies, Thiruvananthapuram, 2003.

Papisetty Rama Mohana Rao, 'Problems of Women Micro

Entrepreneurs in Chennai, with Special Reference to Access to Credit', *Ph.D. Thesis*, Madras University, Madras, January, 2004.

Praveena Kodoth, 'Women and Work: A Study of Female – Headed Households', *M. Phil. Dissertation*, Department of Economics, School of Social Science, University of Hyderabad, April, 1992.

Savithri, M.K., 'Stress Management- A Comparative Study of Women Executives and Women Entrepreneurs', *Ph.D. Thesis*, University of Madras, Madras, July, 2002.

Seenivasagalu, R., 'Women Entrepreneurs and Executives- A Comparative Study', *Ph.D. Thesis*, Madras University, Madras, March, 2001.

Vijayakumar, C., 'A Study of the Hosiery Entrepreneurs at Tirupur, Tamil Nadu', *Ph.D. Thesis*, Kerala University, Human Relations Division, The South Indian Textile Research Association, Coimbatore, August, 1986.

Index